A Dialogue With Death
The Teacher Of Life

Also By Erhard Vogel

Books:

The Four Gates: *A Saga Of The Human Being On The Path From The Pit Of Despair To The Realm Of Fulfillment, From Confusion To Clarity, Culminating In The Deepest Realization*

Journey Into Your Center

Self-Healing Through The Awareness Of Being
(1st Ed. out of print, 2nd Ed. upcoming)

Audio Recordings of Guided Meditations and Teachings:

The Cave Meditation

The Stress Release Response:
Seven Steps To Triumph Over Stress

Guided Meditation For Beginners

Centering

Feelings And Emotions

The Healing Power Of Love

The Silent Observer

Yoga For Life: *Two Hours Of Guided Yoga Classes (Basic And Advanced)*

Advanced Breathing Techniques and The Breath Meditation

Please see back of the book for descriptions of the audio recordings.

A Dialogue With Death
The Teacher Of Life

An Ancient Story For The Modern World

Erhard Vogel

This book is a compilation of the author's teachings
derived from recordings of his stream-of-consciousness discourses
on the Katha Upanisad,
given at the Sivananda Ashram, Rishikesh, India,
and the Nataraja Yoga Ashram, San Diego, California.

Nataraja Yoga Ashram
San Diego, California

Nataraja Yoga Ashram

San Diego, California

Photographs by Erhard Vogel

This book contains two English translations of the Katha Upanisad: The primary translation is from *Eight Upanisads: Volume One: (Isa, Kena, Katha and Taittiriya)*, With the Commentary of Sankaracarya, Translated by Swami Gambhirananda, Advaita Ashrama, Mayavati, Almora, Himalayas, 1972. The second translation is from *The Yoga of the Kathopanishad* by Sri Krishna Prem, London, John M. Watkins, 21 Cecil Court, Charing Cross Road, W.C.2 1955.

ISBN: 978-1-892484-06-2 (sc)
ISBN: 978-1-892484-08-6 (e)
Library of Congress Control Number: 2020901854

Dedication

To the great luminous sages H.H. Swami Krishnanandaji and H.H. Swami Chidanandaji, who have enriched humanity with the light of Consciousness and blessed many years of my life with their devotion and loyal friendship. Also, to Sri Swami Vishnudevanandaji, who revived the ancient teachings of Raja Yoga in India and brought them to the West with his authoritative publication, *The Complete Illustrated Book Of Yoga,* and personally trained me to teach his Yoga Teacher Training Program.

In Gratitude

To my students around the world who have dedicated themselves for years to the experience of the teachings expressed in this book, and sincerely endeavor to live in accord with the reality the teachings represent.

And to those who value themselves sufficiently to respond sincerely to the call within to free themselves and others from suffering by conducting their lives expertly as the real Being they are.

Special acknowledgements with appreciation go to Kathleen McMillen, who dedicated her refined expertise and unnumbered hours to formatting, proofing and editing this manuscript, and Pam Reed, for help in editing and for dedicating expert service to bringing the book to humanity.

A Word To The Wise

These teachings are given to you as lights on the path to fulfillment in the realization of your true identity. They are to be experienced with your full Being, not merely read by your mind. Therefore be deeply focused in Consciousness as you experience each facet of reality presented to you.

Be patient when you come upon ideas new to you; continue steadily, and understanding will grow. Read with trust in yourself and your ability to know and experience what is offered here. After all, it is about you and who you really are, and how to successfully live to your fulfillment.

Contents

Please Be Aware

The sections preceding the story of the Katha Upanisad
contain teachings of fundamental importance
for the understanding of the entire work.

Please absorb them thoroughly.

Luminous Self, Children Of Light, Dear Readers:

The reason and purpose of human life
is to be in the experience of who you really are,
Eternal Consciousness, your true identity.
You are to think feel and act
as the Limitless Being that you are, Self.

Meditation is the experience of yourself as Infinite Consciousness.

But you are conditioned to regard yourself
as severely limited, separate from the whole and isolated.
This false way of identifying yourself is called ego,
and it is the root cause of all your suffering.
Most are so attached to this limited identity,
to all the false ways of thinking and acting based upon it,

and all the dysfunction and suffering resulting from it,
that being in the experience of real Self—meditation—
seems difficult.

There is a great ancient scripture called the Katha Upanisad.
Its purpose is to teach what you need to know
to free yourself from bondage to the ego identity
and experience the limitless joy and love
of self-knowing Being that you actually are.

I first came across this sacred writing while living in the Himalayas.
It was recommended to me
by the luminous master H.H. Swami Krishnanandaji.
As the story revolves around an encounter with Death,
I immediately identified with it—
the Kathopanisad brought me back
to my experiences in childhood during World War II,
when I met Death during a bombardment of our home.
I will tell you that story a little later.
Since my first meeting with him, my relationship with Death
has been a constant touchstone in my life,
and a deeply appreciated friendship.

The teachings of the Katha Upanisad are said to be secret,
for only the properly prepared student will understand them.
I have carefully crafted this work
as a personal experiential learning process,
and included special guided focuses throughout.
As you sincerely apply yourself,
you will come to not only absorb these teachings
with your mind and intellect,
but *experience* them deeply within your whole Being.

Erhard Vogel

P.S. Regarding the Katha Upanisad:

The Katha Upanisad is a concise and beloved ancient Sanskrit scripture, said by scholars to have been written during the first part of the First Millennium BCE. This remarkable text has been translated into many languages and interpreted by sages, teachers and scholars of the world throughout history. My interpretation is based entirely on personal experience. I chose to work with two English translations of the Sanskrit verses, and include them herein: one full translation, and, where I considered it helpful to the understanding of a verse, a second translation.[1] The translations retain some Sanskrit terms for which there are no equivalents in English. I explain and employ certain of these terms for their unparalleled descriptive qualities.

P.P.S. The book's formatting and punctuation, to which you may not be accustomed, have been chosen for emphasis and ease of focus.

I sincerely invite you to share your responses to the ideas in this book by emailing me at eternalconsciousness@me.com

[1] References for the translations are located on the copyright page.

All That Is

Focus

All that is, is Being.
The power to be is the subtle interconnecting substance
linking all expressions, all forms, of Being.
Unbeginning, Being has always been, before all manifestation.
Imminently present, Being is now.
Eternal, Being never ceases to be.
Transcendent, Being is beyond the parameters
of time and space, circumstance and condition.
Being is infinite; you are Being.

This is of fundamental importance, as well as self-evident and simple.

Sincerely and diligently prepare your faculties—
your mind feelings and emotions, your intellect and intuition,
and even your body and senses—
to be fully present unto yourself,
and in constant attentiveness and devotion
to *Infinite Being* that you are.
Prepare sincerely continuously expertly and faithfully
without backsliding, and you will not fail.

Let your faculties be together in your center, the area of your heart,
in a beautiful state of effortless balance.
Be relaxed, be whole.
Have your faculties remain calm and clear—
this is their unmodified state,
the state for which they are intended,
the state of pure Consciousness,
in which they devote their total attention
to the experience of Self Being.

Maintain yourself in the *real* focused state
so that you sincerely take in what you read here
and make it your own experience.
Impress your experience so strongly and deeply
that it will be a permanent part of your life.

May you be inspired
by the joyous and most deeply satisfying consequences
that this will bring about in even a brief time, and for eternity.

May you be empowered to grow
with the knowledge you gain here.
May you open your heart to this knowledge.
May you be strengthened through understanding.
May you gain life in real knowledge.
And may you not cavil within and among yourselves.

May you gain peace in the physical realm.
May you gain peace in the mental realm.
And may you realize fulfillment in the spiritual realm.

The Fundamentals

Establishing Your Understanding Of The Fundamentals

Prepare yourself now for revelations
regarding the mysteries of ourselves in life and death,
individually and collectively,
as the manifestations and the Manifestor,
as the waves and the ocean.
Prepare for the revelations of action and reaction,
cause and effect.

Remember to keep yourself open to the full experience
of this moment of Being.

The Katha Upanisad has come to us
as an inspired record of the luminous seers of ancient times.
These masters of the highest consciousness
and acute perception developed themselves
with rigorous disciplines over a lifetime
into a state of knowledge that was derived from
direct experience far beyond that of ordinary people.
They condensed their knowledge into teachings so pure,
they were considered secret:
you could hear them,
but would not comprehend their real meaning.
Only those whose minds had been trained to a refined focus—
aspirants properly prepared
through the guidance of a real Teacher—
were able to fully understand and benefit from their teachings.
So it is still today.

The masters would deliver a teaching *one time*,
and their students were trained to assimilate the teaching
so completely as to live it from that moment on
and be able to transfer this knowledge to *their* students.
Thus was the Kathopanisad handed down a long lineage,
without losing an iota of its truth.

> You can retain the highest Teachings
> for the rest of your Life
> by completely *absorbing* them—
> not merely registering them in your Mind,
> but wholly *experiencing* and *living* them.

To gain the benefits from the seers' teachings
it is necessary to involve your consciousness.
Be focused clear and present, from moment to moment,
in the way you absorb them and respond.
You are not spoon-fed formulae or rigid rules to follow,
but inspired to experience truth and to live it.
The truths offered here do not belong to this Teacher,
not even to the Kathopanisad, but are reality itself.
The teachings are important guiding lights
on your path to fulfillment;
take them in and digest them,
make them integral to your way of being.
Then you are not merely memorizing words,
but absorbing an integrated experience
with the various points of knowledge interconnected.

This path progresses step by step;
with the relationship between the steps clear,
your journey will be illumined.

What is presented here are *not* some mysterious ideas
or philosophical concepts, but, again, stark reality.

> Reality consists *not*
> of the confused and limited Perceptions and Opinions of Ego,
> nor the incessant Involvement with Phenomena and Details,
> but of what fundamentally and essentially *is*.

This is what those masters experienced
and share with you in the Upanisads,
experiences which you, too, will have
when you clear away the bric-a-brac,
the mental emotional and spiritual baggage
under which most individuals labor.
Clear the way for understanding *real knowledge*—
perception of reality through your own direct experience—
and thus *live* in reality.

Let us look at the word *Upanisad*, for it explains much
about the seers' relationship to knowledge,
which we hope will become *your* relationship to knowledge.
Upanisad is derived by adding the prefixes
upa, which means the intrinsic, the innermost, the essential,
and *ni*, which means certainty,
to the root *sad,* which means to loosen, to destroy, to split up.

It is by the *certain* Knowledge of the *Intrinsic*
that you *loosen* and *split* yourself
from the World of Material Existence,
the World of Illusion and Ignorance—the World of Suffering.
This Emancipation is necessary
for you to come to the Experience of who you really are.

Upanisads are knowledge of reality with certainty
by which you free yourself
from the painful repetitive behaviors based upon ignorance,
mostly ignorance regarding your own identity.

Certainty—this is an important point:
You do not achieve realization by guessing or believing,
but by knowing through direct experience,
which yields certainty.
With knowledge of which you are *certain*, and only with that,
can you eliminate the darkness
of illusion ignorance and false conception,
the root cause of all pain and sorrow.

I always tell my new students,
Do not ever believe a word I say.
With belief you can be misled, and belief is lazy.
But if I can help you experience truth—
and with experience you can say, I know this to be true,
I know this because I experienced it—
then you have knowledge.
Only that which comes from your own direct experience

is knowledge.
Then you are responsible for that knowledge,
and you can use it to liberate yourself from suffering.

What knowledge do you have of which you are certain?
Ask yourself right now, look within:
What knowledge do I have of which I am certain?

You can know with certainty *that you are.*
You are being.
Pause a moment.
Consciously experience this: you are being.
This is obvious, clear and beyond question or dispute.
You *are* due to the ability to *be.*
This holds true for everything that *is.*
Do you know that? With certainty?
Yes, it is possible for you to know that with certainty.

Being is not an object. You are not an object.
The ability to be is not an organ but energy, power.
Being is the power by which you are,
the power by which all is.
Be in the awareness of that.

> You can know with Certainty *that you are.*
> You are Being.
> Being is not an Object.
> *You* are not an Object.
> Being is the Power by which you are,
> the Power by which all is.

Without the power to be, you could not be.
The power to be is what you can *not* be without;
it is your *essence.*
Being is what you essentially are.
And consider this: In the whole cosmos,
can there be being without the awareness of being?
What would be the sense of being,
if you could not experience it?
What *is* the sense of being
when you do not experience it?
Consciousness is integral and essential to being:
Being and Consciousness are one.

The essence of you, that without which you can not *be*,
is your *identity*; you are what you are in essence.
Be clear about that.
Who you are is the power to be, in Self-awareness.
You are the *Power of Being*, *Consciousness*.
Being and Consciousness are your identity.
Know that. With certainty.

To effectively direct your life,
you need to *know* who you *really* are—
know, not believe nor just take for granted.
To live in *false* perception of your identity
is to *not* experience your life as *you*.
Thus it is not a mere philosophical issue,
but the *nitty-gritty practicality*
to consciously conduct your life as who you really are,
and the only way to be really successful.

Be aware of yourself—think feel and act every Moment—
as the Power of Being that you are.
Live in the Awareness of these fundamental Facts:

Power, Energy, is indestructible and indivisible.
You, being the Power of Being,
are indestructible and indivisible.

As Power is indestructible, it is therefore eternal.
You, being the Power of Being,
are eternal.

As Power is indivisible, it is therefore all-pervasive,
the Infinite One.
You, being the Power of Being,
are all-pervasive, the Infinite One.

To be fulfilled, dwell in the Awareness of Being.

Dwelling in this awareness you have knowledge with certainty:
that is Upanisad.

As people are habituated to relating to themselves opposite to this—
'self' as a limited separate disconnected entity—
we use the word 'Self' to refer to your *real* identity.

You are Self:
Infinite Being in Self-experience,
eternal all-pervasive Consciousness.

With the knowledge of reality with certainty
you can destroy your involvement with illusion
and false conception.

Know that.

With the knowledge of reality with certainty
you can destroy all those characteristics within you
that bind you to misery and pain,
and to the recurring cycles of life and death and rebirth
and death again.

With the knowledge of reality with certainty
you can liberate yourself and live in Consciousness,
in union and harmony with true Being,
the essence, the actuality, Self.

How do you actually achieve liberation?

Knowledge alone, even with Certainty,
does not free you.
Only *living* this Knowledge frees you.

As a real spiritual aspirant,
so thoroughly keep the knowledge you gain
in moment-to-moment awareness
that you live it sincerely continuously expertly and faithfully.
As you live true to reality,
you are saved from the fear of Death
and can have a loving trusting relationship
with this great Teacher of life.

The grand teaching of the Katha Upanisad
takes place through a historic meeting between
a representative of humanity, a sincere young man
whose name is Naciketa,
and Death, who is given the name Yama.
Yama has knowledge with certainty of birth and death,
creation and dissolution, reality and illusion.
He can help you attain final liberation
in the infinite bliss of *Self-realization*.

Salutations to Yama, the great master, Death,
my Teacher and liberator,
whom I honor and love.

I will share with you now this tale of Death,
which is a tale of eternal life.

Part I Canto I

Meeting Death The Teacher

Chapter One

The False Sacrifice

Cause relaxation to flow through every part of you
with the impetus to continue deeper and deeper.

Regulate the breath and include a sense of permanency
so it remains steady and calming.

See to it that everything about you
continues to be established in your center,
every faculty in constant devotion and attentiveness
to the Power of Being that you are.

Thus you dwell as self-knowing Consciousness,
limitless eternal and all-pervasive—
your identity, the real Self you are.

It is with this sincere continuous expert faithful focus
that you absorb the knowledge you gain,
and impress it deeply and permanently
as of the moment you experience it.

1. Once upon a time, the son of Vajasrava, being desirous of fruit, gave away everything. He had, as the story goes, a son named Naciketa.

2. As the presents were being carried (to the Brahmanas) faith took possession of him who was still a boy. He thought:

3. *He goes to those worlds that are known as joyless, who gives away the cows that have drunk water and eaten grass (for good), whose milk has been milked (for the last time), and which have lost their organs.*

There once was a wise boy named Naciketa.
One day he watched his father, a highborn person,
make offerings at the temple.
His father was giving away his possessions
to please the priests and propitiate the gods
in hopes of gaining rewards.
As he watches, Naciketa notices
that the cows his father brought to give as sacrifice
are decrepit old and dying—utterly useless.
Being a young man of highly developed spirituality,
Naciketa is struck at this moment by deep faith,
a profound trust in his knowledge of the essential.
He realizes that his father's intention is not so much to *give*,
but to *receive*.
His father is involved with the *results* of his sacrifice,
not with the sacrifice itself.

Real sacrifice is an offering made to acknowledge
the Power of Being, by which we are,
the essence, therefore the unifying factor, of all.
Sacrifice expresses the interconnected wholeness
of all forms of Being.
It burns the dross of attachment to the falsity
of relating to yourself as separate from the whole.

Real Sacrifice is made to acknowledge the Power of Being
that has given us all Existence.
Through this symbolic Act you are saying,
I rid myself of the Conception of *separate Ownership*
and return that which has always been of the creative Source.

Real sacrifice releases your attachment to the material realm.
The material usually so occupies you
that you do not have the time energy or attentiveness left
to experience what is most important about you,
that without which you would not be:
Being.

But the father is involved in an act of deception—
self-deception, the worst kind of deception.
Naciketa, in the inspiration of his spiritual knowledge,
realizes the danger attendant to his father's dishonest act;
he knows you can not fool reality,
you can not fool that which *is*.
By offering a false sacrifice, his father paves the way
...to those worlds that are known as joyless...
Naciketa knows that his father, having damaged his integrity,
is causing himself and his family to live in suffering.
Rather than freeing himself
from the limitations of the material realm,
he is enmeshing himself even more in its bondage.

To ward off this evil,
Naciketa wants to *repair* his father's sacrifice, make it real,

by offering *himself.*
Thus Naciketa faces his father:

4. *He said to his father, "Father, to whom will you offer me?" He spoke to him a second time and a third time. To him (the father) said, "To Death I offer you."*

Second translation:

Therefore he said to his father once, twice and thrice: "To whom will you give me (who also am one of your possessions)?" Whereupon the father replied, "To Death do I give thee."

Naciketa is showing his father the contrast:
If you are giving *useless* cattle in sacrifice to the gods,
to whom will you offer your *precious* son?

The father is stunned by his son pointing out
his obvious attempt at deception;
he just wants to get this sacrifice accomplished,
so he ignores Naciketa.
But the son faces him once more and says,
...Father, to whom will you offer me?...
Again the father brushes him off.
So Naciketa asks a third time
...to whom will you offer me?...

And what do people who want to appear holy do
when the plain truth exposes their fraud?
Naciketa's father strikes out in self-righteous anger:
...To Death I offer you...

The son withdraws in pain to a quiet place to reflect upon this:

5. *Among many I rank as belonging to the highest; among many I rank as belonging to the middling. What purpose can there be of Death that my father will get achieved today through me?*

Naciketa is making a realistic assessment,
one that requires discrimination and honesty.
He examines how he relates to his father,
who in their society is also his teacher.
Furthermore he weighs how he relates to his community.
Appraising himself objectively as a disciple,
one who is committed to being in Consciousness,
a knower of Self,
he sees that he can be ranked either among the foremost
or the middling.

A foremost disciple is, according to the ancients,
one who is engaged in service to his Teacher
by ascertaining and fulfilling the Teacher's instructions
as soon as they are expressed, or before.
Naciketa knows that in his relationship with his father,
his teacher, he is pure;
he has been in disciplined pursuit of reality.
Thus he can say that he is at times a foremost disciple.

A middling disciple is one
who waits to hear the instructions expressed by his Teacher
and then acts upon them.

The lowest disciple is one
who knows or hears the instructions of the Teacher
and disobeys.

He is swayed by pride, thinking he knows better.
She is held back by sloth, forgetfulness
or attachment to old patterns of behavior.
They are stuck in the habit of 'processing',
behaving as if they had no maturity, no potential for growth,
as if the evidence of reality made no difference.

Naciketa knows that he is not of the lowest type of student.
He does not deny reality;
he does not argue with, contradict or disobey his Teacher;
he does not attempt to weaken his Teacher
in order to bring him down to his level;
he does not weave webs of deception within himself
or with his Teacher, and call it spiritual conduct.

Naciketa has been a good disciple.
He is actually highly developed and sincere.
Therefore he knows his father has nothing to gain
by sacrificing him to Death.
It was just an outburst of anger.
He knows his father loves him.
While he also loves and respects his father,
he has to rectify his father's misdeed.

Naciketa's father is now full of remorse for losing his temper
and uttering this curse—it was simply
like saying in the heat of the moment, Go to hell!
But the father has given his word
that his son is to be sacrificed to Death.
Naciketa says to himself,
The veracity of my father must not be damaged,
my father's word is to be kept,
because integrity is of the highest importance.

Yama, the Lord of Death, answers:

6. *Consider successively how your forefathers behaved, and consider how others behave (now). Man decays and dies like corn, and emerges again like corn.*

Second translation:

Bear in mind how went those who have gone before. Note how in the same way go others now. Like grain a mortal ripens and like grain is he born again.

The cycles of cause and effect are interlinked through generations
and succeeding lifetimes.
Are we to be mutely bound to the cycles
of constantly reacting to the consequences of previous actions?
Are we to continue helplessly fettered
to the impressions of past experiences
that carry the latent energy demanding we repeat old behaviors,
no matter how infantile and dysfunctional?
Is this the human condition?

Naciketa visualizes the corn in the field,
sown every spring and reaped every summer,
then plowed under again in autumn to be re-sown in spring,
passively going through the cycles of birth death and rebirth.
What is to differentiate a person's fate from that of a vegetable,
if his behaviors and actions are swayed,
not by knowledge-empowered free choice,
but by outside circumstances
or inner states, such as stress anxiety or fear?
Naciketa knows this world is impermanent.
What is to be gained, he says to himself,
by giving credence to more impermanence?

We will be of the impermanent world if we break our word,
because truth—reality—is permanent.

The honored forebears, Teachers and sages of yore,
lived in a pure relationship with reality;
they lived and acted in truth.
Those who are ignorant of reality—
and even more decidedly, those who knowingly
live in denial and distortion of it—
suffer in the 'vale of tears and sorrow'.
They go through endless cycles of life death and rebirth,
as passive as an ear of corn.
To destroy your relationship with reality, which is everlasting,
for the sake of imagined advantage in this temporal world
is the worst sacrifice to make.

Learn from your learning Experiences.
Learn from the Behavior of the Wise and *emulate* it.
Learn from the Behavior of the Deluded and *be repelled* by it.

Naciketa, prepared to meet Death,
returns to his father and addresses him,
Protect your honor, my father,
and send me to Death, as you said.

Chapter Two

Repairing The False Sacrifice With True Action

Be focused now, effortlessly balanced in your center
with all your faculties in a deeply relaxed state.
Lovingly direct your faculties' attentiveness toward Self,
the Limitless Being that you are.

Thus you sincerely experience the teachings
and impress them upon your systems so deeply
that their positive influence will permanently exert itself
throughout your life.

See everything as the all-pervasive Power of Being
that is the essence, the Self of all that is.
Look around you: whatever you see

is Self-expression of the one underlying essence.
Some expressions are easy to see as Self,
and some are not.
It does not matter; they all are expressions
of the essential Power of Being, which is Consciousness.
Being and Consciousness are one.

Be that.
You are not just learning about It, You *Are* That.

> Your Aim is to be in Consciousness,
> Being in the Awareness of Being.
> That is what Meditation really is:
> continuous undistorted Experience of Being,
> at Will.

Practice meditation only once a day: all day.
You want to be in Consciousness continuously;
it is the most wonderful state of being,
not meant to be a mere momentary thrill.

Naciketa's father has taught him well.
Naciketa not only sees through the false sacrifice,
but when his father loses his temper and curses him,
rather than focus on his own pain,
he determines to save his father
from the additional damage of breaking his word.
Naciketa acts out of great devotion to his father.
He does *not* accuse his father and try to rise above him—

You have finally done something wrong,
now I am better than you—
no, he sets forth to repair the situation, right away.

How do you apply this in *your* life?
Are you, like Naciketa, deeply in touch with the *Inner Knower*?
Or do you sometimes perform actions
incongruous with yourself?
The Inner Knower does not blame, does not accuse,
does not celebrate, but says, We need to fix this.

The Inner Knower is the Way by which you know within, what *is*,
with Certainty.
This takes place in a State of pure Focus,
free of Desire and Aversion,
beyond Wishing and Wanting:
a State beyond the Limitations of Mind.

Naciketa's father, knowing his son is right,
makes the difficult decision to perform a *real* sacrifice.
To preserve the veracity of his word,
he sends his son to the abode of Death.
And Naciketa makes the ultimate sacrifice
by offering his life to repair the negative effects
of his father's false deed.

Naciketa is free of any and all delusion regarding who he is.
He knows he is Eternal Being.
For the sake of his father's integrity,

which is of *permanent* Self,
Naciketa sacrifices his ego aspect, which is *impermanent*.

When you share your Knowledge with others
by living true to Self,
you participate in the sacred Act of Sacrifice.
Giving of who you *really* are
helps others gain Freedom from Suffering.
Such Sacrifice is founded upon
the Recognition of Interconnectedness in Self.
Your Sharing bestows the Experience of All-inclusive Being
to the Recipient,
and in even greater Abundance to the Giver, yourself.

Naciketa's father precipitated a crisis.
The pivotal crises of human existence, even human evolution,
are caused by living in disregard of who you really are,
living in falsity, in opposition to Self.
Through Naciketa's positive response to this crisis
comes the opportunity for the luminous revelations
that lead to liberation, the Katha Upanisad.

The father's sacrifice was destructive
because he gave away what was not precious to him,
but useless.
Attached to the false, he lived as if *that* were precious.
This attachment, the father was *not* willing to sacrifice.

What seem most precious to human beings
are the false ways of thinking feeling and acting

that are predicated on the perception of yourself
as a separate, therefore isolated, entity—ego.

> Ego is the *false* Way you identify yourself
> as separate from the Whole
> and, by extension, isolated weak and flawed.
> Through Ego you remain attached and limited.

The father represents the ego.
Under the sway of ego you engage in actions
that are contrary to the interconnected Being you really are.
In the ego perception of separateness, you feel lack of contact
with the limitless eternal all-pervasive One.
This sense of separateness is the fundamental cause
of dysfunctional relationships with the world,
with others and, most of all, with yourself.

Naciketa represents the real Self.
In the awareness of all-pervasive oneness, he is *unattached*,
therefore willing to make the real sacrifice.
In the awareness of yourself as unending Power of Being,
you are free of attachment.

To free yourself from the bondage
of the false ways of thinking feeling and acting,
consciously and sincerely engage
in the experience of Being you are: that is *meditation*.

Meditation is the active moment-to-moment Sacrifice
of Attachment to the false Perception of yourself
as *separate*, a Fragment disconnected from the Whole.
In Meditation you consciously experience yourself
continuously, at Will, free of Distortion and Distraction,
as interconnected Being, the All-pervasive One.

Yes, the father made a sacrifice, but it was false.
Do not, in the same way, make the mistake
of convincing yourself you are meditating
when you are only going through the motions,
still attached to the ways of thinking feeling and being
to which you are habituated:
regarding yourself as a separate entity.
To make a false sacrifice is destructive;
to sit for meditation in that manner is destructive.

To the degree that you allow your mind emotions feelings,
or any other faculty, to be in distraction or falsity,
to that degree are you precipitating crisis.
What are the symptoms of such crisis,
even with intelligent well-meaning persons?
The consequences of not living true to your real identity are
physical emotional and practical disharmony and dysfunction.
That, in turn, is the seedbed of disease failure and suffering.
Those symptoms are your blessing:
they are notifying you something is awry.

When you perform any Action
or simply sit for Meditation,
let it be the Sacrifice of any and all Perception of yourself
as an isolated Entity apart from the Whole.
False Behaviors are always harmful.

Do you experience this as true?
What follows the experience of truth?
You *enact* it.
Why? Because it is reality, and You *Are* That.
Actions opposed to reality are actions opposed to yourself;
they destroy your integrity and sensibility,
and cause pain and suffering.

As a real spiritual Aspirant—
or even just as someone who wants to make Sense
and be in Integrity—
make the conscious Choice to be true to what you know
by thinking feeling and enacting it,
by *living* it.

Chapter Three

The Universal Law Of Hospitality

Maintain all your faculties and energies in your center
in a state of purity, free of modification,
thereby attending to Self
with sincere and continuous devotion.

Open your heart to respond fully to these teachings.
Be responsive to the subtle vibrations in your core
that reverberate in accord with the truth that is revealed to you,
and be thereby filled with a deep sense of joy and recognition
of the various facets of Self, the infinite Power of Being.
Thus you are at peace.

When Naciketa arrives at the house of Death,
he finds that Lord Yama is not home.
Death is out on an errand.
And so Naciketa sits and awaits Death, unattended,
for three days and three nights.

For how many days and nights—or years—
has Self been sitting in your center unattended?

7. *A Brahmana guest enters the houses like fire. For him they accomplish this kind of propitiation. O Death, carry water (for him).*

A guest entering your home is a blessing,
a purifying influence, as is fire.
The law of hospitality, which is universal,
requires the owner of the house
to bring his guest water, to give him drink,
and in many cultures, to wash his feet,
acts of nurturing and respect.
The urgency of attending with water to a guest
is as strong as the urgency to attend with water to a fire.

The admonition is to honor and nurture the knowledge of Self
the moment it comes to you.
Do not merely collect knowledge of reality
to theorize or even cause distraction;
immediately attend to any ray of illumination
by continuously living true to it.

> Honor and nurture the Knowledge of Self
> by continuously living true to it.

8. *If in anyone's house a Brahmana guest abides without food, that Brahmana destroys hope and expectation, the results of holy association and sweet discourse, sacrifices and charities, sons and cattle—all these—of that man of little intelligence.*

Second translation:

Hope and expectation, friendly intercourse, the merits gained by sacrifice and charitable acts, offspring and cattle—for the foolish man in whose house a Brahman (guest) has to fast all these things are destroyed.

...a Brahmana guest... is of the highest order,
one who is dedicated to living as Limitless Consciousness,
the real Being that we are.
Naciketa, the human representative of Self,
is a true Brahmana guest.
When Self is not properly attended to
all the things important to mortals are destroyed.

...hope and expectation... are destroyed when you neglect Self.
Expecting is not *wishing* for, it is *causing* your facilities
to come together in the state that you intend.
In this sense expectation is a state of *empowerment.*
The destruction of expectation is the destruction of volition—
therefore empowerment—
the destruction of the human experience,
the opportunity to evolve.

> Expect your Faculties to respond to the real you
> when you tell them to respond,
> to function as you tell them to function.
> Expect your Body to relax when you tell it to relax.
> Expect your Mind to be focused present and at Peace
> when you tell it to be focused present and at Peace.
> Expect that you *will* fulfill your Life's Meaning.
> Expect that.

...holy association and sweet discourse... are destroyed.
Relationship and communication,
the positive aspects of being together, unity,
none of that is possible without being in touch with Self.

...sacrifices and charities... are destroyed.
These are ways of paying the debts of cause and effect,
karmic debts.
Karma, the law of cause and effect,
is not some force separate from you;
it reliably applies to all, and all the time.
Giving in interconnectedness establishes karmic positivity:
positive actions causing positive results.
Giving through chosen positive actions
can overcome the harmful effects
of a whole history of negative behaviors.

...sons and cattle... are destroyed.
If losing the higher merits of empowerment and relationship,

communication and giving—functions true to Self—
does not achieve recognition,
then loss on the lowest common denominator,
the material realm, where people usually respond,
will hopefully get the point across.

...all these... are destroyed
for one who is not intelligent enough to welcome Self;
all is lost, even the lowest earthly pleasures.
Consider the illogic of attending to everything else
at the expense of attending to Self,
and thereby losing all.
By placing your attention primarily upon
what promises momentary satisfaction,
you do not attend to the experience of Being that you are.
Thereby you not only lose the relationship with Self,
you lose the lasting satisfaction in all aspects of life
that you reliably experience when you *are* true to Self.

Too often ego's falsity tries to convince you
that living true to who you really are is a harsh discipline,
a hardship.
Attending to Self, being who you are,
is not a burden or imposition, or a task to be performed.
Attachment to the false way of thinking of yourself
is the cause of your dysfunction and suffering,
your inner conflict fatigue and lack.

Living true to Self is the Cessation of Suffering and Hardship.
Hardship is never due to the spiritual Path,
but holding on to the Opposite of it.
You will never suffer or fail by being true to yourself.

When you have the great good fortune
to have the awareness of who you really are come to you,
give it honoring and nurturing—live it.
Cause your faculties to treat the Being that you are
with immediate and continued attentiveness.

Do not delay: When I get through processing about it,
or, When I get rid of my mood,
or, After I've bought my next new toy and played with it,
or, When I grow up.
Do you know when you have grown up?
When you *know* Self
and—most importantly—when you *attend* to Self,
when you *live* as the Being you know you are.
As a six-year-old child you can be grown up enough
to know Self and live It;
you do not have to wait until you are sixteen,
thirty-six, or even seventy-six.

Do not forget:
When Self is in your abode, attend to It every moment.
Keep your relationship to Self from dying.
Self does not die, but your relationship to Self certainly can.
Give consistently to Self from the moment of recognition.

> When the Awareness of your real Identity,
> eternal all-pervasive Consciousness,
> is within you,
> attend to it every Day and every Night.
> Attend to Self in the Way that honors Self:
> *sincerely continuously expertly* and *faithfully.*
> And if at any Time you find you have neglected Self,
> immediately make strong Reparation:
> act in Strength to give to Self purely without Attachment.
> Treat Self as an honored Guest is to be treated;
> do not neglect Self, do not keep Self waiting.

Giving to Self without attachment
is not giving something away or losing it;
it is giving to yourself the experience of reality,
the experience of real you
in the awareness of interconnectedness.
You are highborn Being,
who deserves to be related to with utter honor and respect.
You deserve to attend to Self.

By the choices you make you affect the people in your life.
What is the effect of a negative choice,
the choice of non-being, ego?
It teaches others, especially those closest to you,
to make the same choices:
to be deluded and live in suffering,
to be bound isolated and limited, to fail in life.
This is karmic negativity, a heavy debt to bear.

Knowing this, would you ever make the choice
to neglect your relationship to Self?
Only a self-loathing fool would.

Chapter Four

Three Boons Are Granted

Place your faculties in your center
in the state of effortless balance
and complete attentiveness to the experience of Being.

With sincere determination
experience these teachings in such a way
that they will be powerfully and permanently impressed,
and add to the light by which you are guided
on the path of Self-realization.

When Yama returns to his abode
and is told by his wives that a high-minded guest
has stayed in his house for three nights and three days,
the great Lord of Death rushes to Naciketa,
gives him the proper salutations,
and asks his forgiveness:

9. *O Brahmana, since you have lived in my house for three nights without food, a guest and an adorable person as you are, let my salutations be to you, and let good accrue to me (by averting the fault arising) from that (lapse). Ask for three boons—one in respect of each (night).*

Naciketa is excited and concerned, intrigued and apprehensive
at the prospect of meeting the great Lord of Death.
Thus Yama's greeting floods him with deep relief.

Yama says to him,
We salute you, highborn one, with all respect, though it is late.
I am in your grace as you visit my abode,
and I extend my apologies for not properly attending you
for the three days and nights you have been my guest.

Even to the Lord of Death, the all-knowing master,
it is important to obey the law of hospitality
and show a guest all consideration and courtesy.
He offers Naciketa food and entertainment,
he washes his feet, they engage in sweet discourse,
all so that their relationship is not neglected,
and its benefits not lost.

After all Naciketa's comforts have been provided for,
Death says, I am in your debt for leaving you unattended:
...Ask for three boons—one in respect of each (night)...
Yama wants to make reparation
to free himself from the negative effects
of not fulfilling his duties as host.
Mighty Yama,
the destructive and creative aspect of the cosmos,
endeavors to repair the damage caused by his absence.
This is in his character;
Death is an integral element of the overall harmony.
As quickly as possible, he restores balance and peace.

Death is the great equalizer and ultimate motivator.
Knowing that Death will gather us after this brief span of life,
we are motivated to engage in more
than the mere biological functions.
There is an inherent drive in us
to *realize* Infinite Consciousness.
The prospect of impending death urges you
to break out of your imagined limitations
and attachment to the inertia
induced by a false way of regarding yourself.
Death urges you to expand in Consciousness.

My first meeting with Death began far less calmly,
but may be instructive to you.
As a child, I prepared to meet death
in what I experienced as the final crisis,
when during World War II our home was bombed.

I describe the event in the following excerpt from my book
Self-Healing Through The Awareness Of Being.
I invite you to experience this in a focused state.

Brought up in the midst of the collective outburst of human madness
that was World War II,
I had seen the terrifying effects of death
through years of bombardment:
masses of maimed and mashed corpses,
and the leveling of my world.
I lived in a seemingly endless version of the Apocalypse.

At the age of six I came face to face with death
when our home suffered a direct hit.
I knew in the moments preceding the bomb
that I was going to die.
Impelled by a fervent determination
to remain aware of myself
as my body was destroyed by the explosion,
I prepared consciously for the impending disaster.
In a prolonged moment of stopped time,
I made myself be still to face death
free from the frenzied fear around me and within me.
I had to see what came next.
In the conviction that I would somehow continue after death,
I became stone-cold clear in concentration.
I was determined to experience the transfer
from the present state of being to whatever state would follow.

I focused with such powerful pure determination
that I cleared away everything

so that Consciousness could be uninterrupted.
I determined to be in the continuity of Consciousness
and not have to start over again after death—
not that I knew about it in these words,
but that was the drive and the motivation.
As our home was hit,
the light came on within and all about me.
I was in the state of clear all-inclusive total Being.
'I Am That' was my whole experience.
I was free of fear, at peace, conscious.

The fiercely focused moment was more luminous
than the phosphorescent glare of the bomb's blast
that tore through our house.
The vacuum caused by the explosion
seemed to consume everything, including time.
Death passed me by.
We family members, who were pressed together
beneath a stone arch of the cellar
in the 17th-century Capuchin Monastery we dwelled in,
were spared.
All occupants of the adjoining room died...

This crucial and pivotal experience set my course
for the remainder of my life,
and established my intimate relationship with Death
as my teacher and friend...

Death is impending.
Death is coming for you.
There is no Time to waste,
for this Opportunity of human Life is great.

Though human Life is a great Opportunity,
it is not the Point.

The tenacious deep-seated Directive within
exhorts us to be in the Experience of real Consciousness,
Unending Consciousness, All-pervasive Consciousness,
not the fragmentary Consciousness or *Un*consciousness
that most dwell in.

Death has granted Naciketa the fulfillment of three wishes.
This is a situation many of us play in our imagination,
I know I did as a child.
Many fairy tales are about wishes magically coming true.
When I was six years old, I had to consider,
Why am I still alive? What am I meant to do with this life?
I concluded I had to aim for the highest possible:
the *ultimate*.

If you could have your three ultimate wishes fulfilled,
what would they be?
This is not merely a question for the play of imagination;
it is of profound importance
for intelligently directing your life conduct

to your ultimate fulfillment,
a question of *fundamental practicality*.

After my illumined experience in childhood of Self that I really am,
I knew I deserved the ultimate,
and I knew nothing else fulfills.
In all the deprivation my life offered at that time,
and for years to come,
I was clear I deserved fulfillment.

Yama, being highly motivated to make reparation,
indicates to Naciketa that he can ask for anything.
Death has the potential to fulfill whatever he intends.
So powerful is Death; so powerful are you.

Yama does not advise *what* should be chosen.
Naciketa has free will, as do you.
Be careful here. Death is the great liberator,
but can just as soon leave you in captivity.
If your choices are due to low desires,
they can enmesh and limit you.
The boons you choose can lead to freedom or bondage.
How often have we heard the warning,
Watch what you wish for, it may eventually come true.

> Whatever you intend for your Life will be fulfilled,
> whether it is positive or negative,
> in Harmony or Discord.

Naciketa is very smart, he is highly evolved.
He wants to ask for the absolute best,
the highest that can be attained: Self-realization.
However, there is a catch to these boons:
Lord Yama is only able to give Naciketa
what he is ready to receive,
otherwise it would harm the young man.
Yama has to find out what Naciketa knows,
he has to test him thoroughly.
That test is what drives this dialogue
between the Lord of Death and the human representative,
Naciketa.

Without hesitation, Naciketa addresses Death:
Yama, now that you favor me with three boons,
please grant my first boon as follows:

10. O Death, of the three boons I ask this one as the first, viz that (my father) Gautama may become freed from anxiety, calm of mind, freed from anger towards me, and he may recognise me and talk to me when freed by you.

Second translation:

As the first of the three boons I choose that when sent back by thee, O Death, my father Gautama, his sacrificial intent accomplished, may recognise and welcome me with a mind peaceful and free from the fiery turmoil of the heart.

Naciketa, well aware of the rare opportunity he faces,
and highly developed on his evolutionary path,
chooses as his first boon to heal the relationship with his father.
He wants to share the boons he is about to receive,

well balanced with all facets of his life.
Naciketa is determined to advance to *absolute fulfillment*
in the realization of his true identity: *Self-realization*.
He knows this state to be not of separateness,
but interconnectedness.
Harmonious relationship is of fundamental importance to him.

Naciketa is pure in Being.
He does not relate to his father with blame:
You were terrible, oh highborn Father, my teacher,
you lost your temper; therefore I gladly declare you invalid.
Now I no longer need to live in harmony
with the wisdom you have taught me.
No, Naciketa does not sow discord
or employ ego-serving one-upmanship.
Naciketa is focused in pure love relationship,
in union, with his father.

Love and Union are the Priority in Life.
The rest is the Dregs of the Temporal,
which interfere with the clear Perception
and limitless Experience
of the Joy of all-pervasive and eternal Being.

Naciketa relates in purity to his father, to ego.
This is symbolic of the relationship of pure Self to ego,
not of ego to ego.
He does not blame ego for his behaviors or experiences.

Naciketa causes his ego to function free of discord with him;
he includes ego in his limitless union.

In your quest for liberation from falsity
it helps to have a fundamental understanding of ego.
In its *pure* sense, ego simply acknowledges, I Am,
which is the seed of Consciousness.
This is ego's original state, awareness of the fact that you *are*.
In that state, you experience yourself
as the power by which you are, and ego is calm.

Ego suffers from the complications
of going beyond the I Am, to I am such-and-such:
a man, a woman, angry poor sad, etc.
The pure ego is distorted by modification:
as such-and-such you are limiting yourself;
you regard yourself not as the interconnected Power of Being,
but a separate entity cast adrift in isolation
and therefore lacking and in need.
Ego functioning as modifier is the false ego,
what is typically meant by the word 'ego'.
The modifier ego is false because you are Self, *all*,
not just the modifications—
they are distortions of what the pure ego declares.

> Do not make the Mistake of perceiving a big Ego as powerful.
> An egotistical Person is mired in Falsity, thus insecure,
> suffering from the Weakness of needing constant bolstering.

When ego is distorted by modification, the negative predominates
and prevents you from living the positive.
So while your faculties are meant to serve *you*,
subject to ego they do not.

Be aware: you may use your feelings as distractions.
In the ordinary ego state, your feelings give you false messages
reflecting ego's likes and dislikes:
I fear being empowered and having to be responsible,
I distrust Self.
Consequently your feelings no longer serve you;
they interfere with the true experience of yourself.
When you seek to be in touch with your feelings,
make sure they are the *real* feelings, original and true,
not the feelings of ego: signals in service to falsity.
In the pure state, feelings reflect truth:
I feel the joy of being empowered and interconnected Self.

Modified Ego is the Stance in Opposition to the Truth of you.

For most people the false ego state seems normal;
they have allowed ego to run everything—
ego *owns* their feelings and thinking,
even, by all appearances, their identity.
This false way of living is so familiar
that they think it is comfortable,
even though it is the cause of suffering.
In the false ego identification, the modified you,

your experiences are related to someone you are not,
thus depriving you of your own life experiences.
This explains how people can live in a land of plenty
afflicted with need and want.

How do you give ego the peace Naciketa requests as his first boon?
Ego is only *...freed from anxiety...* when no longer
functioning as the modifier, I am such-and-such.
When ego simply says, as originally intended, I am,
ego will be calm.

Beware: if you try to eliminate the false way of identifying yourself—
eliminate ego, as is the usual spiritual teaching—
your feelings, attached to ego,
will have you feel as if you were trying to destroy *you.*
It is too frightening to do away with
what you have regarded as your identity all your life.
To fight ego only ruins your relationship with yourself.
You can not experience the pure you through conflict.

When you fight Ego, it captures your Energy
and prevents you from experiencing the Being you really are.
Is it not better to make Peace with Ego through living in Reality
than have an Enemy to fight the rest of your Life?

Instead of trying to eliminate the false identification,
or, as you might feel, destroy this *you*,
integrate ego, embrace it,

guide it to its original pure unmodified state.
Peace comes with the recognition that ego is just *I Am*;
the modifications are not real.

> Instead of allowing the habitual negative Monologue—
> I am limited, I am untrustworthy, I am no good—
> proactively cultivate the Positive:
> I know as a Fact that I am limitless Power of Being,
> I Am.

Affirming that you are Being
is not meant to be some empty pat on the shoulder,
something of which you try to convince yourself
in order to feel good momentarily,
but the assertion of knowledge from your own experience
of your true identity.
Constantly acknowledge, I am,
and your ego will be secure and at peace,
free from the need to self-aggrandize
by amassing ephemeral qualities.

Do not blame ego, do not cause anxiety.
Ego has to know you welcome it and are integrating it,
that you are not trying to annihilate it.
Naciketa long ago took charge of his ego;
he is free from its habitual involvement with modification.
His ego is merged in pure Consciousness:
I Am, only that and nothing else.

> The false Ego is not real, it does not exist;
> it is a Figment of mistaken Thinking
> and has no Identity of its own.

Naciketa asks that his father be *...freed from anger towards me...*
The false ego has much anger against Self, enmity, even.
When ego is angry, it *negates* Self, it negates you,
through confusion complication distortion and distraction,
and any other device with which it can perpetuate its falsity.
If your ego is constantly negating you, it is because it is angry,
like the father when he cursed his son to Death.
Ego is angry because it is anxious, not calm.
Ego is anxious when you are *not* asserting
your knowledge regarding Self.

> Anger is but the impotent Expression of Fear
> due to Forgetfulness of who you really are.

Those who perceive themselves
as helplessly disconnected unworthy victims—ego—
erupt in anger throughout their lives.
Anger seems like the only power available to them.
They mistakenly feel empowered, therefore falsely secure,
by anger, not recognizing it is a corrosive power
by which they are eaten up inside
and by which they wreak havoc upon themselves,
and all about them.

Many people have a stranglehold attachment to anger:
I am too unworthy, I can not expect anything
except repetition of my self-abusive behaviors.
They form whole religions around it:
I was born with original sin, it can not be helped.
Only angry people say that—
Christ never said that, Buddha never said that,
Mohammed never did; they were not that angry.
When you live with anger,
at the end of your life as you look back,
all you will feel is sorrow and regret.

Persistent anger causes you to feel so helpless in its clutches
that fear becomes endemic.
Many have lived with such enduring fear
that fear is the familiar, the fabric of their lives.
They even fear being without fear.
You have to learn to actually free yourself
from your *attachment* to fear.
Spiritual teachers throughout the ages have emphasized
the need to overcome fear to be free to dwell in reality.

Free yourself from the cycle of dwelling in ignorance,
leading to the perception of isolation,
leading to fear anxiety and anger,
all leading to destructiveness.
Why else would humanity, with all its talents and potential,
engage in ceaseless war and destruction?
You are in charge; set your ego at ease,
cause it to be in harmony with the Being you are.
That is fundamental to your helping end
the insanity and suffering caused by humans.

...and he may recognise me and talk to me when freed by you...
Naciketa asks that upon his return from Death,
his father will recognize who he really is,
welcome and love him, be in union with him.
In the calmness of mind and freedom from anxiety,
ego will not be blinded by anger and fear
and will be able to recognize true identity, pure Being.
Freed from the turmoil and distortion caused by modification,
ego will acknowledge Self, be a reflector of Self
and relate harmoniously with the Self you are.
...when freed by you... when I am released by Death,
my ego, fortified by the knowledge I have gained,
will be free of modification, the cause of suffering in falsity.
How can *you* be released from death?
By constantly experiencing Self as eternal Power of Being.

To be healthy and beneficial, live as the Infinite Self you are.

Always remember this fundamental Fact:
in Essence and in Reality you are the Power of Being,
which is infinite and indestructible.
Relieve your Ego of Insecurity Anxiety and Anger
by consciously causing your Mind to acknowledge,
I am eternal interconnected Being,
I Am *That*, That I Am.

Please, says Naciketa, grant me this boon so that my father sees me,
and will not say, This is just a ghost, and run away;
that he forgives me, pardoning the cause of his anger;

that he lives in peace—that my ego is at peace.
Does not your ego often say
Self is just a figment of imagination, just a ghost?

Lord Yama is impressed by Naciketa's first request,
and the sincerity of this young man
who has a deep concern for humanity.
Death replies:

11. Having recognised (you), Auddalaki Aruni will be (possessed of affection) just as he had before. Seeing you freed from the jaws of Death, he will get over his anger and will, with my permission, sleep happily for many a night.

Second translation:

As aforetime will that son of ancient Sages behave towards thee. Having seen thee liberated from the mouth of Death and recognising thee as one sent back by Me he will sleep happily of nights, his turmoil stilled."

Yama refers to the father's lineage of *...ancient Sages...*
and thereby Naciketa's. Even the ancient sages had egos—
the ego as pure indicator of *I Am*.
Yama says, Your father *...having recognised you...*
having recalled your real identity—will love you again.
Naciketa's father—the analog
for the common ego-driven human being—
recognizes Naciketa—the Inner Knower, the voice of Self
that permeates and transcends the layers of personality
and reveals true identity—and relates to him in oneness.
When your ego recognizes you, Self,
ego then *knows*—unites with—real you.

You have to go further than having the I-am knowledge;
you have to assert yourself sufficiently as the real you
so that you permanently live and function
beyond the long-ingrained limited beliefs,
and have ego relate once and for all to the Being you are.

In the awareness of the Eternal Being you are,
freed from the fear of Death, ego will *...get over his anger...*
Divest yourself of anger.
Anger keeps you in turmoil and does not allow you to rest,
be it day or night.
Recognize Eternal Self.
Then ego will *...with my permission, sleep happily*
for many a night...

Who gives your ego permission to rest happily? Yama does.
Does this mean when you are dead? No.
Death will give your ego permission to sleep happily
while you are alive, once ego recognizes Self,
and you live as the all-pervasive eternal Power of Being
that you really are.
Free from the fear of Death,
ego overcomes its anxiety and anger, and is calm.
You need not wait until you are dead to sleep in peace.
Why is that such an important point?
Most people, while they feel the urgings
that pull them toward Self throughout their lives,
passively remain in an attitude of waiting until they die.
Many religions are based upon this.

Such Beliefs can be dangerous:
Live a Life of Self-denial Deprivation Anxiety and Anger—Hell—
so you can appreciate Peace in Heaven afterward.
That is how they make Suicide Bombers
and People who conduct lackluster Lives.

Thus by granting this boon,
that his father *recognize* him and live in peace,
Death alleviates Naciketa's first concern:
not his own well-being, but the welfare of his father,
the welfare of the ego, the welfare of manifested humanity.

When the Self-realized human—
one who has gone into the rarefied realm of eternal reality
after the death of her relationship to false ego—
returns to the material human realm,
it is of great importance that she be welcomed there.
Otherwise, what can she accomplish
in terms of helping her fellow manifestations?
It is important for them to not fear her,
but recognize and accept her.

It has often occurred throughout history that one who has gone
through the transformation into the realm of reality
is seen as a threat to the false-ego oriented people,
and sharply attacked.
It requires tremendous strength
to overcome their vilification slander and persecution.
Look at the life of Jesus, the lives of many sages and saints,

who had to—and still have to in this day and age—
overcome the backlash of those they lovingly attempt to help.

Way back in history, thousands of years ago, there lived a great sage,
one of the most accomplished of the ancient seers.
He is reflected through the scriptures of many cultures
through the ages, so great was his influence.
He lived in a cave on a mountainside of the Himalayas,
on the banks of the River Ganges.
This cave is considered a sacred site.

I was privileged to be allowed to visit the sage's cave
and stay in a small cave nearby for an extended period of time.
I dwelled there in the beauty of the Ganges,
with its ivory sand and Banyan trees,
the white heat of the sun, and the ice-cold glacial waters.
All I had to do was be in meditation,
be in the bliss of Being, without interruption.
I had nothing to take care of other than to just be
in the continuous experience of Consciousness.

I lived in silence.
My only contacts were with a tribe of monkeys
that came daily to drink from the river,
and the swami and his assistant
who took care of the sage's cave
and shared their meager food with me twice a day.

My time there was liberating.
I had had such a hard responsible life.
When I was a child I helped keep our family alive.
Along with my older brother,
I started working when I was six years old.

As an adult I became an architect
and designed high-rise buildings in New York City
and other parts of the world,
an enormous responsibility,
as the consequences of the slightest error can be catastrophic.

Here at the cave, all I did was meditate, and for that I was valued more
than if I had created a huge corporation employing thousands.
The tribal people who lived in the surrounding mountains
did not interrupt my silence, out of respect.
In that part of the world they know
that the greatest contribution you can make in life
is to bring the positive force of focused Self-experience,
meditation, into our environment.
It was clear to me that I was now fulfilled,
I had nothing more to do—
dwelling in the deep joy of Self-realization is it.
The experience of yourself not only in relationship with all,
but *as* all, is everything.

It occurred to me that I could stay here forever—
this is the real way to be,
and anything else is painful and unnecessary.
But then somehow the thought arose, almost like an intrusion,
that at home and throughout the world
people are suffering abjectly
because they do not know this is the way to be—
to be joyously free, to be empowered, to be truly conscious.
They do not even know it is possible,
let alone how to attain this state.
I can show them how to no longer suffer.

That is what you do as all-pervasive interconnected Self.
Even though you do not *need* to perform actions,
you do help those facets of yourself living in ignorance
to wake up and be real and be fulfilled.
It is inherent to Being to express Self true to Self.

Humanity suffers terribly.
All the poverty, all the wars
are due to ignorance regarding interconnected Being.
It is a fact that throughout the world the rich are getting richer
while the rest have less and less;
this is a very imbalanced unhealthy and corrosive formula
for humanity.

You can help the World to regain Balance.
Through living real Knowledge you may illumine others
and make a profoundly positive Contribution to Humanity.
Let go of Attachment to the limited Ego;
it is not precious, but an Illness and a Burden.
Let go and live who you really are *now*,
not sometime in the vague Future.

Sincerely continuously expertly faithfully—*really*—
assert your Self-knowledge
and live as the all-pervasive eternal Consciousness
That You Are,
and you are freed from Fear Anxiety and Anger
and can sleep happily for many a Night.

Now Yama says, Please proceed and ask me for your second boon
so that I may quickly grant it to you.
Yama wants to rid himself of his obligations right away;
he does not hesitate, he does not procrastinate.
Death keeps redressing the balance; he is the great equalizer.

Chapter Five

Qualifying For Immortality

See to it that everything about you is deeply relaxed
and effortlessly balanced in your center,
sincerely and continuously attentive to the real Being you are,
with expertise and faith.
Instill this state so that it will be your way of life.
Nurture its continuation
so that you thereby profoundly enhance each moment.

12. In heaven there is no fear—you are not there, (and) nobody is struck with fear because of old age. Having transcended both hunger and thirst and crossed over sorrow, one rejoices in the heavenly world.

Naciketa has a clear purpose for informing Yama of his knowledge:
to earn the revelations of higher wisdom.
He knows Death, in his ultimate wisdom,
will only offer him that for which he is qualified.
Naciketa is determined to prove himself ready.

He says *...In heaven there is no fear...* because you, Death,
are not there.
When you are not afraid of Death,
you are also not afraid of old age.
In their youth, people live as if they were immortal;
when they are old, they think about Death coming for them
and increasingly fear Death.
After Death has claimed them, they no longer fear Death.

Yama is eternal, ever functioning, infinitely patient and impartial.
He will, in time, collect your body.
Learn to love Death.
He liberates you from the limitations of the material realm
and moves you on to greater heights;
he is your instrument of evolution.
Yama is your ultimate Teacher.

This I learned through my childhood experience of meeting Death:

Oh Death,
beloved Purifier,
You cleared the Field with your Fire
to make room for my Birth
into Illumination.
For this I thank you.

Oh sweet Teacher,
you came to me,
a Child of six,
and helped me gather my Forces
and my Attention
unto my Life.
For this I thank you.

You taught me,
oh Death,
to restrain myself from Behaviors and Actions
contrary to myself,
and focus upon my Growth toward Fulfillment.
For this I thank you.

Throughout my Life
You have not let me forget you.
You have been my constant Companion,
my Guide,
who quietly and calmly
nudges me toward ever-greater Heights and Depths
of being in Touch with the Fullness,
the Essence,
the Source of me,
of you
and of all.
For this I thank you.

Oh my sweet Love,
throughout my Life

you have given me Meaning.
You have called me to see beyond my imagined Limits
and gain the Fullness of Life,
oh Death.
For this I thank you.

In your Constancy
you have been my most reliable and loyal Companion.
For this I thank you.

You have held before me, oh Death,
the greatest of all Boons,
that has given my Life Direction and Beauty:
the Boon of merging in Divine Consciousness
to live eternally in the Light
of unending Joy
and the Experience of limitless Union.
For this I thank you.

You oh Death my Love
are the living Promise of my Delivery
to infinite Freedom
and abiding Bliss.
For this I thank you.

Naciketa tells Death what he knows about attaining heaven:

...Having transcended both hunger and thirst...
Gathering imbibing and expelling food and drink
are among our most basic functions.
When allowed to absorb your attention,
these activities keep your experience bound to the grossest,

the material realm.
You are not free then for Self-experience in your eternalness.

The physical state is not your essence, not your identity;
it is a relatively momentary condition.
Thus it is not the reality of you,
but the cause of a disturbing sense of limitedness and lack.
In the death of your attachment to unreality,
you are in equanimity,
you transcend conditions and circumstances
such as hunger and thirst,
and are free to be in the joy innate to self-sufficient Being.

> Transcendence is the required Condition
> for you to be free from the Effects of this material Realm,
> from Circumstances and Conditions,
> the Instruments of your Bondage.
> When you identify as your Body,
> you regard yourself as extremely limited
> and are bound by the physical Realm.
> This Attachment to the Material at the Expense of real Being
> you need to transcend.

...and crossed over sorrow...
You transcend sorrow
only when you have eliminated its root cause—
not circumstances and conditions,
not having or not-having,

but false conception regarding your identity.
You might wonder,
Does a Self-realized Being still feel sorrow?
She may *feel* sorrow, such as in empathy, but not *be* in sorrow.

Normally your feelings and actions
are responses conditioned by ignorance and illusion.
Contrary to the experience of real Self, they harm you.
When you overcome your conditioned responses
and do not regard reality as other than what It is,
you are free to dwell in the realm of the heavens,
the realm in which you gain immortality.
In Self-realization, as in death, you are freed from sorrow.

Now Naciketa asks for the second boon:

13. O Death, such as you are, you know that Fire which leads to heaven. Of that you tell me who am full of faith. The dwellers of heaven get immortality. This I ask for through the second boon.

To further qualify himself for Yama's secret teachings,
Naciketa says to him, I am *...full of faith...*
I am ready to receive your instructions *without doubt.*
Naciketa knows that faith, trust in Self, is fundamental,
the necessary condition
for the aspirant to learn from the Teacher.
Not blind faith, but faith founded upon experience
by which you gain and live knowledge of who you really are,
thus intelligent knowing participatory faith, real faith.

Faith is Trust in the Reality of Being.

Only living *...full of faith...*
is Naciketa ready to receive his great Teacher's instructions.
He will receive the teachings fully—
not picking and choosing what seems convenient or palatable,
not somewhat attentive, half asleep, or in partial response,
but *fully*.
Ask yourself, What has been *my* usual response
to my Teacher's teachings, to Self's urgings?
How many times have you thought,
I am not worthy of living the highest teachings?
That is not trust in the Being you are.
Self is absolutely worthy.

Tell me, he says to Yama, about *...that Fire which leads to heaven...*
What are the disciplines, the acts I need to engage in
to attain the heavenly realm?
Only those who live in heaven achieve immortality,
and immortality is what everyone wants.

The Quest for Immortality is a driving Force in Humanity.
Immortality is innate to Being.

This is what Naciketa's father was aiming for with his sacrifice,
which is accepted practice in exoteric religions.

Exo is from ancient Greek for *outer*.
The exoteric is the popular, the commonplace.
Exoteric religious practices focus on external expressions,
such as rituals, like the father's sacrifice.
The exoteric is not necessarily superficial or bad,
but exoteric religions create difficulties when they
exhort their followers to adhere to their way
to the exclusion of all else:
If you do not follow this, you will go to hell.

Opposite of the exoteric is the internalized approach to reality,
where you observe and respond to inner, subtler,
therefore more secret, experiences—thus called *mystical*—
in your drive toward the realization of Infinite Consciousness.
Naciketa is the representative of the *esoteric*,
the subtle experiential way,
whereas his father is an example of the exoteric.

In exoteric religion, the focus is on the afterlife:
the hope is that in the hereafter
the individual's soul will unite with the Infinite.
The Infinite is seen as *exo*, *outside* the individual.
In the internalized approach, the focus is on
attaining the experience of union *in this life*
with the services of all the fine faculties
with which the human being is endowed.
The Infinite is not considered as other, but inherent to you.
The union is not seen as *created*, but *realized*,
because it already exists, always has and always shall.

Waiting to unite with the Infinite in the Hereafter is a false Hope.
Focusing your Faculties on the Union
between individual Soul and All-inclusive Self
in this Lifetime
asserts your Ability to respond to the Call of Conscious Being
by the Power of your divine Free Will,
and to realize yourself as integral to the Infinite One.

The *...Fire which leads to heaven...* is the fire of transformation
by which the ego transcends its modified state.
It is the sacrifice that burns all attachment to past conditioning
and returns ego to its original purity.
It is the fire of purifying knowledge
that the ancient sages considered the greatest secret,
to be given only to well-prepared initiates,
for it is so powerful
that those who do not respond with proper conduct—
pure determination to live accordingly from that moment on—
can be severely burned.
The fire to heaven raises the individual
from *personal* consciousness to *All-embracing Consciousness*.

Those who receive higher knowledge
and violate their relationship to it
by continuing to conduct their lives
as if they had never learned anything,
will experience severe detrimental effects.
Beware. You are through this process
exposed to the knowledge by which you can attain

the heaven of immortality.
If you do not live true to what you know,
it will strike you like a bolt of lightning
and sear your innermost heart.

> You who truly seek the Heaven of Immortality in this Lifetime
> must invite the Cooperation of Death, you must die while alive:
> die to Falsity,
> die to the limited Perception of yourself as an isolated Personality,
> die to your Attachment to Behaviors conditioned in Ignorance,
> and live in the fiery Knowledge of Truth.

Yama now answers Naciketa's request
for the boon of teaching him about this fire:

14. O Naciketa, being well aware of the Fire that is conducive to heaven, I shall tell you of it. That very thing you understand, with attention, from my words. That Fire which is the means for the attainment of heaven and which is the support of the world, know it to be established in the intellect (of the enlightened ones).

Second translation:

Knowing that Heavenly Fire, I explain it to thee. Do thou therefore, O Nachiketas, understand it well of me. Know that that Fire, the means of the attainment of unending being, the Support or Basis of all the worlds is hidden in the Cave of the heart.

Yama first acknowledges Naciketa's awareness
and the young man's readiness
to receive Death's further teachings.
But he alerts Naciketa that he will only understand
with his full attention, not with mind in distraction.
You can only hope to absorb these teachings
by *experiencing* them fully right here and now,
and impressing them permanently.
The ancients did not have recordings
or books to which students could refer;
you got it the first time, or not at all.

That is the way you must respond
to the word of an enlightened Teacher,
or you risk being severely burned from lack of self-respect.
Naciketa responds to Yama's teaching
with immediacy expertise and integrity.
I do not think Naciketa plans to be a permanent guest
in the house of Death.

Yama will teach Naciketa
about the fire that conducts you to the heaven of immortality.
He describes it as *...the support of the world...*
Support is the underlying—that which stands under,
the substance—not the appearance, the superficial.
The substance out of which the world is created
is reality, Being.
What brings you to the heavens and leads to immortality
is the knowledge of the truth, of what is.

The knowledge of reality is a fire
that burns up the dross of ignorance falsity and illusion,

and the attendant misery and pain.
It consumes all attachment to the fruits of the ego realm.
That is what Naciketa's father's sacrifice was meant to do,
but instead it was a sham to gain benefits for ego.

The inner Fire of Reality
burns out Falsity and leaves Purity.
To realize your true Identity, to realize Self,
you must throw into this sacrificial Fire
all Attachment and Involvement with the illusory Ego Perception
and the Tradition and personal History thereof.

This fire of purity and light
is *...established in the intellect (of the enlightened ones)...*
It is permanent in the *purified* intellect of illumined beings,
abiding in their core, their center,
named by the ancients *...the Cave of the heart...*
The pure intellect does not function in service to ego;
it does not distract from reality or rationalize.
Intellect in service to Self is not in the head,
but *illumines* your core, the cave of the heart.
The means to the attainment of *...heaven...*
the realm of immortality,
know you, it resides in the intellect of men and women,
in the cave of the heart of beings of real knowledge,
realized beings.
Open your heart to the fire of Self-knowledge.

Here again this dialogue with Death
spoke to me with such familiarity.
My early experience of meeting Death
had me intuitively go to the cave of my heart
to cope with the enormous moment;
thus it has been my point of focus since.

Established in the Intellect of enlightened Beings is *Tapas*,
the Purity of being honest, being real,
always, in all Actions, all Moments.
To attain Immortality,
live purely as who you essentially and really are.

With the fire of the inner discipline of purity
you are not attached to anything
that distracts from what is, what you are
and what you are meant to experience.
Distraction takes you away
from the experience of the *allness* of Being.
Freed by the fire of purity, you are qualified to attain
the heavens that provide immortality.

On your path you can gain much knowledge of Self.
You can learn how to live in accord with that knowledge
from deep experience of the positive and the negative,
and from great teachings and techniques.
However, there is one final task
to which the real Teacher will persistently guide you:

Bring all your Knowledge and your pure luminous Intellect
into the Cave of your Heart,
and make one final absolute real Decision
to give your Loyalty, all the Energy of your Faculties,
and all your Love and Devotion,
to the Reality of Self
and not to the Falsity of Ego.

For this Determination to be real
it has to be made with utter Finality Sincerity and Permanency,
free of any and all Backsliding,
and with absolute Trust in the Being that you are.

Make your determination with such integrity
that you will always and forever live true to it.
This is a most important point in relation to all the teachings.
To make your liberation come true,
you must take this practical fundamental step.
The knowledge you gain means nothing
without the determination to be true to yourself.
Only you can make real your learning, by living it.

When, in the core of your heart,
you make the determination of permanent loyalty to Self,
you will be purified as by Yama's fire.
You will be freed from the dross that has cluttered
distorted blocked and distracted your life force
under the dictatorship of false identity.

Responding from the Cave of your Heart
with the fiery Determination to live in the Truth of Being
henceforth and without Variation,
you reach a Zenith in Life:
all your Questions are answered,
the Complications disappear,
and the Path to Success is decided.
You have the guiding Light and the Touchstone
for all your Decisions,
all your Actions and Behaviors,
all your Moments.

Once you have made the decision to live true to Self,
and fulfilled it,
you are in the realm of the real, you are Self-realizing.

15. Death told him of the Fire that is the source of the world, the class and number of bricks, as also the manner of arranging for the fire. And he (Naciketa), too, repeated verbatim, with understanding, all these as they were spoken. Then Death, being satisfied with this, said again:

Second translation:

Then He told him of that Fire which is the creative power that builds the worlds, with what kind of bricks its altar is to be made, both how many and how they are to be arranged. And Nachiketas repeated whatever was told him by Death, so that the latter, satisfied with the pupil, spoke again.

Yama gives Naciketa specific instructions
on how to establish the fire of pure reality within himself.
He tells him in detail how to create this fire
and how to relate to it.
Naciketa repeats the instructions perfectly,
in complete understanding, missing not one detail.

True aspirants value the teachings, and themselves, so clearly
that they retain the specifics as well as the wholeness
of their learning experience.
These ancient teachings were passed on
by word of mouth directly from master to disciple.
It was important to assimilate the knowledge in purity,
and hand it on to the next generation without distortion.
This teaching is not to be treated like a telephone game,
where you whisper a message to someone,
who whispers it in a slightly different manner to another,
and the message is passed on this way
until it reaches the last person as something entirely different.

Have the teachings of reality in your heart.
Learning is not merely being able to recite something,
but experiencing and impressing it so deeply
that you live it and benefit others, as did the ancient sages.
Their teachings are presented in a concise manner
to inspire you to *experience* truth through your own process,
your own investigation, your own living.
Keep the teachings pure, know their real meaning
and live them clearly from your heart.

Misrepresentation of the teachings of reality
can not be tolerated on the spiritual path.
This knowledge is so powerful

that if not related to truthfully, without distortion,
it can be of great harm instead of profound help.
To have some truth mixed in with lies
so they seem less dishonest
is more harmful than just plain falsity.

> An Element of Truth combined with Falsity
> causes more Damage than an outright Lie;
> it gives Credence to the Deceit.

Now Yama describes the fire to the heavens as
...the source of the world...
This fire is the beginning of creation, the first vibration,
the first expression of the *...creative power...*
by which the all-pervasive underlying power of all that *is*
reveals Itself, the cosmic energy in its purest form.

Death instructs how to be in direct relationship with the fire of reality,
to work with it consciously.
...the class and number of bricks...
concerns the elements for building this fire within yourself.
...the manner of arranging for the fire...
refers to upholding this fire of knowledge as an eternal flame.

Knowing who you are and having your faculties relate to you
in terms of your true identity, faithfully and continuously,
is the first of the fundamental components.
Next is the determination to live congruent to yourself
sincerely continuously and expertly, without backsliding,
and with trust in the Power of Being that you are.

The final step is to *follow through.*
Most people are good at making determinations
but not at fulfilling them.
They may even make them with full inspiration
and intent to keep them, and all too often fail.
What is required to fulfill your determinations?
Integrity self-trust loyalty focus continuity love: living it.

Integrity: Establish yourself unconditionally in the state in which
you unhesitatingly and always put into action
what you determine.
Do not procrastinate, do not complicate.

Self-trust: Once you know your real identity,
you can have full confidence in the power and reliability
of Self.
Respect Self's abilities.

Loyalty: In the awareness of your true identity
and in the knowledge of the wholeness of the real you,
keep your mind feelings emotions intellect and intuition
deeply in oneness with Self.

Focus: Gather all the energies of your faculties
and apply them full force onto what you determine.
Have this be the given course of action
and you will gracefully succeed on the path to fulfillment.

Continuity: No matter what the circumstances or conditions,
keep feeding the fire and do not leave it unattended.
Let this be your constant way of being,
free of the stops and starts
of the unsuccessful and frustrating life.

Love: Relate to yourself in these reliable and respectful ways,
attentive to who you really are,
and be suffused with an all-filling experience
of unconditional agreement with yourself.
That is the seed of love.

> Unconditional Agreement with yourself
> is the Seed of Love.

Yama, the noble high-spirited Teacher, not being narrow-minded,
is so pleased by the purity of his disciple's understanding
that he spontaneously offers him two extra boons.
Once you ally yourself with reality sincerely and loyally,
more and more boons will come to you.

CHAPTER SIX

Identifying With The Fire

With everything about you relaxed
and gathered in your center, the cave of your heart,
be aware of the Eternal Consciousness that in essence you are,
free of distortion,
and be filled with devotion.

The whole universe is a manifestation of the Power of Being.
Limitless Consciousness in Self-expression
is the essence of all that is.
You Are That.
When you truly live as Limitless Consciousness,
eternal and all-pervasive,
you are forever free of the pain and suffering
attendant to ignorance regarding Being.

Thus freed, you realize your highest potential,
to experience Self in all
and all as the Self that you are.

Because Naciketa has so expertly learned
and sincerely responded to the teachings,
Yama spontaneously gives him additional boons:

16. Feeling delighted, that high-souled one said to him, "Out of favour towards you, I now grant again another boon. This fire will be known by your name indeed. And accept this multiformed necklace as well.

Second translation:

Being pleased, the Mahatma said: here and now I give to thee another boon. In thy own name shall this Fire be known in future. Accept from me also this Garland of many forms.

Naciketa, in the purity of his aspiration,
in his knowledge of and adherence to truth,
is being identified with *...this Fire...*

It is quite an honor that this fire, which is the spirit of the world,
the first expression of the Absolute
in the materialized universe,
shall be named after Naciketa.
Naciketa means 'the unperceived'.
The perceived is the phenomenal.
Phenomena are ephemeral, passing;
they are only manifestations, momentary expressions,
thus *not* reality.
The fire that burns in the cave of the heart,

in the center of Consciousness,
is beyond the perceptive powers of the senses;
nor can it be perceived by the mind; it is transcendent.
Reality—Self—is unperceived;
that is why most people do not believe It exists.

Yama offers Naciketa yet another gift: *...this multiformed necklace...*
What is the meaning of this gift from Death?
What has many forms? The multiple manifestations.
A necklace, or *...Garland...* is made of things strung together.
What momentary manifestations are strung together?
The succession of lifetimes.
Yama is so pleased with his student that he presents Naciketa
with the remembrance of his past lives, his past manifestations.
This only makes sense:
Naciketa has evolved to no longer regard himself
as merely the personal consciousness of the manifestation,
but All-pervasive Consciousness, Continuous Consciousness.
He can now remember what transpired in his past lives
as ordinary persons may remember events of their present life.
This does not mean that all who are Self-realized
remember past lifetimes,
though many will remember knowledge gained in past lives.

> Limitless Consciousness experiences all in the Continuum of Time:
> past Lives merge with the Present, Moment to Moment.
> Just as you can remember what has happened in this Lifetime,
> Consciousness is aware of what happens in all Lifetimes.

Yama's necklace is made of many-colored jewels,
symbolizing the patterns of action, the karma, cause and effect,
leading to each manifestation.
Manifestation and action are synonymous: karma.
Naciketa is offered the knowledge about actions
and their results, throughout the universe.

The *mala* is a representation of this garland.
It consists of 108 beads strung upon a unifying thread.
Malas are utilized by Buddhists, Hindus
and practitioners of various other disciplines.
New monks and initiates are given malas
as a symbol of their union with the Teacher.
The mala is also a reminder of the multifarious mortal desires.
Aspirants hold the mala during *mantra meditation*
in their quest for *enlightenment*.

These are two beautiful awards for Naciketa.
He is identified as the eternal fire of Self-knowledge,
the luminosity of the enlightened soul,
and he is granted the recognition of cause and effect, karma.
By whom? By Death.

> It is only when you die to your Attachment
> to the limited Identity, Ego,
> that you achieve Illumination, All-pervasive Consciousness,
> in which you experience all spontaneously.

These great gifts Naciketa receives
because he is a purely responsive student
who lives and functions true to his purpose.

Now Yama teaches Naciketa about the *...connection with the three...*

17. "One who getting connection with the three, piles up the Naciketa fire thrice, and undertakes three kinds of work, crosses over death. Getting knowledge of that omniscient One who is born of Brahma, and realising Him, he attains this peace fully.

Death says to Naciketa, Once you get *...connection with the three...*
set *...the Naciketa fire thrice...*
and engage in *...three kinds of work...*
you overcome death.

Three is an important number,
a symbol in many cultures and disciplines throughout history.
It is the fundamental point of balance.
A duo does not provide balance.
Three, a tripod, is the beginning of structural balance,
it is the dynamic balance.
Four is the number for completion.

There are three modes of energy vibration: *static*, *dynamic* and *pure*.
In Sanskrit, these three states are called the *gunas*:
tamas, *rajas* and *satva*, respectively.
Everything is in a state of vibration:
in the static state, tamas, there is no movement;
the dynamic, rajas, consists of movement, changes,
creation destruction and preservation;
and transcendent to those two is the pure state, satva—

balance, equanimity, true expression of Being.
When you are in union with the three vibratory modes,
you are in balance.

There are three planes of Consciousness:
material, which is comprised of all the objects of the cosmos,
including earth planets and galaxies;
astral, the principles by which manifestations function
in the cosmos, such as gravity attraction and repulsion;
and *spiritual*, the pure essence, the Power of Being,
beyond and underlying all, transcendent.
When you are in union with the three modes of Consciousness,
you are in balance.

There are three dimensions of time: *past*, *present* and *future*.
You set the *...Naciketa fire thrice...*
unbeginning past, imminent present and eternal unending,
the continuum of time.
When you are in union with the three dimensions of time,
you are in balance.

You undertake *...three kinds of work...*
to accomplish the Naciketa sacrifice,
to burn away all attachment to non-being
and dwell in the continuity of Eternal Consciousness.

...work... is karma, action.
The three Naciketa fires of karma
are the actions that accomplish living in reality:
you first *prepare* the fire—*study*—
then *live with* the fire—*sacrifice*—
and finally, *realize* the fire—*charity*.
These three works give you balanced completion.

Undertaking *study* is to seek real knowledge,
knowledge of the permanent underlying foundation
of all that is, not the momentary show.
Amassing knowledge of the ephemeral
does not yield any real benefit,
only bric-a-brac to store in your mind
and use to play out ego patterns.
Ultimately, the only knowledge relevant to your fulfillment
is of truth, the experience of Being.

> Real Study is to expand your Base of Knowledge of Reality,
> to realize the Omniscient, the All-inclusive One,
> and attain perfect Peace.

Beware: there are many who amass knowledge of reality
and do not gain the benefits; they relate it to ego,
using their knowledge to intellectualize and rationalize.
They turn real knowledge against themselves,
like a snake eating itself from the tail on up.
For real knowledge to benefit your life,
you have to relate it to who you really are,
not to someone you are not.
This is of vital importance
regarding the sacred knowledge you are gaining here.

You attest to your authentic relationship
to real knowledge through *sacrifice*.
This is not the sacrifice made by Naciketa's father,
not burning butter or pouring milk over statues,

but the Naciketa sacrifice,
burning out the false idea of ego as your identity.

Free of ego identification, you are delivered from
the mistaken perception that someone you are not, ego,
performs your actions. Ego is not the doer of action;
the Power of Being is the originator of all action.
Give up the doership of action in the ego sense,
and acknowledge your every action as
expression of self-knowing Being.
It is difficult to be responsible as the ego doer,
because ego is frail and temporary, thus doomed to failure.
It is easy to be responsible
when you relate to yourself as Power of Being
and thus have the limitless ability to respond.

As you perform sacrifice with the Naciketa fire—
and remember, this is not a physical fire,
but the burning light of pure truth—
you give the Creator His due, you detach yourself
from ego ownership of actions and objects,
which you know to be only momentary and illusory.

There is a story in the Old Testament
about God asking Abraham to sacrifice his son.
God, Infinite Consciousness, is meant to be related to
with continuity and loyalty, as the meaning and focus of life.
Abraham's challenge is to be loyal to God's word
and sacrifice his filial attachments, ego attachments to family.
It is a terrifying story.
Perhaps a few words were left out at some point—
a just God would not put you in the position

of holding a knife over your son to kill him.
Even after God stops him and says, You have passed the test,
Abraham must have felt guilty for the rest of his life.
But the story still has merit,
as it illustrates the ultimate test for a parent:
to relate to an offspring not as your separate child,
but as a facet of all-pervasive Power of Being.

Be careful here: ego likes to claim you are acting on God's word.
Many egomaniacs have used such rationalization
to commit mass mayhem and murder, and still do—
look at all the religious zealots who kill in the name of God.
The story of Abraham urges sacrificing attachment to ego
and being in exclusive loyalty to the Being of all,
which includes understanding
that the Power of Being chooses to express Self
through His manifestations.

Sacrifice attachment to anything that is not Essential Being.
You can attest that everything is Being,
but still relate to an activity, person or thing in separateness—
that is the attachment from which you need to free yourself.

Give the Creator His Due,
detach yourself from Ownership.
Do not attach with the Ego to anything.

Sacrifice all that has to do with ego-identification:
ways of thinking and feeling, habits and conditioning,

the actions of your faculties,
the objects you are surrounded by in life,
any sense of ego-ownership or -doership.
Acknowledge that all is but expression
of the creative aspect of Consciousness.
When you do this, you are acting with truth,
you are acting with the Naciketa fire.

> Every Day throughout your Day
> acknowledge all as being of Self,
> and do not allow Ego to take Credit.

Freely and willingly sacrifice your attachment to illusion,
to the material realm and all its limitations.
People have such difficulty cutting their attachment
to the familiar momentary and superficial.
Imagine a newborn not having its umbilical cord cut
out of fear for its survival.
What would happen? It would die of poisoning.
You trust that the baby can survive
without being attached to its umbilical cord—
and that is the only way it *can* survive.
Cut the umbilical cord.
All living according to false conception of your identity
throw into the sacrificial fire named after Naciketa.

You who are blessed with the attainment of real knowledge
yet do not dwell in the joy and peace thereof, note this now:
The reason you are not deeply satisfied and fulfilled,
in spite of all your privileged knowledge of reality,
is not that you are unworthy,
and not that you are incapable,
but simply and directly that you have not
sacrificed your attachment to a false idea of your identity.
Now you have this powerful purifying Naciketa fire
into which to throw your attachments.
Sacrifice them into the inner glow,
and the fire becomes most luminous.

Unless you burn the attachments all the way down to the roots,
they will spring up again.
There was once a beautiful gigantic pepper tree
that stood near the gate to the Nataraja Ashram.
Years ago, a great firestorm swept the land
and completely burned the great tree.
You can cut a pepper tree down to the ground,
and within a few weeks it will sprout up again.
This fire burned the tree so thoroughly
that for weeks after, smoke rose from the ground;
the roots were burning all the way through.
There has not been a single sprout of that pepper tree, since.

Your Opportunity, your Mission,
is to burn down through the very Roots all Attachment to Falsity,
and all Behaviors that are Part and Parcel of it:
Ways of thinking feeling and acting,
Ways of emoting,
Ways of tasting seeing and hearing,
Ways of intellectualizing,
Ways of relating to your Intuition,
even Ways of relating to your Body—
in all Ways, and always.

Is it possible to do that permanently?
The ego will let you make some advancement,
because it knows that most likely
you will not go all the way down to the root.
There may be stages of processing,
first pruning and then cutting down;
but unless you burn up the roots
and even the seeds in the field—in the energy field of you—
the false ego will take hold again.

Sacrifice is mistakenly thought of
as giving something of yourself away.
Real sacrifice is respecting the highest in you,
the highest in the universe,
and not giving credence to the lowest, the false.
Your tendencies are often in response to the lowest.
When you have an opportunity
to be in contact with the highest,

seize this opportunity every time.
Is there ever *not* such an opportunity?
Be in relationship with the highest, the true, in you,
which is the highest in the universe, every time, all the time.

The last of the three actions, but certainly not the least important,
is *charity*.
To live in quest of *knowledge* regarding real identity
and *sacrificing* ego are not enough.
Charity is the natural consequence of Self-knowledge
and sacrifice of falsity.
Giving is recognizing and expressing your real identity
in the interconnectedness among us all.
We all share the same source, the same essence.
Thus, we share our talents and abilities,
our gains growth and knowledge.
We share all we have in essence
because of the fact of our underlying union.

There are many cultures in which sharing is the natural way of living.
Most indigenous cultures lived communally
and still do in various parts of the world.
The Yurok Indians of the Pacific Northwest, for example,
teach that being true to yourself
means giving your best to help a person in need;
being true to yourself is a principal Yurok law.
Service, or *karma yoga*, is action in the perception of our unity.
You serve, not to receive thanks or approval,
but for the simple reason that you are interconnected Self.
Some elements of our culture hold the ego principle sacred
and are opposed to the sharing way of life.

This is what is meant by accomplishing the three works
and burning the Naciketa fire *...thrice...*:
gaining knowledge of reality,
sacrificing your attachment to a false identity
and sharing yourself in egoless service.
When you faithfully perform the three works,
you are in balance.

With fiery determination, once and for all and forever
acknowledge your real identity,
burn out all ego behavior patterns,
and purposefully express yourself
in actions that reinforce your interconnectedness in Self,
without backsliding.
It is important to have continuity;
backsliding easily revives
what you have worked so hard to overcome.
Relapsing is severely damaging:
it corrodes your enthusiasm and faith in your upward thrust.

So powerfully and devotedly ally yourself with your real Identity
by melding your Faculties and Behaviors with real Self,
that no Energy is left or ever will be again
for anything else.
Firmly establish the Impression of your true Identity
so that it makes such a deep Groove for your Behaviors,
nothing else can take place.

Like in the Grand Canyon, where the Colorado River
running persistently over hard stone
has carved such deep straight walls
that there is not a chance for the river, no matter how mighty,
to flow anywhere else,
so must you deeply impress your real identity
upon your faculties,
if you want to be safe from the affliction
of ego sprouting up again and again like weeds in a field.

Your loyalty to Self has to be independent of
whether the feelings want to or not,
or what is called for by time circumstances or conditions,
or the people around you.
You have to be independent of your past as well.
Then learning takes hold through your *own experience*,
whether you study with books or with a master.

The result of burning the Naciketa fire thrice
is that you will *...[cross] over death...*
you will be done with the fear of Death ruling your life
as it does for so many.
This freedom from fear came to me when I met Death
as a child, when the bomb hit our home.
I decided to face Death, met him, and was free of fear.

Death does not really have a Sickle to chop you down,
he does not cause you to *not* be;
Death just helps you to be done with this Cycle
and have the Opportunity of another Start.

Overcoming death, you can rejoice in immortality
and be free from ego's tricky snares:
free from greed jealousy rationalization attachment
hypocrisy self-deception and deception of others,
free from constant conflict.

...Getting knowledge of that omniscient One who is born of Brahma...
Who is *...that omniscient One...* and who is *...Brahma...*?
They are facets of the Power of Being.
The Absolute is simply Being,
Absolute Being in the unmoving state—
Consciousness just is—in Sanskrit called *Brahman.*
From the Absolute comes a pure potential state,
the Unmanifest, the creative force or the Creator,
in Sanskrit called *Brahma* or *Hiranyagarbha.*
From Its unmanifest state
Being expresses Self through creation
as the infinite interconnected One, the Universal,
the *...omniscient One...* the All-knowing One,
which in Sanskrit is *Mahat.*
You will learn more about these facets as we progress.

Realizing *...that omniscient One...* born of the creative force
one *...attains this peace fully...*
You attain the peace for which manifestations yearn—
heavenly peace,
the cessation of lack need anxiety fear and depression—
by realizing Self as the interconnected One.
In this peace you experience the calm joy
of the harmonious confluence of Being.
What a beautiful statement *...he attains this peace fully...*

Sincerely continuously without Backsliding and expertly,
with utter Faithfulness and with everything that you have,
proactively cause your Mind to think of you
only in terms of the one limitless all-pervasive Being that you are,
and your Feelings will reflect
the resulting Ease Confidence and Balance,
you will be flooded with Joy, with Bliss,
and all your Behaviors and Actions will express only that.

Then, and only then, will you live in the purity of the Naciketa fire,
the fire of true Self.

18. "One who performs the Naciketa sacrifice thrice after having known these three (factors), and he who having known thus, accomplishes the Naciketa sacrifice, casts off the snares of Death even earlier and crossing over sorrow rejoices in heaven.

Second translation:

The wise man who having kindled the triple Naciketas Fire and known this Triad, builds up that Fire in meditation, he having already (that is, while still living) destroyed the bonds of death, gone beyond sorrow, enjoys the bliss of the Heaven World.

In meditation you dwell sincerely and free of distraction
in the experience of Conscious Being.
Thus you build up the Naciketa fire.
One *...accomplishes the Naciketa sacrifice...*

by not merely *knowing* the secret teachings of the sacred fire,
but actually *implementing* them.
Implement the teachings of reality in your *whole* life,
not just as a ritual now and then,
not just for meditations, no matter how many or how long.
Live the truth of Self
that you experience in real meditation.

As you implement the knowledge of your real identity,
you *...[cast]off the snares of Death even earlier...*
meaning, in this lifetime, you rejoice in heavenly experience.
What are the *...snares of Death...*?
All the ego tricks that make Death so fearful,
that have you perceive yourself as condemned to annihilation.
Instead of fearing Death,
you can have a wonderful relationship with him,
as has Naciketa, and as have I in my life—
as I can, anyone can.

...and crossing over sorrow [one] rejoices in heaven...
This is a beautiful phrase.
Give up your habitual attachment
to your precious suffering and sorrow.
Can one actually be attached to sorrow and suffering?
Yes, it is the big melodrama cultivated in many a life.
Often spiritual aspirants look like they are
slumping through hell, not rejoicing in heaven.

> Many claim that the Path of Reality is fraught with Difficulty;
> quite to the Contrary, it is filled with Grace and Joy.
> The Difficulty lies not in Allegiance to Reality
> but in Attachment to Behaviors in Falsity.

Symptoms of this chronic attachment may be familiar to you.
When you learn about reality and naturally feel uplifted,
but then resort to behaviors that dampen the vibrant energy—
smoking, or drinking and eating too much,
or even eating unhealthy food,
or cultivating conflict instead of love—
what does this accomplish?
It dulls your experience and diminishes your learning.
As you repeat the harmful behaviors,
you extinguish the positive energy;
instead of blossoming in Self-knowledge, you wither.

Do not fall for ego's predictable tricks:
have some success and then lessen it right away,
or even worse, go in the opposite direction and create disaster.
You deserve success, and to keep advancing.
Ego will act as if your success were a fluke
and pull you back into unworthiness.
Inherent to the ego state is a timidity,
an attitude that safety lies in the habitual misery
because it is familiar.

Do not punish yourself if you fall into ego snares.
Instead, assess the situation dispassionately,
and draw from that the energy of loyalty trust empowerment

and enthusiasm:
I can learn from this.
I see now that I fell into the false patterns again,
so I will counteract my mistake
by applying more intelligent consistent positive force.
I am not here to just meander from crisis to crisis.
I will dedicate my energy to enacting and living my life
empowered by the Naciketa fire.

Make real your relationship to what you are learning,
to what you know from your own experience.
It is not sufficient just to say,
Yes, I understand, I know this to be true.
If you want the ultimate, you need to go further:
immediately implement what you learn.
Go with what helped you gain clarity, and add to it.
You do not advance to the next step
by disregarding what you have learned:

> Implement your learning Experiences.

The four major elements of success on the spiritual path—
or with anything—are
sincerity expertise faith and continuity, without backsliding.
Remember, continuity is vitally important;
without it ego will play you like a fish on a hook,
letting you make some progress in reality
and reeling you back in to falsity.

While it is counterproductive for you to struggle with ego,
you want to be clear that you are the one in control.
The reason people have so much difficulty
and feel they have to fight false ego, and for so long,
year in and year out,
is that ego has picked up the message that *it* can choose.
It has not received the message that *you* are in charge,
you choose your actions and behaviors.
If you leave the door open even just a little,
ego will sneak in and take over like poisonous fumes.

When your life is not led by loyalty and devotion to Self,
it is extremely restricted by your dysfunctions:
you do not have the relationships you want,
you can not go where you want or do what you want.

> When you devotedly conduct your Life loyal to who you really are,
> Immortality will be yours, now—
> not sometime in the Future.

And thus it is, says Yama to his worthy disciple, Naciketa.
Through the triple combination of study sacrifice and charity,
in the meditation in action,
one attains the state of *...the Heaven World...*
One who has real Self-knowledge
and lives it with determination
...accomplishes the Naciketa sacrifice...
and rejoices in the immortal world, even in this lifetime.

Now there is one more boon to gain;
otherwise the story would end here.

19. "O Naciketa, this is for you the boon about the Fire that leads to heaven, for which you prayed through the second boon. People will speak of this Fire as yours indeed. O Naciketa, ask for the third boon."

Yama affirms that he has granted Naciketa his second boon,
knowledge of *...the Fire that leads to heaven...*
and the honor he has conferred upon Naciketa
by naming the fire after him.
He says, And now you may ask for the third boon.
Please get on with it, otherwise I am still indebted to you.
I want to complete this,
and attend to the many other tasks that await me.

You might wonder what more could be asked for.
Naciketa has already received
some of the highest possible boons:
He has forged peace between ego and Self
with his father's acceptance,
as well as his elders' and society's.
He has succeeded in his duties as son and disciple,
as a seeker of true knowledge—a significant accomplishment.
He has gained the honor
of having the great sacrificial fire named after him,
and been gifted remembrance of his past lives,
knowledge of karma.
And finally, he has received freedom from fear of Death
while still in this life,
the assurance of immortality,
of overcoming ignorance and illusion

and dwelling in the heavens of reality.
Is there anything else to ask for?

Learn to ask for the ultimate, for it is said,
Ask and you shall receive.
What is the *ultimate* to gain?
Throughout life the opportunity is presented
to ask for the ultimate boon,
yet most people waste their opportunities
by craving the lower.
They seek momentary titillation of the senses
or perhaps removal of the irritation caused by old habits.

Naciketa does not cease his quest.
There is still something missing in his life,
thus his pursuit of a third boon.

CHAPTER SEVEN

Death Tests Your Readiness For The Ultimate

Bring all your faculties together in your center
and have them be attentive to the experience of real Self.
Burn the Naciketa fire sincerely with continuity and expertise
and trust in the Power of Being that you are.
Dwell in equanimity, in peace and the deep subtle joy of Self,
who expresses through all manifestations.
Be aware of Being that you are—
from moment to moment, free of distraction.
Keep your focus alive as you continue,

remaining determined to live true to the teachings
that you experience.

Now Naciketa requests from Death the final boon:

20. This doubt that arises, consequent on the death of a man—some saying, "It exists", and others saying, "It does not exist"—I would know this, under your instruction. Of all the boons, this one is the third boon.

Second translation:

There is this doubt about a man who has gone Beyond, some saying that he exists, others that he exists no more. This I desire to know as thy disciple (literally, being taught by thee). This the third of my boons.

Most people wonder,
After death do I still exist in some form?
Do I leave the body and go on to other realms?
Some say there is an entity
distinct from body senses mind and intellect,
who is connected with the body before birth,
separated after death,
and connected with another body in a next life
to go on through evolution.
One might think from the evidence of the many
who walk mindlessly through life
that death means the end of being.

It is said the Buddha refused to answer that question.
Because, he explained—and this is not a direct quote—
whether I said yes or no,
either answer would give rise to false interpretations.

So forget it, I do not know.
Remember, these are secret teachings.

When I was about to meet death as a child during the war,
I prepared myself with sheer determination and focus
to be conscious of whatever came after death.
When death arrived with the bomb striking our home,
I was inundated by the experience
of continuous conscious Being.
I did not say it that way to myself,
I could not put it into words as I can now,
but there was the utterly clear experience of me continuing
after the body was destroyed.
I knew what it is like to *be* forever.

Naciketa, through his disciplines
and the boons already granted him by Yama,
has attained immortality;
he is free from ignorance, the seed of mundane existence,
of living on the material level as an ego entity,
isolated limited and in fear and need.
However, in spite of all you know and gain,
you may still *experience* yourself as a separate individual,
not as the All-pervasive One.
Self, pure energy, pure spirit,
is the one Being that *all* is, and *you* are.
When you superimpose separateness or agency,
you are in disequilibrium;
there is no contentment, something is wrong.
You could go on through eternity in the knowledge of Being
and still feel beset by a sense of lack.

For his final boon, Naciketa seeks to realize the knowledge
of Transcendent Self, the illumined state.
This is what is missing in Naciketa's life.
That subtle knowledge you can *not* acquire
through mental perception, nor by inference through the senses,
and yet the supreme goal is dependent upon it.
Since you, O Yama, are the greatest Guide, Naciketa says,
I want to know this finally *...under your instruction...*

> Infinite Being expresses Self in innumerable Ways
> while remaining the totally united independent One.
> Realizing this, you gain absolute and final Liberation,
> the Emancipation for which your entire Life strives,
> for which all Evolution strives.
> Without Self-realization there can not be real Satisfaction,
> even if the Heavens of Immortality are attained.

Death hesitates, and says:

21. With regard to this, even the gods entertained doubts in days of yore; for being subtle, this substance (the Self) is not easily comprehended. O Naciketa, ask for some other boon; do not press me; give up this (boon) that is demanded of me.

Naciketa has asked Death how to gain the ultimate:
identification with Infinite Being through his direct experience.
Living in the fiery knowledge of Eternal Consciousness
is the consummation of all.

To realize the Knowledge of Self is the highest Boon.
Self-realization is the ultimate Consummation:
uniting with All-pervasive Reality.

The Lord of Death tests Naciketa's resolve:

Even the gods have doubts about Self;
It is too subtle to be known *...not easily comprehended...*
Buddhists claim It is beyond description, calling It 'the Void'.
In many of their teachings the yogic seers do not even name It, calling It 'That'.
Yama says, Please do not ask for this.
Ask for any other boon; I will give you anything else.

What Naciketa seeks to realize in the third boon

is so subtle that our senses can not perceive It,
mind can not comprehend It,
none of our faculties can grasp It.
Naciketa wants to know the most subtle. Why?
I will give you a clue:
What is more pervasive, the subtle or the gross?
The subtle is more pervasive.
Pervasiveness is the ability to penetrate,
which is also the ability to merge with, to be one with.
By wanting to *know* the most subtle,
Naciketa is asking to be one with that which permeates all.

What is most subtle and pervasive?

Yama refers to It as *...this substance (the Self)...*
Usually substance is thought of as something material.

Here the concept of substance is much more profound:
substance is what 'stands under'.
The ultimate support of all that *is*, is the Power of Being.
Being, that which is most subtle and most pervasive,
is the substance of all, the Self of all, pure Consciousness.
And at the same time Being—absolutely independent—
is not *contained* in any.

Having heard Yama's entreaty, Naciketa replies:

22. Even the gods entertained doubt with regard to this thing; and O Death, since you too say that It is not well comprehended and since any other instructor like you, of this thing, is not to be had, (therefore) there is no other boon comparable to this one.

Naciketa says that if even the gods are uncertain about *...this thing...*
it must be very high knowledge.
Even you, Yama, the most knowledgeable of all,
say It is not easily comprehended.
And since there is no teacher more qualified than you,
I require your teaching.
...there is no other boon comparable to this one...
Thus I insist you grant me this as the third boon
you have promised.
There is no higher goal for me.

Naciketa is not cowed by the fact that something is difficult;
he appreciates it as a test.
How many times have you wanted the Teacher to say—
or life to proclaim—This is too difficult,
you do not have to do it?
The ego often argues, This is too hard, I refuse to do it,

I will just suffer misery, it is too difficult to be joyous.
You may not wish to be treated as so incapable.

Naciketa does not accept difficulty as a deterrent:
Because it is so difficult I have to pursue it—
with your guidance.
Even when this great authority tries to discourage him,
he is not swayed from his purpose.
Naciketa will not be intimidated by Death.
He recognizes his right to know
and will let nothing hold him back.
He is practical and Self-empowered:
I will not take 'no' for an answer.

Naciketa regards Yama as the most knowing Teacher.
What better Teacher is there throughout life?
If it were not for Death, what impetus would you have
to get yourself together and move ahead?
Death is a great boon, your great Teacher.
Naciketa willingly accepts Death as his Teacher;
he deeply appreciates and esteems him,
and he is willing to qualify for his entire teaching.

> Once you have a Teacher
> by whom you have gained Experience of your essential Identity,
> do not let go.

The boon asked for by Naciketa is important to Death,
he is very protective of it.
Since this is the highest attainment, and difficult to achieve,

Yama will only give it to those who are absolutely ready.
He does not want to throw precious seeds of knowledge
onto fallow ground to be trampled into oblivion
through disregard disrespect neglect forgetfulness
or living the opposite.
Acutely aware of the great power of this subtle knowledge,
Yama must make sure that Naciketa is worthy and prepared.
He is still testing the young man
after whom he named the fire of truth,
a rigorous qualification indeed.

You may wonder,
Why are you giving this knowledge to me,
how do you know I am ready?

> Knowledge is always available, Reality is always present.
> Living in Accord with what you know to be true
> qualifies you for Knowledge.
> The more true to all Levels of Reality you live,
> the More will be revealed to you.

Be sure to prepare yourself for this advanced knowledge
with complete sincerity and integrity.
Beware of appropriating higher knowledge
and applying it to the lower levels of life.

Yama tests Naciketa's resolve with worldly delights:

23. *Ask for sons and grandsons that will be centenarians. Ask for many animals, elephants and gold, and horses, and*

a vast expanse of the earth. And you yourself live for as many years as you like.

Death is pulling Naciketa's human strings.
He tempts him with sons and grandsons
who live to a ripe old age.
In the culture of that time, to survive infancy was a feat;
to become a centenarian—live a hundred years—was rare.
Death offers: Your lineage will be assured.

Ask for *...elephants and gold, and horses...*
They represent power wealth and warfare,
which the common folk, as well as great leaders, would want.
...and a vast expanse of the earth...
He will be a great king of an enormous realm
with immeasurable wealth in perpetuity,
continuing generation after generation.
...And you yourself live for as many years as you like...
the great temptation, to live a long vibrant life.

But Naciketa persists and lets nothing distract or detain him;
he knows there is only one goal for him.
Naciketa is established in the certainty
that Self-realization is his birthright.
He will not let fancy promises of sensual delight distract him.
He will not waste this most important boon
on momentary thrills.
How secure and Self-empowered he is;
the highest authority can not waylay him.

Death has been regarded through the ages as *the* authority figure.
Generation after generation, the fears and sins
of the forefathers are visited upon their descendants,

making it possible for Death to tempt people
with the supposed comforts
of a long life, social position and material wealth.
Subject to social conditioning
and habituated to the input of the senses,
most regard physical well-being as their highest priority.

Afraid of dying, people hold on to the familiar for supposed security,
no matter how fraught with disappointment and suffering.
When they are offered the prospect of eternal Self-realization,
as opposed to remaining attached to the ephemeral
by which they have been repeatedly let down,
some individuals respond with, I have to think about it,
I have to process this. Come back to me in ten years, Yama.
Let me enjoy worldly goods and conditions for a while.
Maybe in the last moment of my life
I will aim for Consciousness.
That is not how it works, though: you drive away from the ball
with the vehicle that brought you there.

You can learn from the example of the *misguided.*

A Life conducted in Disregard of Consciousness
results in future Lives lacking in Consciousness.
A Life devoted to Consciousness
continues into future Lives in Consciousness
until Self-realization is gained.
Cause and Effect.

What would *you* choose if you were Naciketa?

Be realistic; look at your daily life:
Right now I can not be focused in Consciousness,
I have a telephone call to make.
I can not be real, I prefer to be in sloth for a while.
Do you really prefer the misery of nescience, not-knowingness, over being in the illumined state?

Naciketa's attitude is,

Look Death, do not try to tempt me.
I only want the highest: the realization of Self.

Yama thinks this over—and Yama is quite wily.

He says:

24. If you think some other boon to be equal to this, ask for that. Ask for wealth and long life. You become (a ruler) over a vast region. I make you fit for the enjoyment of (all) delectable things.

Death says, Look Naciketa, this last boon you request is too much.

I can not do that for you; you are not ready for it.
If you can think of anything else
that you want equally as much, ask for it—
I will give you anything of this world.
I will even keep your senses and faculties intact,
totally unimpaired, to enjoy your dominions
long into the future;
you need not worry about the ravages of age.
You will rule without strife and be a legend for ages to come.

Since many trade illumination for misery,

Yama's deal is quite appealing:
he offers all these great riches, and the ability to enjoy them—

what more could you want?
I will give you whatever could be of possible earthly attraction.
Truly, I can do all this for you,
because I am the deity who never fails.
Death is completely dependable.

Now Yama ups the ante:

25. *Whatever things there be that are desirable but difficult to get—pray for all those cherished things according to your choice. Here are these women with chariots and musical instruments—such are not surely to be had by mortals. With these, who are offered by me, you get yourself served. O Naciketa, do not inquire about death.*

Second translation:

Whatever desires are difficult of attainment in this mortal world; ask for all desires at thy will. See these desirable maidens seated on chariots and with instruments of music—their like cannot be had by man—by them, as my gift, be waited on and served; O Nachiketas, do not ask about (the Great) Dying.

By way of temptation, Death gives Naciketa
visions of the most beautiful celestial nymphs
such as no man has ever known.
Driving their chariots with wild abandon,
while playing lovely string instruments
and chanting seductive songs,
they offer themselves to Naciketa,
who in his great kingdom can zestfully enjoy all pleasures
even when he is over a hundred years old.

Yama is urging Naciketa to desist his quest:

I can give you all things divine as well as human,
everything that is *...desirable but difficult to get—*
pray for all those cherished things...
and you will have them at your disposal,
for I have the power to totally implement my will.
Asking to know about life after death is useless.

...O Nachiketas, do not ask about (the Great) Dying...

Naciketa is not just asking about death of the body and mind,
but what is there after the false ego identity
is thrown into the sacrificial Naciketa fire.
He is unruffled by Yama's temptations and subterfuges.
Certain of the necessity of understanding what is *...Beyond...*
he persists:

26. O Death, ephemeral are these, and they waste away the vigour of all the senses that a man has. All life, without exception, is short indeed. Let the vehicles be yours alone; let the dances and songs be yours.

The things that you offer me, Death, they do not last,

they are not worth it,
they would just waste my attention.
...All life, without exception...
no matter for how long you promise it,
...is short indeed... on the scale of eternity.
Keep the nymphs and elephants and lands for yourself
...let the dances and songs be yours...
They are impermanent, therefore not real. I do not want them.
They will all vanish; they belong to you, Death.

27. *Man is not to be satisfied with wealth. Now that we have met you, we shall get wealth. We shall live as long as you will rule it. But the boon that is worth praying for by me is that alone.*

What wealth do I need, Death, but the boons I gain from you?
I am not satisfied with earthly wealth, it is not a boon.
I am content to live as long as you say
...as long as you will rule it...
The boon I pray for is the realization of Self.

28. *Having reached the proximity of the undecaying immortals, what decaying mortal who dwells on this lower region, the earth, but knows of higher goals, will take delight in a long life while conscious of the worthlessness of music, disport, and the joy thereof?*

Having reached the realm *...of the undecaying immortals...*
and knowing now of the infinity of Being,
how could this temporary mortal state on earth be satisfying?
What enjoyment is there in this realm of death and decay
with its distractions and enmeshment in falsity?
What delight could I take in a prolonged attachment to illusion
...while conscious of the worthlessness... of the passing music
name and fame, the short moments of happiness?

> We have an inherent Drive to go higher
> until the Ultimate is reached.

29. *O Death, tell us of that thing about which people entertain doubt in the context of the next world and whose knowledge leads to a great result. Apart from this boon, which relates to the inscrutable thing, Naciketa does not pray for any other.*

Second translation:

> *Tell me, O Death, of that Great Passing On, concerning which people have such doubts. That which is wrapped in such great mystery (literally, that has entered into secrecy), that and no other boon shall Naciketas ask.*

Naciketa appeals to Death again: Tell me now, please,
that which I really want to know,
for I am one of faith and I *shall* know.
What is different from all things mortal, or immortal,
so subtle, and difficult to understand and attain?

Naciketa is making it clear that this is his ultimate aspiration.
He wants to be free of encumbrances,
of the binding attachment to passing phenomena,
and give all his attention and energy, his full worth,
to the one thing that counts: the realization of Essential Being,
the full experience of oneness with the infinite source.

The Ultimate in human Endeavor
is Evolution toward the Realization of Perfection,
the Realization of Being in Consciousness,
being Consciousness,
relating in Union with the Infinite recognized as Self.

Naciketa is in harmony with the people
with whom he has been involved in this life cycle,
his family and society. He is at peace.
He has immortality, freedom from fear and need.
But he knows that the highest attainment lies in this final boon:
total clear continuous *realization* of Self,
the Essence that we are.
Nothing will sidetrack him from his quest;
nothing will tempt or dissuade him; nothing else will satisfy.
That is the determination and purity of the Naciketa fire,
that is the pure determination you must muster
to be Self-realized.

There is nothing more to be gained in all existence
once you have the boon of Self-realization.
It is the goal of life, and it is the purpose of evolution,
for the manifestations to realize themselves
to be All-pervasive Self.
That is the reason for your being, that and nothing else.
You want to live Self fully, without distortion,
and spontaneously, as well as continuously.
Remember, Self-realization is gaining what you are,
in conscious experience.
When you are Self-realized,
you can say with full understanding:
I am eternal all-pervasive Power of Being,
and I express the Limitless Essence that I am.
I Am That, That I Am.

Naciketa, possessed of Self-knowledge through living with Death,
acts accordingly, and has thus progressed toward the ultimate.
He is filled with beautiful attributes
and has become praiseworthy.

Do not create Difficulty for yourself
by gaining Knowledge of Reality
then regressing to Ways of thinking and acting dictated by Ego.
Through the sincere and immediate Enactment
of what you know to be true,
thereby alone do you achieve Peace
and the Cessation of Suffering.

That is the way it is.

Here is how I, as a child, qualified myself for the ultimate
(from *Self-Healing Through The Awareness Of Being*):

After I had met Death during that direct bomb hit of my home,
I had to know why I was still alive.
My life became purposefully absorbed in such questions as,
What is my life for?
Why did I not die like so many I have seen killed
in this slaughter?

These were not questions of intellectual curiosity,
but of survival.
In order to healthily and meaningfully survive
the mayhem and murder I had witnessed,
I had to know *who and why I was.*
That was my quest…

However, I knew not how to know.

In attempting to derive the knowledge by means of mind
I found mind to be lacking in focus—
my mind would jump to irrelevant details

as I was attempting to focus it on the question of my identity
and my reason for being...

So I developed practices to keep my mind on task.
My concentration practices ranged from
simply focusing on things in nature,
to the more complex,
like attempting to absorb the nature and essence of a saint
as I looked upon his wooden likeness,
or stimulating within myself
the experience contained in each and every word
of a prayer or poem...

My practice was not play; it was hard work.
I saw no other choice. I had to know why I am.
Since my mind did not automatically cooperate,
I had to train it, to learn to strengthen and direct it.
The more I practiced, the easier it became
to keep mind steadily focused.

This practice was something that I engaged in over a period of years.
Although I did not practice in a systematic way,
I practiced frequently.

After I had been doing the focusing exercises
for about a year and a half, at age seven,
I had a real breakthrough,
an experience of brilliant clarity.
One night, just before going to sleep,
there came to me a moment of profound serenity
in which I had a luminous experience of Being:
simple direct all-embracing Being.

A gentle flood of peace flowed through me.
Deep tranquility washed away
my inner response to the turmoil and destruction of the past.
I was aware of myself in the pure experience of Being.
It was wholly clear to me:
I am Being; this is what I really am.

The moment was at once radiantly clear and utterly simple.
It had not announced itself with fanfares
or with fancy miracles.
The moment was sufficient unto itself,
because in it I experienced myself to be.

I was at peace with the spontaneous state of being,
and I was at peace with myself.
There was no doubt, no fear;
there was no anguish and no need.

The moment did not yield to intellectual explanation
nor idle curiosity.
The moment just was.
I just was.

It was what I called my This-Is-It experience,
direct and beyond the linear quality of thoughts and words.
I was fully focused
in the expansive and clear experience of Being.

There was the immediate knowing:
This is what I am. This is why I am. This Is It!
Being, complete and beyond words—
no matter how many words are said about it,
they still can not explain Being.

I was aware that I simply was.
This is the reason for being in this life:
to experience and express Being
That I Am.

The moment continued with luminous realization.
It was as bright as the moment when I had met Death
during the bombardment.
The experience was much gentler, though,
the light not harsh.
I was deeply in touch with myself
and blissfully content in a quiet, calm way.
Right there and then I knew
that this was what life was really about.

The moment eventually yielded to more ordinary ones.
The experience, however, remained with me
as a wonderfully nurturing and enriching gift.

After this luminous experience my life was transformed.
The experience of Being
provided me with the reason for being in this life...

Naturally, I felt inspired to give myself
more of the wonderfully luminous experience...
By now, keeping mind in sustained focus on a series of ideas
and expanding my experience in the process
was not hard work, but an exercise I relished.
I enjoyed being able to direct my mind
into ever more encompassing experiences.

Thus the experience of myself in the state of tranquil luminosity
repeated itself.

I had learned in the first experience of undistorted Being
that this clear and direct way of being
was the answer to my question, Why am I alive?
I had discovered not only the purpose *of my life,*
but also that the fulfillment of that purpose
is the meaning *of life...*

The experience of Luminous Being
inspired me to continue with renewed ardor
in training my mind and living in focused awareness.
I did not realize it at the time,
but the hard work I had invested in disciplining my mind
had paid off in a way I had not at all anticipated.

As a boy I did not know that mind alone
could not give me the answer to my urgent question,
Why am I alive?
However, through my intense attempts
to force mind to give me the answer,
my mind became focused enough to let go and transcend itself.
Thereby it allowed something greater in me
to provide the luminous experience
that not only gave *the answer,*
but is *the answer I had so devotedly been searching for...*

Impress what you have learned so far in this dialogue with Death
so that you have a firm base of understanding
for the experiences to come.
Let it empower you for the rest of your life.
That is your task now, if you so choose.

Have your faculties dwell in your center sincerely and expertly
with continuity and faith,

and relate to your knowledge of the Being you are, really—
loyally wholly and lastingly, with certainty.
So deeply impress your Self-knowledge upon every faculty,
that you will never forget it.
Expect your faculties, led by the mind, to be
proactive empowered perceptive balanced incisive and flexible.
Do not allow dullness to overcome mind, nor distraction;
have it remain in an effortlessly balanced state.
If you leave this state of Consciousness, you will be met again
by closets full of litter from the past.
Let it be your mission to be uncluttered
and in a pure relationship with reality.

Let everything about you remain in your center, attentive to Self.
When your faculties devotedly attend to Self,
when they treat Self with honor and respect, in sweet discourse,
they gain the highest reward: union with the Limitless One,
Eternal Consciousness, who is all-pervasive.
Relax and trust in the eternal continuity of reality
and its all-pervasiveness.
Self is who you really are.

Be content to be in pure relationship with reality.
Let this relationship empower you.
By living reality that you know,
you loosen your enmeshment with modes of being
that bind you to misery and pain.
Remain focused in the knowledge that you have with certainty,
which, when lived, frees you from bondage.
Integrate this knowledge so that you ensure
you will live in the continuity of Consciousness
and non-forgetfulness of Being.

You are Being.
Being is.
Being is to be experienced as Being is.
Being is indivisible and indestructible.
You are to experience yourself
as indivisible indestructible Powcr of Being,
all-pervasive and eternal.
You Are That.
Experience that in Reality—in Wholeness and Continuity—
and you are fulfilled.

Part I Canto II

Gaining The Ultimate Boon

Chapter Eight

Choosing The Preferable Over The Pleasurable

Thoroughly relax your faculties
and bring them together in your center
in a state of effortless balance, harmony and continuity.

Cause your breath to flow in easy rhythm.

Sincerely have all your faculties in true relationship with Self.
Divest yourself of any vestiges of false ego attachment.

Simply and humbly be attentive to Being
with an attitude of unconditional acceptance,
love and peace.

Make the strong determination to be focused and continuous
in the wonderful experiences that Yama is offering
to help you respond to the invitation to fulfill your evolution.

1. The preferable is different indeed; and so, indeed, is the pleasurable different. These two, serving divergent purposes, (as they do), bind men. Good befalls him who accepts the preferable among these two. He who selects the pleasurable falls from the true end.

To achieve his final boon, Naciketa has to be free of attachment
to factors that would bind him to a lesser state.

We have the right of freedom.
In life, our faculties are constantly called to respond
by many forces.
We are called to respond to the objects of the senses,
what we see touch hear smell and taste;

we are called to respond by our ambitions and drives,
inspirations and aspirations, desires and aversions;
we are called to respond by our society,
its laws and edicts, unwritten as well as written,
its beliefs knowledge and illusions;
we are called to respond by the patterns of the past,
our good habits and bad,
and our fears of the future and the present;
we are called to respond to the divergent energies
of our faculties,
body senses mind feelings emotions intellect and intuition.
All these forces combine in competing
for our response, throughout life.

There is one more force who urges our faculties to respond:
the Inner Knower, who is of Self.

Keep in mind, in the all-pervasive Power of Being
there is no inner or outer.
For convenience here, we denote Self's knowing as 'inner',
and the pull of the myriad distractions as 'outer'.

> The outer Pull involves you with Ego—
> relating to Objects and Entities with a sense of 'other'—
> thus results in Isolation.

From the illusory perception of yourself as separate,
you relate to the cosmos as many distinct parts.
Enmeshed with attraction and repulsion,
your mind's attention is habitually pulled

from one object or event to the next.
You even identify *yourself* as an object
and experience yourself as isolated from the vast cosmos,
in spite of the innate knowledge
that it is one interconnected wholeness.
You feel unique in your isolation—
the whole cosmos is interconnected except for little me—
which causes you to be filled with intense existential fear.

People attempt to free themselves from fear
by amassing as many parts of the universe as possible,
hence the pervasive object fascination and entrapment,
and the consequent neediness.
The result of amassing things—you hope—is pleasure,
the cessation of the fear and irritation of your isolated state.
However, contrary to this hope,
you only gain disappointment and more anxiety.

> The Quest for Pleasure is based upon the Illusion of Separateness
> and is an Attempt to reconnect yourself with the Whole
> through its Parts.

In this object mentality, people relate to things in illusory ways,
as if they were permanent and separate.
Objects and events are only momentary eddies
in the continuous stream of energy;
they are like waves in the ocean, not discrete entities.
Thus the pleasure you seek through the pursuit of the outer
is fleeting, not real.

Temporary Pleasure is a Contradiction in Terms:
you know you will lose it,
thus the Pleasure is not *really* pleasurable.
Pursuit of the Pleasurable is frustrating and disappointing.

The person living in illusion pursues *...the pleasurable...*
in spite of consistent and predictable disappointment.
The person of real knowledge, however,
prefers what is fulfilling *...the preferable...*
that which is in accord with reality.
Both the pleasurable and the preferable *...bind men...*

This is due to the immutable law of cause and effect—karma:
all actions cause re-actions of their kind.

When you engage in behaviors
dedicated to the pursuit of pleasure,
you suffer disappointment,
because pleasure is temporary and illusory.
Responding to the latent power of impressions,
you will repeat those behaviors,
thereby causing an ever-increasing tendency
toward further dysfunction
and a life of failure and suffering.

You have been misled by a society that is almost uniformly dedicated
to the pursuit of so-called pleasure.
You have been brought up to follow its social precepts
of 'ought-tos' or 'ought-not-tos',
'thou-shalts' and 'thou-shalt-nots', rights and wrongs.

There is heavy social and peer pressure to follow these edicts
as if they were the laws of nature,
or—even more detrimental—ethical and spiritual laws.
That leads not to discernment, but blind following.

This is not to say you should not have or obey laws;
the caution is to relate to laws
with conscious and responsible understanding,
not blind obedience.
Some societal and religious elements
would consider this attitude heretical.
However, as St. Paul wrote in his Letter to the Corinthians,
By the law alone shall you not attain the kingdom of heaven.

A responsible relationship to the law requires discrimination.
You have to exercise your ability to discern
the true and the false, the real and the illusory.
And please do not ask whose reality we mean, mine or yours.
There is only one reality, the one that *is*;
all else is interpretation at best,
opinions likes dislikes prejudices and manipulations at worst.

Discrimination involves responsibility.
If the law includes, for example, killing to steal land,
you have to set yourself above it.
However, making your own choices is not a license
for behaviors contrary to our ultimate well-being.
You have the responsibility not to fall
for the tricks and snares of ego
and become a law unto yourself, a self-righteous vigilante.
It is important to exercise your ability to respond to reality.

You are not helpless nor need you feel hopeless.
You can discern the Effects in Relation to their Causes:
A Relationship with Reality causes Functionality Liberation and Joy;
with Illusion, Dysfunction Bondage and Frustration.
A Relationship with Virtue causes Harmony;
with Vice, Disruption and Disintegration.
A Relationship with the Lasting causes Fulfillment;
with the Temporary, Disappointment.

The preferable and pleasurable serve *...divergent purposes...*
The preferable reveals the way to Self-realization—
it is the positive;
the pleasurable conceals or obstructs it—
it is the negative.
These paths are 180 degrees opposite each other.
If you try to do both, you will fail.
When you sit on the fence,
you eventually fall into the realm of the negative.
You can not serve two masters.

The pleasurable and the preferable
...serving divergent purposes, (as they do), bind men...
The pleasurable binds you to the meandering path
of hope frustration disillusion and dysfunction,
and thus depression and anger.
Many are so attached that, rather than face the difficulty
of overcoming their bondage to the pleasurable,
they settle for the difficulty of living in hell.

The pleasurable binds you with great force
to profound difficulty and suffering.

The preferable also binds you, but to the path of Consciousness.
This is an even firmer union,
your faculties in union with Self, in yoga.
Yoga means yoked—faculties to Self, Self to all.

The ability to discriminate is good, but not enough.
Many have gained the knowledge by which to discriminate
between reality and illusion
yet throughout their lives continue to suffer.
They continue with the negative patterns of the past
as if the knowledge available through repeated experience
made no difference.
They do not learn from their learning experiences.

> Knowledge and Discrimination are not enough.
> When you have had learning Experiences
> yet still suffer as if you had not,
> you are not implementing what you learned,
> you are continuing to act in Response to the Pleasurable
> instead of the Preferable.

As an intelligent discriminating responsible individual,
you can *choose* the preferable
over the illusory pleasurable and its misery.

Sincerely and continuously
with Loyalty Expertise and unswerving Trust in Self,
and with the full Force of your Will,
direct your Faculties to live in Accord with who you really are,
Limitless Being.
This is what you *really* prefer; it fulfills you.

The enactment of the preferred is utterly necessary for Self-realization.
Live in accord with your knowledge of reality
lest you treat it as fantasy, or outright deny it.
Having knowledge of reality and not living it
is even more detrimental than living in ignorance.

You always make a Choice
but the Choice is not in Words,
it is not even in Determinations,
it is in your Actions.

They say Knowledge liberates,
and they are wrong;
only living it, enacting it, liberates.

...Good befalls him who accepts the preferable among these two...
Choosing and enacting the preferable, you gain the good.
You are in harmony with who you really are,
in harmony with all,

and therefore dwell in the luminous experience
of unitive limitless Being, in lasting bliss.

...He who selects the pleasurable falls from the true end...

The person attached to illusory behaviors
is enmeshed in a downward spiral of negativity
and *...falls from the true end...*

What is your true end?

We are all engaged in evolution.
The thrust of evolution is to develop to more advanced states
until the ultimate is attained:
manifestations achieving Infinite Consciousness,
experiencing and expressing as the unitive whole.
Your evolution is complete
when you experience and express yourself
as the all-embracing Power of Being—
not just now and then when you think about it,
not just when you sit in meditation,
but continuously, permanently.

2. *The preferable and the pleasurable approach mankind. The man of intelligence, having considered them, separates the two. The intelligent one selects the electable in preference to the delectable; the non-intelligent one selects the delectable for the sake of growth and protection (of the body etc.).*

Second translation:

The better and the more pleasant both approach man. Having examined them from all sides, the wise man discriminates between them. He chooses the better rather than the more pleasant, while the foolish, through desire to have and hold (objects of desire), chooses the more pleasant.

...*The preferable and the pleasurable*... the good and the pleasant always present themselves as choices.
Many individuals perceive no difference between the two, in spite of the fact that they are diametrically opposed causes that have profoundly differing effects:

> The Preferable, or the Electable,
> leads to Satisfaction and Joy, the Realm of lasting Fulfillment.
> The Pleasant, or the Delectable,
> leads to Suffering in the Non-experience of Being.

While most people relate to the preferable and the pleasurable as if they were the same, individuals of *real* intelligence treat them as different.
They regard the morass of stimuli calling for their response, with discrimination.

> The really intelligent Person separates
> the Permanent from the Momentary,
> the Revealing from the Concealing,
> the Beneficial from the Harmful.

Really intelligent individuals expertly direct their actions
in accord with what they have learned.
They not only differentiate
between the preferable and the pleasurable,
but choose the preferable consistently.

When you identify with the material world, you favor ego
and select *...the delectable for the sake of growth*
and protection (of the body etc.)...
This is not saying you should not take care of your body
or that you should shun all pleasure,
but rather that you should not focus on the body or on pleasure
to the forgetfulness of Self.
In Self-awareness you are in harmony with what is,
in distraction you are in *dis*harmony with what is—
the merely pleasant or delectable is only an appearance,
a fantasy image of ego based upon false conception.

...non-intelligent... persons act as if they did not perceive
a difference between reality and illusion.
Focused exclusively on the physical and material,
they habitually gravitate to the pleasure principle
in deciding what to do, no matter how often disappointed.
They may even recognize the painful effects
caused by acting in pursuit of momentary pleasure,
but nevertheless repeat this behavior over and over,
as if the predictable suffering would not persist.
The deepest form of ignorance
is repeating actions predictably harmful and hurtful to yourself
when you know better.

That which momentarily titillates the senses *...the delectable...*
tends to bind you with its seduction,
enmeshing you in irritating urges
to attain more of what has you suffer.
You do not have to be controlled by those false seductions.
You can objectively look at your life and see that
...the delectable... delivers suffering,
...the electable... fulfillment,
and *elect* intelligent choices in response to your learning.
The electable is the preferable;
it unites you with deep satisfaction and lasting joy,
as well as nurturing and effective functioning.

You can also make the choice of *...the electable...*
in response to the knowledge that you are not the body.
As Self, you *elect* what really serves you:
to live true to the all-pervasive eternal Being you are.
Apply your intelligence as free and knowledgeable
Power of Being.
Consciously select those options that are in accord with Self.

Throughout the day, focus on the real Being you are, Infinite Being.
This is not a mere philosophical or spiritual notion;
something in you knows this is true:
you are Being, and Being is limitless.
Many try to relegate the responsibility for their behaviors
to a god figure.
It is dangerous to relinquish your life decisions
to what you regard as an outside authority.
Relate to the real you, the Divinity that you, Self, are.
Remember, the Divinity does not reside in you—
or outside you—You *Are* That, just like the wave is the ocean.

The intelligent Person responds to her learning Experiences
and thereby guides her Path of Progress
toward her Goal of final Fulfillment
with Dedication Devotion Continuity Expertise and Faith.

3. *O Naciketa! you, such as you are, have discarded, after consideration, all the desirable things that are themselves delightful or are the producers of delight. You have not accepted this path of wealth in which many a man comes to grief.*

Yama acknowledges Naciketa's intelligence and integrity.
He informs his prized pupil of what has saved him:
his sincere relationship to what he knows.
Yama is the Inner Knower speaking,
Self acknowledging Self.

What saves you from repeatedly falling into
downward-spiraling cycles?
Consider what is really good for you
as opposed to what is merely pleasant,
choose to invest in the long term, the Eternal Self,
give yourself the ultimate joy,
do not shortchange yourself with cheap momentary thrills.

Naciketa has concluded that
only what is in harmony with Essential Being
is good, is electable, is the ultimately desirable.
He has not tied himself to the delectable that so many desire.
He wants to keep his energies free for the fulfilling,
not occupied with the disappointing.

Yama says the *...path of wealth...*
is where *...many a man comes to grief...*
This is not to say you should not take care of
your material or physical needs;
they have to be taken care of to facilitate the spiritual path.
However, to pursue wealth for its own sake is to court failure;
it results in poverty, internal poverty.

In our culture we are conditioned to hold the pursuit of wealth
as noble and commendable,
and to look down on those who want something different
as dreamers or even fools.
But the pursuit of the lowest level of manifestation
at the rejection of all the other levels,
at the expense of being conscious in reality—
the real identity, oneness—is the ultimate foolishness.

> Those who follow the Path of Wealth
> at the Expense of being consciously in Reality
> suffer Failure.
> They run away from their own Light
> and mistake the ensuing Shadow for their Identity.
> Their Lot is Grief.

Chapter Nine

The Divergent Consequences Of Knowledge And Ignorance

Consciously place your body
into the deepest attainable state of relaxation,
while causing the breath to flow in effortless rhythm.
See to it that the entire body remains fully relaxed.

Pull all your faculties into your center, your very core,
the cave of the heart.
Let them remain there feeling at home
in a state of effortless balance and absolute equality
as they turn their full attention toward the Self that you are.

As your faculties are gently and persistently focused,
they experience you, the Being that you are;
they experience Consciousness.
Consciousness is the constant and most subtle
experience of Being.
It persists on every level.
Every level of your faculties can experience Consciousness.
Consciousness is eternal and all-pervasive.
Have your faculties continuously experience you
as Unlimited Consciousness.

4. That which is known as knowledge and that which is known as ignorance are widely contradictory, and they follow divergent courses. I consider Naciketa to be an aspirant for knowledge, (because) the enjoyable things, multifarious though they be, did not tempt you.

Real knowledge is not of mere things of the world—
the lower level, the material—
but of the cosmos and our place and meaning in it, and beyond.
Knowledge concerns our relationship to reality, to what is.

How do *you* relate to reality?

You can relate to the holism of the cosmos and yourself.
In holism you perceive and relate to the universe
with the recognition
that the whole is greater than the sum of its parts.
Another characteristic of holism is that every facet
contains all the information of the whole.
Our DNA serves as an analogy:
in each one of our tiny cells is the information—DNA—
to construct our entire body.

Thus you can relate to reality in interconnectedness,
experiencing yourself congruent with the overall harmony.
Such a relationship to reality is of real knowledge.

Or you can relate to reality
in terms of a mistakenly perceived fragmentation
that yields the experience of isolation and conflict.
Such a relationship to reality is of ignorance.

Here is an example of knowledge versus ignorance:
In ignorance you see a rock as separate and solid,
contained within its perimeter, and even permanent.
Knowledge has you regard the rock as a phenomenon
caused by a momentary vibratory constellation of energy.
Remember, three vibratory modes of energy make up
all *forms* of Being: static dynamic and balanced.
Energy vibrating in a certain combination of these modes
causes a particular event that is called rock.
With knowledge you perceive the rock
as neither solid nor separate nor permanent,
but as integral to the limitless ocean of energy:
an eddy of particles dancing in space, coming and going,
forming the momentary appearance of a rock.

The ignorant consider their body,
and by extension themselves since they identify with the body,
as solid and separate and relatively permanent.
In knowledge you regard the body as a momentary event
caused by the oscillations of atoms,
the basic building blocks of nature, which are but energy
in various combinations of the vibratory modes.

In ignorance you see yourself as separate from the whole.
This causes a mistaken perception of fragmentation,
from which emerges the false perception of isolation,
which gives rise to fear and need,
which in turn lead to desire and aversion,
competition conflict anxiety and depression,
all of which results in widespread dysfunction throughout life.
Of course the more dysfunctional an individual becomes,
the more difficulty does he have conceiving of himself
as the holism of Being.
Thus ignorance is the root cause of human suffering.

Only when a life in ignorance
is replaced by a life in accord with knowledge,
do you see yourself as the unified whole.
Then you experience yourself as interconnected
and are free of the vicious cycles of suffering.

The Ignorant see only Diversity;
the Knowledgeable see the Unity
that is the underlying Reality of all.

As knowledge and ignorance are diametrically opposite
...they follow divergent courses...
We can discern the difference between the two causes
by their effects:
the course of knowledge is toward the permanent—fulfillment;
the course of ignorance is toward the momentary—discontent.
When you acknowledge cause and effect,

you receive feedback quickly;
the more attuned to karma, the more immediate the feedback.

The life of ignorance is one of failure on every level,
from the grossest material to the subtlest spiritual.
That is highly divergent from the path of an Expert In Life[2],
who is devoted to living in accord with knowledge,
who *regards* herself as nothing less
than the unified limitless whole, the One,
and *expresses* himself as nothing less.
The *...aspirant for knowledge...*
does not perpetrate dysfunction and failure.

The course of ignorance and the course of knowledge being opposite,
you can not live true to some of each.
Yama, the Master Teacher, drives home this lesson again:
You can not serve two masters.
You can not sit on the fence
when it comes to living in reality or illusion,
knowledge or ignorance, Self or ego.
You can not be loyal to both.

> Knowledge and Ignorance are mutually exclusive,
> like Light and Dark.
> The Life of Knowledge is diametrically opposite
> to the Life of Ignorance.

[2] Reference to the Expert In Life™ Program, which is an experiential learning course created by the author.

Many choose to continue in behavior patterns based upon ignorance,
while, at the same time, they want to respond to Self's urgings
toward relief of suffering, and liberation in Self-realization.
Such dual loyalty is the offspring of self-delusion
and is not achievable in reality.
Those who attempt it are lying to themselves
about their continued attachment to the unreal, the false.
Their deception does not affect reality in any way,
but injures the individual gravely.

> Your Life is dedicated either to Reality or Falsity.
> When it comes to living in Accord with Reality
> does the Matter of Degree really matter?

I once visited an old picturesque part of India
where there is a beautiful tranquil lake
that nourishes the small villages scattered around it.
Every day the women come to the lake
to bathe themselves and the children and do their laundry.
Now imagine if one village became angry at another
and poisoned their water. What would happen?
The toxins would soon spread poisoning the whole lake;
the angry village would kill everyone,
including their own people.
Similarly, if you live contrary to your knowledge
perpetrating such behaviors as competition anger or hatred,
you poison the life of everyone around you,
and also your own.

> Since Ignorance and Knowledge are opposite of each other,
> you can not do some of each and hope to succeed in Life.

Yama gives a clear description of the real spiritual aspirant:

...I consider Naciketa to be an aspirant for knowledge,
(because) the enjoyable things, multifarious though they be,
did not tempt you...
The aspirant must not leave the door open
for the tendencies toward the momentary,
as they distract from the course of emancipation.
The temptations are multifarious; they come in many guises:
shifting moods, impressions and resistances,
pressures of what the family demands or society proselytizes.
No matter what the distraction, the real aspirant is not tempted.
Is it possible to be so empowered?
Yes, but it requires self-respect self-appreciation
and Self-honoring.
Maturity also helps, but I have known eight- and ten-year-olds
who already had the maturity to proceed so independently,
and seventy-year-olds who did not.

Think for a moment, what are *your* temptations?

What do you choose, the pleasurable or the preferable?
What do you live *with* by habit
rather than consciously elect to live *by*?
As a real aspirant, see to it that you never fall for
the temptations that seem so pleasant and are so destructive.
Direct your energy in self-determination—commit yourself.

> When you become aware of dysfunctional Patterns of Life,
> instead of placing your Focus and Power into stopping them—
> a negative Approach—
> dedicate your Energy and Consciousness
> to initiating purposeful positive Behaviors
> that are opposite to the negative ones.
> This is the 180-Degree Rule.

To implement the 180-Degree Rule, start by sincerely asking yourself,
Who owns this life, I or my old patterns?
Ego does not want you to oppose its urgings,
so you have to stand on the battle line
and commit as to whose life this really is.
When you decide *you* are the director
and willing to be responsible,
act 180 degrees opposite of the temptations.

Yama repeatedly poses the challenge: Where is your loyalty?
Which are you choosing, not by your words,
but by your actions?
An aspirant for knowledge does not vacillate,
does not get distracted over and over again, disloyal to Self.
Knowledge is not just being able to recite all the right words.
As you perceive your unity with the holism of the cosmos,
you act free of fear or anxiety,
unobstructed by depression slovenliness forgetfulness
and unconsciousness.

Determine that you will relate to yourself with such loving and valuing
as to give yourself the very best

and not sell yourself short for that which is only momentary
and guaranteed to disappoint.
You deserve to realize the fullness of the Power of Being.
Face yourself and say, I am not to be distrusted,
I am not innately limited or incapable.
I am Self—I have strength integrity and intelligence.
I deserve to be treated by my mind and all my faculties
with respect trust and love.

With the foundation of being true to yourself,
whatever you do, whatever decisions you make in life,
will be successful and fulfilling in reality, thus permanently.

5. *Living in the midst of ignorance and considering themselves intelligent and enlightened, the senseless people go round and round, following crooked courses, just like the blind led by the blind.*

Second translation:

Revolving in the midst of Ignorance, wise in their own conceit,
considering themselves learned, wandering hither and thither,
the fools go round and round like blind men led by the blind.

This describes the opposite of the aspirant for knowledge:
the ignorant *...the senseless...*

Symptomatic of the Ignorant
is the blithe Conviction that they are not ignorant.
They even believe they are better off
than those who have real Knowledge—
Conceit goes Hand in Hand with Ignorance.

The deluded regard their ignorance as knowledge.
Can anyone really be so innately and hopelessly
out of touch with what is,
or is there an Inner Knower who knows better?
We *know* that there is an Inner Knower.
Thus *...the senseless...* who act in denial of reality
but consider themselves intelligent and even enlightened,
are lying to themselves, they are denying their Inner Knower.

> When you deny the Inner Knower
> you are lying to yourself and the World.

The Inner Knower is a facet of Self.
It is the pure power by which you know the unity of all—
know with certainty, not guess or believe.
It is so pure and continuous that there is no separation
between the knower and the known;
the Knower knows He is also the object of knowledge,
that which is known.

> With the Inner Knower,
> the Knower the Knowing and the Known
> are One.

When you respond to the Inner Knower
and act according to its message, you succeed.

As the principal power by which you are able to lead your life
true to the Being you really are,
the Inner Knower is utterly reliable
and will never lead you astray,
will never take you away from fulfillment in Self.

> The Inner Knower is utterly reliable.
> It is to your Faculties as the Stars are to the Navigator,
> as the Compass is to the Explorer,
> as the Homing Instinct is to the migratory Bird.
> The Inner Knower is your infallible Direction Device
> through the Shoals and Vicissitudes of Life.

Those who live and act contrary to the Inner Knower
are throwing away any sense of direction
by which they could lead a meaningful life.
The sage Death is unambiguously emphatic about such people,
calling them *...fools...*
They are like people without senses,
unperceiving and insensible on every level.
They live in a thick darkness, entangled by fetters,
stumbling aimlessly.
Lost in life without direction,
they *...go round and round...* in a rut.
The path to Self-realization is not revealed to them.

Such individuals are heavily invested in self-deception,
a product of ego falsity.
Ego prevents them from admitting their lies,

even when they are suffering horrendously.
They know they are out of integrity
even as they attempt to deceive themselves that they are not—
you may obscure or disregard the Inner Knower's message,
but you can never really silence it.
Thus they suffer from shame, which they act out
through self-denying and self-destructive behavior,
which makes them even more shameful: a vicious cycle.

> When you act in Opposition to the Inner Knower,
> you are betraying yourself.
> From this arises Shame
> and the Urge to get even for the Self-betrayal
> by harming yourself and others.
> As the Self-betrayal grows, so does Self-hatred,
> resulting in an increase of Violence.
> The Evidence of the vicious Cycle
> of Self-betrayal Shame Hatred and Destructiveness
> is overwhelming throughout Humanity.
>
> The other Option is Harmony.

There is yet a deeper level of living in the midst of ignorance
while considering oneself intelligent and enlightened:

The subtlest most deep-reaching and destructive Form
of living in the Midst of Ignorance
is having the great Blessing of Teachings of Reality
leading to Knowledge from direct Experience,
and knowing how to live according to that Knowledge,
but choosing to maintain the Life of Ignorance.

Remember, knowledge and ignorance are mutually exclusive.
Having knowledge but living contrary to it
is a life of ignorance—and a form of self-hatred,
of purposefully hurting yourself:
You stupid fool. You have been so ignorant for so long,
you do not *deserve* to live better,
even though you *know* better now.
Like a blind man
who has purposefully gouged out his own eyes,
you knowingly condemn yourself to a life in chains,
filled with emptiness cravings anxiety fear
self-loathing and self-disrespect,
and afflicted by disease, old age and death.

Then you not only blind yourself to truth,
but, by your example, encourage others
in the life of self-deception.
You are responsible not only for your own demise,
but actually fuel the demise of many.
You might think, I can treat myself like a good-for-nothing,
that's just between me and myself.
No, you do great damage to many others

by making false thinking and negative behavior
prevailing influences in humanity.
Through this you accumulate enormous karmic debt.
The realization of Limitless Consciousness,
the realm Naciketa values so much—and claims—
will not be yours.

In such senselessness,
your actions are consistently twisted and complicated.
If the energy and dedication applied to self-opposing actions
were to be turned toward the positive,
you would be in a wonderful state
and enjoy an easy successful life.

6. *The means for the attainment of the other world does not become revealed to the non-discriminating man who blunders, being befooled by the lure of wealth. One that constantly thinks that there is only this world, and none hereafter, comes under my sway again and again.*

It is inherent to human nature to rail against the limitation
caused by the material world,
to rail against the perceived annihilation by death.
It also is inherent to humans to seek the means
to attain immortality, and finally, transcendence.
This is a call in all cultures throughout history.

However, the ignorant are *...befooled by the lure of wealth...*
They are fooled by the profusion of temptations
of the lowest, the material realm,
and cultivate an attachment to their siren song

guaranteed to bring disappointment.
As a result they blunder through life
bereft of their true powers:

> As Human Being we have the Powers of
> *Discernment* to appraise ourselves and our Conduct,
> *Discrimination* to distinguish between the Real and the False,
> the Beneficial and the Harmful,
> and *Choice*, our Prerogative, to give ourselves what we *really* want,
> as well as *Will*, our Birthright, to *enact* our Choices.

The *...non-discriminating...* suffer from desires
because of their false conception of separateness.
When you identify yourself as a body,
you are a fragment in your perception,
isolated needy and endangered,
driven by burning urges that must be fulfilled
for you to survive, to not be annihilated.

Perceiving yourself as finite and doomed to decay,
you only experience the lowest level of existence.
You *...constantly [think] that there is only this world...*
Habituated to your self-imposed limitations—tendencies,
slovenly habits, self-negation and self-destruction—
you reinforce that thinking by acting repeatedly as if it were so.
Your suffering will have at its zenith the fear of Death
constantly terrorizing your life.

Death says that such a one *...comes under my sway again and again...*
You will be living under the influence of Death
from moment to moment.

Chapter Ten

Finding A Real Teacher

You are Consciousness,
who through Self-knowledge
experiences Self as unbeginning.

You are Consciousness,
who through Self-knowledge
experiences Self as imminently present.

You are Consciousness,
who through Self-knowledge
experiences Self as eternal.

You are Consciousness,
who through Self-knowledge
experiences Self as transcendent.

You are self-knowing Consciousness
in the bliss of your own luminosity, *Satchidananda*:
Existence-knowledge-bliss-absolute,
the unitive state.

7. *Of that (Self), which is not available for the mere hearing to many, (and) which many do not understand even while hearing, the expounder is wonderful and the receiver is wonderful, wonderful is he who knows, under the instruction of an adept.*

Most people live in such a morass of ignorance,
the pervasive societal droning of falsity,
that they never learn about their real identity.
They are so tuned in to the discordant noise,
that they do not hear the harmonious symphony
that underlies it.

Appreciate how truly blessed you are to have the unique opportunity
to hear about the Power of Being that you are.
Only a few out of scores of millions achieve this.
The rest of humanity suffers terribly,
because they do not recognize the benefit
of being exposed to the knowledge of Self.

Among the very rare who get to hear about Self,
even rarer are those who understand
and respond by sincerely living in accord with their knowledge.
Those receivers, Yama says, are *...wonderful...*
and *...the expounder is wonderful...*

There is an innate yearning in man for a Teacher, a Guide.
Various cultures throughout history
have made attempts at systems of mentoring;
people constantly search for guidance,
but to find a real Teacher can be difficult.

When you seek a Teacher in Ignorance,
you will find an ignorant Teacher.

False teachers promise to produce—
through sleight of hand, magical words or intense emotions—
that which the aspirant needs to attain
through her or his own workings.
They appeal to ego, leading students to think
they have accomplished real learning and are spiritual adepts,
when they are still attached to their familiar delusions.

Who is the Teacher?
The Representative of Reality,
Eternal Being in the Awareness of his Infinitude
guiding those Aspects of Himself
who are in the Illusion of Separateness
toward the Realization of their Interconnectedness.

Who is the Student?
Eternal Being in the Guise of Separateness
being guided by Infinite Being
into the Experience of Interconnectedness.

How do you know who is a real Teacher?
You allow yourself perception of reality.
The old cliché is that the Teacher appears
when the student is ready.
The Teacher may be right in front of you,
but if you are not conscious, you will not recognize him or her;
if you are not loyal enough to yourself to let go
of attachment to the illusory, with which you are so familiar,
you will reject a real Teacher.

A woman came to me crying out for help:
If only God were to give me a sign,
I would follow His law to the letter every day and night.
I said, I will show you signs:
look at this grass at your feet, and that bird in the sky,
look at that horse, this ant, or a whale, look at you and me,
all are signs from God.
Now that you have seen God's signs,
follow His law to the letter, as you said you would.
That was too simple and obvious for her;
she was looking for miracles.
She would not allow herself to see clear evidence of Him
nor to follow His word or her own.

So it can be with relationship to a Teacher.
People yearn for the Teacher to reveal himself,
yet often when he does, they put him down,
deny him as they have denied themselves.
To recognize a real Teacher you have to have enough sense
to perceive what is real.

A real Teacher teaches from his own experience.
He has *realized* what he teaches;

he does not merely *know* it, he *lives* it.
The Teacher has traveled the path—not just studied maps of it.
He guides the real aspirant by illumining the signposts
that make progress on the path straight-forward and decisive.

The Teacher knows how to share her light;
she communicates knowledge
so the sincere aspirant can experience it within.
The Teacher speaks to your core, the Inner Knower,
and lights the treasure of knowledge,
causing it to vibrate into cognition from a latent state.

> The real Teacher knows the three Worlds:
>
> The World of the Power of Being,
> Infinite Being knowing Self in Interconnectedness.
>
> The World of All-embracing Being's Manifestations
> in their Misperception of Isolation and Separateness.
>
> The World of the Teacher knowing himself
> as Being manifested in His self-knowing Aspect,
> guiding the Aspirant,
> who is Being manifested in His not-knowing Aspect.

In the Teacher the divine light of knowledge shines brightly,
whereas in the aspirant it is hidden under the veil of ego,
the enmeshment with self-negation -doubt and -distrust.
Between ego's self-aggrandizement and self-belittling,
the individual is lost in confusion and indecision.

The Teacher knows the pitfalls, detours, false directions and obstacles
that waylay the person who lacks a Guide.
He is not only helpful, but—
according to the persistent teachings
of illumined masters through the ages—indispensable.
Unattached to the wiles of ego, the Teacher has deep insight
regarding your strengths and aspirations,
tendencies and hindrances.

However, no matter how enlightened a Teacher you may meet in life,
no matter how fully and effectively
you are exposed to knowledge,
you can distort the teachings of reality
by persisting in the limited perception of a separateness
of world, and of Being.

The concept of a Teacher guiding individuals to the realization of Self
is difficult to accept in a society under the sway of ego.
There is fundamental disrespect and distrust
of the individual and his power to make choices,
to choose and determine his own path.
It demeans the human spirit to say aspirants are deluded
or controlled by a real Teacher;
you can not be controlled
unless you create the delusion of an outside authority.
In the ego-oriented society, the Teacher may be negated,
even demonized.

Relationship with a true Teacher threatens ego's false kingdom.
Many will not accept
that without a Teacher they are unable to reach Self-realization.
It is simple cause and effect: the Teacher is the link

to overcoming ego isolation and being in union with reality.
If the aspirant can not be in union with one facet of reality—
the Teacher—he certainly can not do it with the All.

> The Task of the real Teacher
> is to cause the Reverberations of Truth
> to be experienced in your Faculties,
> for Truth is your very Core, your Essence.

When you sincerely realize what is expounded here,
you experience Self clearly and purely.
Honor these teachings;
it harms you and others to deny or abuse them.
The Teacher's guidance aims to free the heart
from the addictive layers of doubt confusion and distraction
so that your knowledge can shine brightly
and illumine your path to Self-realization.
You earn having a relationship with a real Teacher
through long struggles over lifetimes of evolution;
it marks your opportunity for Self-realization in *this* lifetime.

There are some rare individuals who have through previous lives
developed to be close to, or already in, Self-realization,
and they return for another life.
They may not need the direct relationship with a Teacher,
yet out of respect and as an example to others,
seek him out to receive initiation.
But it is rare. Christ perhaps was such a one.

> An Aspirant relates to the Teacher
> in the way she relates to Self.

This Teacher has enjoyed a loving relationship with Yama
since childhood.
I am grateful for the early life experiences
that brought me to him.
Yama has been with me ever since,
and I have conducted my life with deep affection and respect
for my luminous Teacher.
I do not see Death as the grim reaper,
but as the luminous transforming power
in which death of the body is just a momentary event.

8. The Self is not certainly adequately known when spoken of by an inferior person; for It is thought of variously. When taught by one who has become identified with It, there is no further cogitation with regard to It. For It is beyond argumentation, being subtler even than the atomic quantity.

It is not through words alone that I teach;
when you are sincerely focused in the teachings,
you are in an almost palpable vibratory state
of union with the Teacher.

The words of a real Teacher open avenues
for your vibratory systems to unite with the truth of Being,
which is always alive in you.
You may have heard the words before—they are not the point.

You may even think you already know a teaching,
but if you are not living it, you do not truly *know* it.
Each teaching I offer is an opportunity
to experience the truth so deeply
that you live it permanently, really.

Self is not your body; the body is but an ephemeral event
of particles dancing around in space, coming and going.
Most interpret this momentary image falsely
as a solid and relatively permanent object,
and, even more mistakenly, as their identity.
Therefore they suffer from the
fear loss lack anxiety depression and dysfunction
of someone who innately is eternal
and all-pervasively interconnected,
but lives the life of one who is convinced
that he is an isolated material fragment doomed to decay.
This false conviction is the normal way of thinking.

Many a person whose development is *...inferior...*
attempts to explain Self
from the perspective of the isolated individual,
who perhaps has a soul, something idealistic
and separate from themselves.
They regard Self as a glimmer of something
that is even more removed from them than the soul.
They may relate to the source
as the distant one with the white beard.

Self-awareness can be witnessed throughout this world:
the energy underlying everything including you
has the ability to know Self.

What good would all this Being be
without the ability of Self-experience?

> The Power of Self-awareness,
> by which the Energy underlying everything knows Self,
> is Consciousness.
> Being and Consciousness are inseparable, they are One.

Consciousness is the subtlest, most refined energy
...subtler even than the atomic quantity...
It is not only vibratory, but also non-vibratory.
That limitless indivisible indestructible
power of Self-expression and Self-experience
through all manifestation
is the essence, your identity, Self that you really are.

Self is what all your experiences are meant to be related to
and from which all your expressions, all your actions,
are meant to come forth.
It is the cause of human suffering
that Self is not recognized by most:
they are too busy with their distractions from,
and distortions of, reality.

However human beings have a persistent inner urge to experience Self
and to live as the Consciousness they are.
This is the deeply moving impetus to live authentically,
to live congruently,

and the only way to be at peace and finally fulfilled.
That is the motivating force of the entire evolutionary process.

Through the ages there has been much discussion regarding Self,
but most speak from ignorance.
Even learned philosophers psychiatrists and psychologists
labor under false ideas regarding Self.
Many religious and spiritual leaders teach about Self
from a lack of experience and therefore a mistaken standpoint.
Thus there are many misleading ways
of thinking speaking and learning about your identity.

...It is beyond argumentation...
Many so-called teachers engage in competitiveness
regarding spiritual knowledge.
They practice one-upmanship, censure
and other ego-centered methods
to prove they are the more advanced.
Real teaching is not an arena for scripture quoting;
the illumined experiences encapsulated in scriptures
are not instruments for ego battles.

The ultimate Reality is no Matter of right or wrong.
Reality is what is.
The ultimate Reality is not Matter,
nor even the subtle constituent Particles—
Reality is not even on the atomic Level.
Matter does not really matter.

Being so subtle, Self, Consciousness,
can not be grasped by the linear-functioning mind;
It is beyond mental and intellectual analysis.
Unitive Self is not to be realized by posing and dissecting
the pros and cons, likes and dislikes, good and bad,
belief and dogma, the fragmentary and the fragmented.
These are fabrications of the limited mind,
the mind of disintegration,
which is contrary to the wholeness of Being that really is.
Many a teacher and student resort to those mental processes
in teaching and learning about Self—
they predictably fail.

All the Complication and Confusion regarding Self come to an End
when sincere Students are guided to experience Self
by one who has the ultimate Advantage:
Realization of himself as the Power of Being
that is the all-pervasive eternal Source of all.

When you are taught about Self
...by one who has become identified with It...
not merely reads or hears about It
and then theorizes or intellectualizes,
but one who thinks of herself as Infinite Consciousness,

feels as Self, lives as Self,
then you have an authentic Teacher of Self.

This Teacher identifies not as a Mary or a John,
but only as Limitless Consciousness.
He does not see other people or entities,
but only Being and Its manifestations.
She regards herself not as a wave, but as the ocean,
and all the other waves as the ocean as well.
The real Teacher does not think of herself
as contained within the perimeter of her skin
or within the operations of her mind,
or confined by any other faculty.
He experiences himself consistently
as eternal all-pervasive Being that is the One of all that is.

When this Teacher speaks of Self,
the true student no longer has to attempt
to grasp the concept of Self through thought processes.
By proactively participating in what the real Teacher evokes,
you not merely *believe* in it,
you *experience* it for yourself in the unitive knowledge
deposited within you and each one of us.
This experience can be nurtured into such fullness
that you no longer cogitate about Self,
but *live as Self sincerely and continuously*.

When you are taught by such a one, you will know:

> I am not this Body,
> nor am I the momentary Energy Fluctuations called Mind.
> I am the Energy that is the Source
> of the very Atoms that compose the Appearance of Body,
> I am the Energy that is the Substance of Mind
> and the Foundation of everything about me.
> I am the underlying substantive Energy that experiences Self
> through everything I think feel and enact.
> That Energy is continuous—indestructible and indivisible—
> infinite.
> That is what I am.

9. *The wisdom that you have, O dearest one, which leads to sound knowledge when imparted only by someone else (other than the logician), is not to be attained through argumentation. You are, O compassionable one, endowed with true resolution. May our questioner be like you, O Naciketa.*

Second translation:

> *This wisdom which thou hast attained is not to be gained by any process of logical thought (nor is it to be destroyed by such either). Yet when taught by another it is easy to be known. Thou, O dearest Nachiketas, art of true resolve. May we have such another questioner as thee.*

This verse paints a beautiful portrait of the successful aspirant:

sincere compassionate and determined,

not someone who plays word games or politics,
or just pays lip service.

Yama calls Naciketa *...dearest one...*
Think of Yama not only as
the one who delivers us from this life cycle,
but lovingly guides us through it
as the force of transformation,
of which the process of dying is a minor part.
This wonderful power of transcendence
addresses the true aspirant as, My dearest one:
a declaration of love.

And he says *...you are...endowed with true resolution...*
The persistent defining factor of a real aspirant is true resolve.
True resolve is lasting;
false resolve is implementing what you know
only sporadically—now and then.

...The wisdom that you have...which leads to sound knowledge...
solid lasting real knowledge
...is not to be attained through argumentation...
Yama repeats this lesson:
The holism of Being is not understood by the linear mind,
which goes from point to point—
the process used in argumentation.
Real knowledge is not of the mind,
but of the *experience* of reality.

As the Self that you are can not be embraced by mind,
It also can not be disproved or negated by mind;
nevertheless, many try.
Renowned psychologists warn that attempts to understand Self
can result in losing touch with your identity.

Others even try to disprove the 'concept' of Self,
claiming it is the word of the devil.
In their limited understanding they confuse it
with raising ego to a divine level, competing with God.

The true Teacher is not a mere logician.
Self-knowledge lies in experiencing
the unity of the knower the knowing and the known.
Who is the *knower*? Self.
What is to be *known*? Self.
All objects, all events are but manifestations of Self.
Manifestations are expressions of the Power of Being:
Self expressing Self, thereby Self knowing Self.
The *knowing* of Self is Consciousness.
Consciousness is Self, Self is Consciousness.
The Teacher identifies himself—and the aspirant—
as the knower the knowing and the known.

Often, through the false perception of separateness—ego—
the aspirant considers herself far removed from her Teacher.
Keep this in mind:

The Light of Knowledge that is the Teacher
is to the true Aspirant like the North Star,
the constant Illumination on your Journey.
Hold fast to the Light in the Storms that cloud the Vision,
for Relationship with the Teacher helps you accomplish
the final evolutionary Goal: the Transformation
from false Self-perception to real Self-experience,
from Bondage to Liberation,
from Ignorance to Enlightenment,
from Suffering to lasting Joy of Being.

This transformation is resisted by ego, the false identity.
Falsity usurps your faculties:
your mind habitually thinks of you as limited
and separate from the whole,
your feelings reflect the alienation and unease
of the perceived isolation,
and your emotions express the resultant
fear frustration anger depression and desolation.

Habituated to ego, you protect it from change
as a creature protects its survival.
You may even maintain this protection after learning
that attachment to false identity is the cause of your suffering,
that it is the moment-to-moment annihilation
of not living as who you really are.
Annihilation is the foundation of all your fear.
What an irony: *causing* from moment to moment
that which you *fear most*
out of fear of changing the destructive ego patterns.

It takes true resolve in the aspirant to persevere
amidst the clamoring demands of the false ego patterns.
It takes true resolve to weather the dark storms
and keep charting the course of life
toward the light shed by the Teacher.

...O compassionable one...
Yama acknowledges the compassion that led Naciketa
to go to Death in order to save his father's integrity.
Thus, implies Yama,
you are qualified to receive compassion from me.
There is a beautiful love relationship
between the aspirant of true resolve
and that wonderful power of transformation, Death.

...May our questioner be like you, O Naciketa...
May you, the witness to this discourse, be like Naciketa,
so the grand Teacher Yama may speak to you
as one who is capable of receiving compassion.
May you, too, be Yama's dearest one.

May you, through the ardent fire of true resolve,
awaken the Naciketa within
and establish yourself in an eternal relationship
with the true Teacher.
May you earn his compassion love and admiration.
May you dwell in the bliss of realizing
eternal infinite limitlessly interconnected Being that you are.

Chapter Eleven

Attaining The Permanent

Sincerely open your heart and mind,
as well as the rest of your instruments of perception,
as Naciketa is open, to the realization of Self
and to the relationship with the Teacher,
which is relationship with Self.

Open yourself to the experience of the teachings,
the experience of the Being that you are.
Be at ease in the simple clear joyous experience of Self.

Impress this learning experience so indelibly
that you vibrate in accord with it throughout your days,
throughout your life.

Establish yourself in a relationship of love,
the unconditional agreement with Self,
utterly open and accepting.
Be at peace.

Now you will be invited—
and challenged in the most empowering way—
to attain much higher and subtler levels of experience.

Prepare yourself.
Work with true resolve to bring about
the transformation of your faculties
to benefit from more expansive knowledge;
otherwise you will miss it all.
Bring the highest resolve to this most precious opportunity.

10. (Since) I know that this treasure is impermanent—for that permanent entity cannot be attained through impermanent things—therefore (knowingly) did I pile up the Naciketa fire with impermanent things, and have (thereby) attained (relative) permanence.

Second translation:

I know that what is known as the Treasure-house is also impermanent; nor, in truth, is the Eternal to be gained by that which is temporal. Therefore by me has been laid the Nachiketas Fire and with transient things I have attained the Enduring.

Remember, by setting the Naciketa fire thrice
through the three functions of study sacrifice and charity—
gaining real knowledge, sacrificing the ego identity
and sharing oneself in interconnectedness—
one passes beyond the cycles of birth death and rebirth,

one gains immortality
and becomes an inhabitant of the Great World beyond.
In this ...*Treasure-house*... is experienced the Cosmic Unity.
Here resides the wisdom of all that is
and of all that has ever been.
Therein lies the cessation of perceived lack and need.

It is important to understand, however,
that the means employed in the Naciketa fire are temporal,
and the Great Treasure attained thereby
also ...*is impermanent*...
The cosmos, a manifestation, is impermanent;
it comes forth from something and will dissolve again,
albeit in eons of time—a ...*(relative) permanence*...
Western culture does not have much of a history
of learning about the coming and going of the cosmos,
but the Vedic system, the Sanskrit teachings,
have taught since ancient times
that there are epochs upon epochs
of the universe being manifested and then reabsorbed.
If there is manifestation, then there is something beyond it.
The Cosmic Union therefore is not the final goal.

When Naciketa gained the second boon, we posed the question,
What else could he ask for?
He has immortality, he reached ...*the Treasure-house*...
realized the Cosmic Union, became one with all manifestation,
and yet he asked for more.
There is something beyond the cosmos—
that is the permanent, the Unmanifest Eternal,
the Unbeginning:
that which is there before—and after—manifestation.

Feel this, experience this.

The Cosmic Experience that can be attained through temporal means
endures for eons, but is not eternal.
The cosmos will eventually be reabsorbed into *...the Eternal...*
The Eternal is the absolute source, Brahman,
the ultimate goal of all your desires and aspirations.
It is not to be attained by any means that are of manifestation.
That is why It is not attained through the mind or the intellect
or any other faculty.

> What you ultimately seek is not Immortality,
> but the Eternal.
> The Eternal is beyond the Great Treasure-house,
> beyond the Great World of the Cosmos.

Let yourself experience that for a moment:
the Eternal, beyond the cosmic manifestation,
the source of all, yet beyond all, contained by none.
The Eternal is beyond objects and events,
beyond time—beyond beginning and end—
beyond being and beyond non-being.
This is the final goal.

Now the question is not why Naciketa asked for the third boon,
but why he asked for the first two boons.
Attaining the experience of Cosmic Union—
liberation from the material-bound life in human form—
can be seen as an intermediate step to the subtler level,
the realization of the Eternal.

One could argue about an intermediate step:
you either go to Self-realization or you do not,
there are no intermediate steps.
However, here it is said that through reaching immortality
you become an adept for the ultimate realization.

> Immortality is not the final Goal,
> but is an intermediate Step to the Ultimate:
> Realization of Eternal Consciousness.

To the human mind this all seems so vast
and beyond comprehension—the churnings of eons of time,
manifestations and dissolutions of universes
culminating in the realization of the Eternal in and beyond all.
Mind can not grasp this.
However, sincerely devoted to reality, you can *experience* It!

The Eternal Consciousness that you are,
while incomprehensible to the faculties
through which you normally function,
is the focus with which you navigate your path
to final realization.
Cosmic Union is on the way to the ultimate goal—
realization of the Eternal—and is even integral to it,
for it takes place within the context of the Eternal,
albeit momentarily.
It may be in the state of Cosmic Union
that you traverse the final facet of the path of Self-realization.
You can see the star, but how do you navigate your path to it?

Your faculties, while limited, can still assist you in experiencing Self.
Your feelings and emotions, for example, although ephemeral,
and certainly not the Being you are,
can help reveal your true identity.
The feeling and emotion most congruent with Self is love.
Love is the unconditional acceptance of Being, your identity,
and the identity of all.
You *Are* That, That You Are.

> Love is a great Power.
> When Love suffuses your Feelings and Emotions,
> they become ardent Instruments toward Self-realization.

Thus, the transitory—even feelings and emotions—
can serve you in the realization of interconnectedness,
which can in turn lead to the realization of your identity:
Limitless Consciousness.

Cosmic Union is the threshold to the experience of the Eternal
for the sincere intelligent expert student.
It is a necessary stage for those who find it difficult to grasp
all the aspects of realizing the infinite Power of Being.
Through experiences of interconnectedness
you can advance to Cosmic Union,
where you hone the ability to deeply understand,
and ultimately realize, Limitless Being.
However, the separation between the intermediate step
and the ultimate goal is an artificial one:

it can be at the moment you realize Universal Consciousness
that you realize Eternal Consciousness.

Now a warning regarding an intermediate step,
which can be an argument against it:
desire for union with the Universal
is an attachment that distracts you
from the ultimate aim.
You could, in the ego sense, desire union with the Universal
just to be free from feelings of lack need and separation,
and not extend yourself further into the realization of Self.
Desired union is a tainted mindset, an ego delusion,
because, after all, you *are* the Power of Being—
we are not talking about *attaining* something
or *becoming* something.

The Infinite Eternal is the ultimate source of all,
including all your experiences.
The infinite absolute Eternal just *is*;
It is on all levels and is ultimately *experienced* on all levels.
Focus now on experiencing the hierarchy of Consciousness
from the grossest to the subtlest:

The material, which includes your body, is the grossest level.
Gross is dense, not very pervasive.
For a moment allow yourself to experience this gross,
material level with its severe limitations and clumsiness.
Notice in you an objection to remaining so limited.

Subtler than the material are the senses.
Being subtler, they are more pervasive.
Your senses gather information regarding the material world.
Experience yourself now as subtler, more pervasive.

Subtler than the senses—therefore more pervasive—is mind.
Your mind takes the information gathered by the senses
and interprets and correlates it.
Experience yourself now in terms of the mental level,
subtler, more expansive, more pervasive.
However the mind has its limitations, too.
Notice, for example, how someone can be talking to you,
and you may not hear a word,
because your mind is somewhere else.
For a moment, let yourself experience
such a state of absentmindedness.

Mind has another limitation:
it habitually misinterprets sense information,
proclaiming the objects sensed are solid and permanent,
not momentary events, appearances.
You could call this a disorder of mind.
Let yourself notice this mental disorder consciously now.

Subtler than mind—therefore more pervasive—is the intellect.
Your intellect makes inferences deductions and conclusions
from the information mind garners through the senses.
Experience the intellect now,
more empowered, more pervasive, subtler.
Yet even the intellect is limited in its pervasiveness
and its ability to comprehend what is.
If your intellect is dull or dysfunctional,
it will fail to make proper judgment about what you perceive;
you will not know whether it is real, whether it works.
Sometimes you have experiences that you know to be true,
but your intellect can not grasp what your intuition knows.
Let yourself experience, for a moment,
the intellect's limitations.

Subtler than intellect—therefore more pervasive—is intuition.
We usually can not explain what we perceive intuitively,
but can say with certainty, I know it is so.
Be trustingly open to the experience of intuitive knowledge.

There is a knowing that is subtler than the intuition's,
more pervasive, therefore superior.
It is the Cosmic Intelligence,
capable of asserting itself within you beyond all your faculties.

This Cosmic Intelligence is the Mahat,
the Greater World, the Cosmic Experience,
the Grand Treasure.
The Mahat is not only the summation of all intelligence,
but a whole that is far beyond those parts.
The Cosmic Intelligence is of an entirely different quality
than human understanding:
far subtler and more pervasive, therefore far superior.
Open yourself to the experience of this whole intelligence,
the intelligence beyond all intelligences.

Now you are ready to understand and experience:

The Cosmic Experience is not yet the final evolutionary level.
It is a manifestation of that from which it comes forth.
Therefore, although it endures through eons, it is not eternal.
The universe was caused by something.
This ultimate cause is the ultimate *Is*, the Power of Being.
To experience this *Is*,
expand into your subtlest powers of awareness.
The ultimate Is, is the subtlest and most pervasive.
Experience ultimately subtle and infinitely pervasive.

Consciousness is contained by none, yet is the source of all,
the original and final cause,
and yet neither a cause nor a source.
It is in and beyond all,
the ultimate void and fullness.
Experience yourself as the ultimate void
and thereby become open to experiencing yourself
in absolute fullness.

That is what Naciketa seeks to realize,
what the true aspirant seeks to realize:
the reality, Limitless Consciousness, Eternal Self.

Let yourself dwell in the experience of reality:
limitless eternal all-pervasive Consciousness.
It can not really be described, It can not be taught,
It can only be known by *being* It,
by realizing It through luminous experience.
Experience.
Expand in your experience.
Let your experience become ever subtler, purer,
more expansive.

Make Eternal Consciousness your unremitting focal Point.
Constantly relate yourself to the Power of Being
even if It seems vague or distant.
The more you nurture that Relationship,
the more familiar will the Infinite be,
and the more will you experience It as the Self that you are.

11. *O Naciketa, you, on becoming enlightened, have rejected (them all) by examining patiently the highest reach of desire, the support of the universe, the infinite results of meditation, the other shore of fearlessness, the extensive course of (Hiranyagarbha) that is praiseworthy and great, as also (your own) state.*

Second translation:

Thou, O Nachiketas, art wise; for having seen the fulfillment of all desire, the Foundation of the world, the infinity of creative will, the fearless other Shore, the Great One, mantra-bodied (stomam), the Wide-extended, that in which all is established, thou hast with firmness put (this great attainment) from thee.

...you, on becoming enlightened...

Naciketa is enlightened,
he has realized himself as Self-luminous Being.
Experience this: self-luminous—
you do not *take* light from anything,
you do not *have* a light within you,
you *are* the light by which you are illumined.
You are luminosity, you are Consciousness.

Naciketa, freed from the cycles of birth and death and rebirth,
having attained immortality,
has the wisdom to go beyond even that.
He has accomplished this by divesting himself of attachment
to objects and experiences of the temporal world—
that includes the material sensual and mental realms,
even the higher subtler intellectual and intuitive realms.

He has rigorously and continuously
refused to be seduced and imprisoned by
...the fulfillment of all desire...

You must learn on your path to reject attachment to objects of desire,
certainly on the material level, but even on subtler levels,
such as the highest knowledge or great states of being:
...the infinite results of meditation...
Most get attached to much less than infinite results:
feeling good, seeing lights or hearing bells.
To be free for the ultimate realization,
you must be unattached to luminous insight,
powerful confidence, abiding peace, effortless success—
these may come about, or not; do not let it matter.
You have to be willing to be true to yourself
even when you are feeling poorly,
when your body is aching, your mind is out of tune
and your emotions are rebellious or distraught.
Accept yourself even if none of your faculties are cooperating.

> All Attachment limits you.
> Give up your Desire even for great States.
> To be true to yourself,
> live free of all Attachment.

So discriminating is Naciketa that he refuses *...fearlessness...*
The basic human fear is of annihilation, of not being.
Along with that comes the fear of change.

Fear stems from limited ego perception.
A conscious participant in evolution embraces change—
many on the spiritual path have not freed themselves from fear
and thus resist growth and continue to suffer.
Realizing yourself to be immortal, you lose all fear—
a wonderful reward,
to which Nacikcta feels no attachment.

Naciketa refuses all the high rewards of Cosmic Unity,
of realizing *...the support of the universe...*
He knows the cosmos is manifestation.
He wants to go beyond the created
...the infinity of creative will...
...the extensive course of (Hiranyagarbha)...

Naciketa from the beginning on has said he wants the realization
of the permanent, Eternal Consciousness.
You may by now have this perception:
he already has that, he has realized it—
it is as if this entire discourse were simply for your benefit,
for getting Death to reveal his secrets to you.

There is one overriding principle that Naciketa exemplifies:

Go for the Ultimate,
do not get stuck on the Lesser.
Do not attach yourself
to any of the Rungs of the evolutionary Ladder,
or even the Ladder itself—
choose that to which the Ladder leads.

I learned early in life through my war experiences,
through deprivation and starvation,
not to settle for the lesser.
I was starving and freezing,
yet I knew I deserved the ultimate—
not just food survival or safety, but the ultimate.
My meeting with Death taught me that.
I decided as a little boy to dedicate my life to the ultimate.
This is a vitally important lesson:
do not shortchange yourself by attachment,
even to Cosmic Union,
let alone to your moods fixations conditionings and habits
by which you make life miserable.
Involved with the lesser,
you are not free for the ultimate fulfillment.

Always remember, you are not aiming to *become* Eternal Self;
you already *are*.
The Eternal is not *in* you or *about* you,
but what you essentially are: your essence.
The aim of the real aspirant is to *realize* your eternalness—
not to *make* your eternalness real,
but to make your *experience* of it real.
Your eternalness *is* real, always has been, always will be,
even if you think you are mud or frog or person.

While Eternal Self can not be realized by your instruments,
for they are manifestation, therefore temporal,
you can draw upon them to help you experience who you are,
for example through focused love upon the reality of you.
Ultimately, your faculties are meant to merge
into the experience of Self.

When facing death in my childhood during the bombing of my home,
I prepared myself to continue consciously
even as my body was going to be destroyed.
That was based upon the inherent knowledge of being eternal.
As a six-year-old boy
I had had no previous teaching about that;
I drew upon something invisible and mysterious,
yet established, existing:
the Consciousness that I would go on beyond this body.
Consciousness is absolute, all-pervasive,
so why would I be excluded? Why you?

It was an established experiencing, not a mental knowing.
I could not talk to anyone about it;
I could not even talk to myself about it.
I did not have the words, only the experience of it.
I was in the experience that I am Eternal Consciousness.

Ego, the limited self, is a false perception.
There is something secret in you that knows of
your Eternal Beingness, although your mind can not explain it.
That is the light, the star, by which you navigate your path,
if you are wise like Naciketa.
That secret knowing allows the grace of Self to take over,
and the ego to stand aside.
It is the real 'leap of faith', or 'blind faith',
a knowing that transcends the linear functions
of the mind and intellect—it is trust in the Being that is.

When you are attached to false conceptions regarding your identity,
Consciousness does not come through to your cognition,
your '*re*-cognition'.
Confused by ego, the faculties are in turmoil,

they are under the subjugation of the static or dynamic.
Their form is gross, thus not conducive
to the experience of the subtlest, Eternal Being.

How do you bring your faculties into the experience of Self?
You transform the faculties.
Your faculties take on the form
of whatever vibratory state they are in.
You want your faculties to take on the form of—to merge in—
the subtlest vibratory state, pure Consciousness.
All the practices of yoga have that as their real purpose:

The practice of restraining yourself from ways of being
that are contrary to your true identity
has the continuous experience of Eternal Consciousness
as its purpose.

The practice of purposefully choosing behaviors—
ways of thinking feeling and acting—
that are in accord with who you are
and cultivating those behaviors purposefully and loyally
has the continuous experience of Eternal Consciousness
as its purpose.

The practice of adopting the stance
of effortless balance and purity—satva—
has the continuous experience of Eternal Consciousness
as its purpose.

The practice of regulating the rhythm of your breath
to be in attunement with the universal flow of energy,
free of conflict and distraction,
has the continuous experience of Eternal Consciousness
as its purpose.

The practice of purposefully withdrawing mind
from its outgoing tendencies
and all its involvement with falsity and distraction
has the experience of Eternal Consciousness as its purpose.

The practice of focusing the mind onto your core
and bringing all your faculties
into the state of pure concentration
has the experience of Eternal Consciousness as its purpose.

The practice of dwelling in a focused state, in continuity, by will,
with the sincere intent of making that state permanent,
not just a practice for an hour now and then,
has the experience of Eternal Consciousness as its purpose.

All these practices help you keep your faculties tranquil, calm,
and eventually so refined as to merge with pure Consciousness.
This is superconsciousness, *samadhi*,
the zenith in which you experience union with the divine.
Samadhi means both the state of death—dying to your ego—
and the state of bliss, as all your needs desires and aspirations
are fulfilled, finally.
In samadhi, your mind feelings emotions
and everything else about you merge in Being.
There is a beautiful ancient analogy for this:
it is like a man made of salt walking into the ocean.
When you maintain samadhi, it becomes illumination,
Self-realization.

Realization of the Infinite Consciousness you are
is the purpose for engaging in yogic behaviors.
Through them you purify all your manifested facets
with sincerity continuity and expertise.

A yogi is an expert in action.
You might wonder, Why does the Teacher bother
about this thing I do and that thing I do?
You can not advance unless you are an expert in action, a yogi,
for whom the most mundane activity is a divine expression.
With sincerity continuity expertise in action
and trust in the Eternal Consciousness that you are,
you transform all the manifested facets called faculties
into *realized Consciousness.*

Then you will know the Self that you are,
and you will know Self manifested as a creation
with your name attached.
Self, Power of Being, is who you are in essence,
thus your true identity.
The body-mind complex
by which you are habituated to identifying yourself
is mere momentary manifestation.

...the Great One, mantra-bodied... is the Cosmic One,
the unifying principle of all creation, Mahat.
It is composed of vibration:
the creative (rajas) brings about manifestations,
the destructive (tamas) dissolves the creations,
and the pure (satva) maintains the balance
beyond creation and destruction.

Sound is a manifestation of vibration.
In the creation chapter of the Bible, Genesis,
it is said, In the beginning was the Word.
The Vedic scriptures also refer to the first-created as the word.
The beginning act of creation is the word, vibration,

from which all springs forth.
Pure sound represents the creative source most directly, truly.
There are pure sounds, known as *mantras*, passed on to us
from the luminous experience of the Rishis,
the great seers in clear Consciousness.
These pure sounds are direct representations
of the creative source, and certain qualities thereof.

Mahat is *...the Wide-extended...* expansive and permeating,
pervading the three worlds of past present and future,
of creation maintenance and dissolution.
Refuse attachment to this *...Great One...*
for your aim is beyond: the Absolute.

Be careful here.
The Absolute is in everything, yet not limited to anything,
and is not anything at all—
this is an apparent paradox
the mind and intellect can not overcome;
only your experience in pure Consciousness
reaches the Absolute.

Aim for the Experience of the Absolute:
all is established in the Absolute,
the Absolute is in all
and yet contained by none.
The Absolute is the Star by which to chart your Course
to Self-realization.

The great attainment of the fulfillment of all desire,
the foundation of creation and the will which causes it,
the Great One of subtle vibration and wide extension,
freedom from death and fear—Cosmic Union—
Naciketa refuses as his final reward.
He firmly says, This is wonderful and generous, Yama,
but since you offered me a third boon,
the ultimate is what I shall have.

And how pleased is the great Guru Yama with his disciple, Naciketa,
calling him *...wise...* and *...enlightened...*
The great Teacher affirms through these passages
that a real aspirant on the spiritual path is sincere and steadfast.
He strongly asserts the loving loyal relationship
between the aspirant and the Teacher,
between Naciketa and the Lord over Death, Yama.

CHAPTER TWELVE

Concentrating On Self

Sincerely and expertly create the conditions
that maximize your ability
to be in clear and uninterrupted Consciousness,
your faculties in direct relationship
with the Being that you are.

Create relaxation throughout your body
from the top of the head to the soles of the feet,
inside and out.
Bring all your faculties into that state of release.

Regulate the breath to be attuned to the universal flow of energy.

Cause everything about you to be in effortless balance in your center,
the area of your heart,
and to remain there sincerely and continuously attentive
to reflecting the experience of Consciousness
free of distortion, with utter devotion
and with trust in the Power of Being that you are.

Affirm that determined Consciousness now,
so it will be with you throughout this discourse
and beyond, permanently.

12. The intelligent man gives up happiness and sorrow by developing concentration of mind on the Self and thereby meditating on the old Deity who is inscrutable, lodged inaccessibly, located in the intellect, and seated in the midst of misery.

Second translation:

Having known by means of the union with the Inner Self (adhyatma yoga), that Shining Power, very difficult to see, present in the Darkness, dwelling in the Cavern of the Heart, abiding in the Abyss, Primaeval, the wise one abandons joy and sorrow.

Naciketa *...the wise one...* experiences within his core
his real identity, Self.
He is blessed with this experience
because he sincerely and continuously devotes
the full power of his will and mind,
the finely honed skills of all his faculties,
to one focus: All-inclusive Consciousness.

Naciketa lives in meditation:
he is in the experience of Self-effulgent Consciousness
from moment to moment,
whether he sits stands walks or lies down,
whether he is working playing or resting.
When he arises in the morning,
he experiences himself as Consciousness,
and as he goes about his day,
he performs all actions as Eternal Consciousness.

Naciketa does not indulge in the hypocritical practice
of sitting for meditation one hour a day,
or two or three or any amount,
and returning to the accustomed life in ego.

> Once you know the Clarity Ease and Joy of living Self,
> why would you choose even for one Moment
> to live in the Dysfunction Confusion and Suffering of Ego?

...*The intelligent man*... does not delay:
I'm too busy to experience myself in full Consciousness
as the Power of Being that I am.
He does not rationalize: I'm not feeling well today,
or, I forgot to be real, or, I don't know how,
or, I'm confused about reality.
He never wants to take a 'vacation' from Self.
He is not fool enough to think
he can sincerely begin living true to himself sometime later.

Naciketa does not seek refuge in deferring life in reality—
illusion offers no advantage, no gain,
neither safety nor succor, pleasure or joy.
All the suffering and confusion
due to enmeshment with illusion is over and done with
once and for all,
as far as the manifestation called Naciketa is concerned.

Naciketa knows himself, he lives true to himself.
Naciketa is your model of the ideal aspirant
blazing forth on the path trod by the soul.

> The Power of Being experiences and expresses Self
> through any and all Manifestations,
> including you.

...The intelligent man gives up happiness and sorrow...
The normal human attachment is to dualities:
right and wrong, good and bad, happy and sad.
Dualities appear only in the illusory context
of separate entities.
To dwell in the purity of Self,
you have to surrender the illusory dualities,
no matter how deeply impressed.
When you know that you are not separate,
that you are interconnected Being,
there is no question of allowing mind
to think according to dualities.

To free your mind and all your faculties
from their enslavement to false conditioning,
rigorously cause them to operate from the foundation
of reality.
Relate to yourself as an intelligent adult—
not an inexperienced child—
who knows how to gather the divergent energies of mind
and concentrate on Self,
keeping mind on this chosen point of focus at will: meditation.

...meditating on the old Deity who is inscrutable, lodged inaccessibly,
located in the intellect, and seated in the midst of misery...
Self is before creation, therefore *...old...* and beyond.
Experience yourself as unbeginning.
Self is the Supreme Being, the *...Deity...*
Experience yourself as unbeginning supreme Being.
Self is not knowable by the mind, intellect or any other faculty,
therefore *...inscrutable...*
Experience yourself as unbeginning supreme
inscrutable Being.

Self is what you are, your origin and substance,
yet is as if hidden behind your faculties and their activities;
It is *...lodged inaccessibly...* and
hidden *...in the midst of misery...*
Your faculties are of the material realm,
and attachment to the material realm is the source of misery.
The faculties are conditioned to a seemingly endless
enmeshment with the changing, the ephemeral.
As a consequence, they tend not to respond
to the far subtler influence of Self,

even though it is infinitely more pervasive
than the material realm.

Most people keep their body and senses so involved
with matters of the physical realm,
that they are preoccupied when it comes to responding to Self.
Mind and intellect are habitually so mired
in constantly changing events and phenomena,
that they have no attentiveness left
for experiencing and reflecting the permanent, the Eternal.
Surrounded by so much loud noise, people are unable to hear
and respond to the subtler sound of the universal symphony.
The loss is profound.

All-pervasive Consciousness, the Self that you are,
is most subtle, thus can not be seen in ordinary ways.
The experience of Self is to be found not in the objects outside;
Self is to be found within.
Be careful with the term 'within'.
To Infinite Self there is neither inside nor outside.
'Within' indicates here, within Self.
Self is to be found within Self, not in ego or its instruments.

Self is to be found *...dwelling in the Cavern of the Heart...*
You gather the divergent rays of your mind
and bring them into effortlessly balanced focus
in the area of your heart, which you relate to as your center.
However, remain clear that your center is not a physical place.
Where is the center of the Infinite? Anywhere, everywhere.
Your center is the point of focus of a mysterious energy
that is so pure, it empowers your faculties
to come into the experience of the Infinite.

Self is *...located in the intellect...*

Infinite Being, the origin and substance of all that is,
yet not bound to nor contained in any,
can not be fully grasped by the intellect;
however, the intellect is required to perceive Self.
To unite your intellect with Self,
you need to bring your intellect into its pure transcendent state.

13. After hearing this, grasping it fully, separating this righteous thing (from the body etc.), and attaining this subtle thing, that mortal rejoices, for he has obtained that which is the cause of delight. I consider that the mansion (of Brahman) is wide open to Naciketa.

The reality of Self is the eternal symphony
that is constantly playing, yet few hear.

> Most fail to hear the eternal Song of Being
> not because they are mortal,
> but because they are distracted.

The true aspirant, through the favor of the Teacher,
does hear the eternal song,
and through sincere continuous expert and faithful
application of the teachings,
flourishes in the knowledge and experience of Self.
Such aspirants clearly know
that Self is other than your body and mind
and the false identity associated with them.

Knowing aspirants live in accord with their perception of Self
and experience themselves truly as this most subtle identity.

Thus, even as a mortal you can dwell in Eternal Consciousness
and be filled with joy again *...rejoice...*
This joy, this bliss is inherent to you:
bliss is inseparable from Infinite Being in Self-experience.

Naciketa is a true aspirant who is fully open to the Teacher
and to the experiences he offers.
He does not separate himself or conceal anything,
but reveals himself fully to his Teacher, and thereby to himself.
A responsible seeker,
Naciketa does not interfere with his Teacher's gifts
by arguing distrusting disregarding or forgetting,
or by attempting to find fault.
As Naciketa is open to Self,
the realm of blissful eternal Consciousness,
which is *...the mansion (of Brahman)...*
is *...wide open to Naciketa...*
Naciketa is ready to dwell in the house of Consciousness.
If you are open trusting and expert like Naciketa,
the house of eternal Power of Being is wide open to you;
otherwise, it is not.

Qualified to dwell in the bliss of self-knowing Being,
Naciketa again appeals to his beloved Teacher, Yama:

14. "Tell (me) of that thing which you see as different from virtue, different from vice, different from this cause and effect, and different from the past and the future."

Why does Naciketa pose his question in this way?
When you allow your mind to settle upon it,

your faculties will become absorbed in the experience
evoked by this entreaty
until they are open to a deeper vision.
The faculties will go beyond the usual processes
with which they relate to the world.
For example, when you engross your faculties in
that which was before a beginning,
they also experience the never-ending and the eternal now.

Questioning what is beyond the ordinary person's concerns,
the dualities of virtue and vice,
cause and effect, past and future,
can only be accomplished by a sufficiently advanced aspirant
who acts in the responsibility of Self.

> We live in a World of Phenomena
> created through Differences in Vibration.
> Some Vibrations reveal Reality, they are harmonious—
> we consider those to be of *Virtue*.
> Other Vibrations distort or obscure the Experience of Reality,
> they distract and confuse, they are disharmonious—
> we consider those to be of *Vice*.
> Yet even these vitally important Distinctions
> are only from the Point of View of the Manifestation
> and in the Context of the Momentary;
> that which underlies Creation does not have Dualities.

...different from this cause and effect... These events occupy lives
in an apparently ceaseless succession.

However, even cause and effect
can be experienced in their unity:
an effect becomes a cause for another effect.

When the mind and other faculties open themselves
to the apparent oppositions, without judgment,
something unique happens:
the line between the opposites blurs, then disappears,
and you encounter the underlying unity.
You no longer experience differentiation,
you experience unified Being.
Your faculties merge with that which underlies all creation.
That is what Naciketa wants, final liberation in Self-realization.
That is what you want.

So persistent is Naciketa in wanting to realize the Absolute,
that he aims at it from all directions, in all contexts.
He repeatedly rejects that which is normally considered
important in this world, in favor of what underlies it:
the source and essence of all.
So persistent must you be in wanting to be truly liberated
that you divest yourself of attachment to the world
even on its highest and subtlest levels.
Naciketa is the quintessential human soul
on the path to final emancipation in Self-realization.
Emulate his example.
So devoted to Self is Naciketa that he knows
he deserves the highest, and he will settle for nothing less.

This is what I decided amidst the horrors of war.
Imagine the audacity of a little boy
who had endured so much deprivation
determining not to accept anything less than the ultimate.

The successful aspirant navigates his path faithfully
with his sight firmly set on Eternal Consciousness, Self.
He never veers from his path.

Because Naciketa is such a determined loyal expert pure aspirant,
Yama has no choice but to grant him
the greatest of all possible boons, the final achievement:
Self-realization.

Determine to give yourself the Ultimate.
Do not take 'No' for an Answer,
do not shortchange yourself,
'I can't' is not in the Dictionary.
Otherwise you will not be on the Path to Self-realization.

Your sincerity leaves fate no choice but to give what you determine.
Naciketa is courteous respectful and cultured
in his own simple way,
as he demands the ultimate,
and he will accept nothing less from the great Lord Yama.

If you are determined to claim the ultimate, Self-realization,
then you must, like Naciketa, steadfastly refuse
any further attachment to the realm of murk—
as if that were your home.
You must give up all attachment in the behaviors
of your mind emotions feelings intellect intuition
senses and body.
You must cut off once and for all any enmeshment
or investment in ego—as if that were really you.

If you do not, you are knowingly lying to yourself,
for it must be clear to you now who you are.
As long as you are lying to yourself,
you can not be in Consciousness,
and Consciousness *is* your real home,
is who you really are.

To be Self-realized in this lifetime, you must *now*,
with single-minded devotion,
focus on living sincerely and continuously
as the Power of Being that you really are.
Do not delay living true to Self—
not one facet of falsity is preferable.
If you know who you are, why condemn yourself
to even one more moment of living contrary to yourself?
If we were talking about *becoming* something,
that might take a while, but that is not the case.
Your quest is to live true to who you really are
always have been and will always be.

To tread the spiritual path to reality takes courage,
you can not run with the herd.
You have been conditioned to find safety in numbers
and be a follower;
whether you accept the conditioning is up to you.
The only reason I can teach what I teach
is that I have *experienced* it.
And the only reason I have experienced it
is that I have consciously refused to follow the herd
since early childhood when I witnessed everyone around me
in the throes of self-induced mayhem.
This is not to say you should stand in opposition

to the world around you, but do not follow its patterns,
and do not identify yourself by it.

Functioning in the herd mentality and being in universal union
are diametrically opposed.

> Those running with the Herd have sold out what is within:
> the Ability to respond to Self,
> Response-ability.

Attendant to not responding to Self is a sense of shame,
a terrible thing to bear
therefore covered up by mutual agreement—
never expressed, never allowed to come to the surface.
The societal cult of denying true identity is most vicious:
you are discouraged from thinking for yourself,
and persistently pressed to be a follower.
Even the leaders are followers.
That is what attracts many to military service:
you can be a general and still be a follower,
because everything is prescribed for you.
That is not responsibility but assigned duties.

Someone who on his own
succeeds in living a meaningful productive life
is offensive to those running in the herd.
They feel threatened: here is a living example
that you can be balanced happy successful healthy and decent
without selling out.
That is an irritant the herd has to kill—and often does.

Many spiritual aspirants remain attached to the herd mentality,
even when they know better.
As a follower, you suffer terribly.
To free yourself, you need not oppose the herd,
nor consider yourself superior,
but simply be secure in Self.

The Path of Self-realization is not for the Weak;
it is for those who are determined
to claim a functional successful fulfilling Life
in the Freedom of Self-empowerment.

Chapter Thirteen

Meditating On The Supreme

Open your heart to Yama as fully as has Naciketa.
Be receptive to the full experience of these teachings.

Sincerely determine to impress the teachings indelibly
upon all your faculties, so they will be transformed
and behave and act only in accord with the knowledge gained.

Maintain yourself in Consciousness that in essence you are.
Have all your faculties in direct relationship with It,
devoted and determined, pure whole and continuous.

Yama responds now to Naciketa's request
to know that which is the essence and identity of all that is,

the meaning and purpose of all manifestation,
including you.

15. *I tell you briefly of that goal which all the Vedas with one voice propound, which all the austerities speak of, and wishing for which people practice Brahmacarya: it is this, viz Om.*

Second translation:

> *That word which all the Vedas declare, which all inward-turnings (tapansi) sound forth, desiring which men lead the Mystic Life (Brahmacharyam): that Word I tell thee briefly: it is Om.*

Yama's answer to the entirety of Naciketa's request is
...I tell thee briefly: it is Om...
There is no need for further talk, Om is it.
That is all you need to know.
What Naciketa has been asking for,
what everything about us yearns for and drives toward,
is indicated by the sacred syllable Om.

The word Om is what *...all the Vedas with one voice propound...*
All the scriptures in the world, all teachings,
spring forth from Om, the primal vibration of creation.

...all the austerities... have Om as their goal.
Austerity, tapas, is not only
the discipline to forgo negative behaviors,
but the internal fire, the deep glowing warmth
of Consciousness turning inward toward Self:

In your Center, the Area of the Heart,
is the ardent Passion that heats and illumines your very Core,
Passion of the Power of Being experiencing Self:
I am aware of being aware of Being.
This is Satchidananda,
Existence-knowledge-bliss-absolute,
your real Identity.

How pale are the ephemeral obsessions that people pursue
at the expense of this all-consuming passion:
Eternal Consciousness aware of Self,
not in a deferred eternity, but in the present moment,
aware of having always been,
before a beginning, before creation,
and aware of being without end.
What an indefinable richness.

It is for the realization of Om, eternal all-pervasive Consciousness,
that individuals *...practice Brahmacarya...*
Some interpret the word 'Brahmacarya'
as restraint from sexual conduct.
However, its true meaning is subtler:
to live in the knowledge and purity of Brahman,
the Supreme Consciousness.
In Brahmacarya you cultivate the life of balance,
live in association with a real spiritual Teacher
for the purpose of sincere study,
and dedicate your life to the experience and expression
of Essential Being.

16. *This letter (Om), indeed, is the (inferior) Brahman (Hiranyagarbha); and this letter is, indeed, the supreme Brahman. Anybody, who, (while) meditating on this letter, wants any of the two, to him comes that.*

Om symbolizes and is the Supreme Consciousness,
and Om symbolizes and is the first vibration of Being,
the beginning of all creation.
Om is the source and originating impulse
from which all manifestation—this whole world—arises:
In the beginning was the Word.
Om is *...the supreme Brahman...* and
Om is also His mode of Creator *...the (inferior) Brahman...*
When you meditate on Om,
you will be united with either the inferior or supreme Brahman,
according to your focus.

Be not confused by the words inferior and supreme—
they are the same One.
'Inferior' does not have a negative connotation here.
It is not a lesser meditation to relate to Om as the Creator.
However, you are fundamentally Transcendent Consciousness,
and everything about you is evolving to experience that—
until then, you will not be at peace.

This is powerful information not to be taken lightly.
You have been told the direct way to realize your true identity
through the sounding of Om.
Your focus must be profound, clear and free of distraction,
such as special pronunciations or rituals.
From your core, with sincerity and determination,
you vibrate in union with All-pervasive Essence.

Meditating on Om you harmonize your faculties
to take on the shape of Om
on the level for which you are ready,
be it in relation to manifestation
or identifying with the Ultimate.

Experience Om, Supreme Consciousness,
the infinite reality of all, therefore free of lack or need,
including the need for movement vibration manifestation.
However, though eternally in quiescence,
Supreme Consciousness does move vibrate manifest.
Let your experience embrace both aspects of Om:
Eternal Consciousness that *moves not*
and Eternal Consciousness that *moves*, expresses.

Om is the subtle Self-expression of Consciousness
who also does not express at all.

Om is the name of that which is unbeginning, ever-present
and eternally unending;
as well as that which is timeless and conditionless,
transcendent.
Relate to yourself as Om, Eternal Consciousness
expressing through creation by Om.

17. This medium is the best; this medium is the supreme (and the inferior) Brahman. Meditating on this medium, one becomes adorable in the world of Brahman.

There are many means by which you can focus for meditation:
observing the breath, chanting mantras,
gazing at a chosen point of focus, such as the light of a candle
or a mandala, a complex symmetrical graphic design.
These are methods to help retain
the attentiveness of your faculties.
Of all the different ways,
focusing on Om is said to be *...the best...*
whether it is representing the Supreme Consciousness
or the Manifestor of Universal Consciousness.

In the throes of ego, many aspirants think
they must have Om for their personal mantra;
anything else is not good enough.
There are *many* 'bests'.
The mantra with which the real Teacher initiates you
is what is best suited for you as an individual.
Every mantra comes from Om,
every manifestation comes through Om.
Om is the foundation of all.

Om is the support of meditation, of experiencing yourself
as that which is the essence and foundation of all.

Om is the Support for the Experience of yourself
as the essential Force,
the Cause Foundation and Substance of all.

Meditating on the imperishable medium, Om,
you become *...adorable in the world of Brahman...*

Here again is the deep affection
that echoes throughout this dialogue with Death:
love between the Lord of Death and humanity,
love between the Teacher and aspirant,
love between Self and ego,
love between the Manifestor and the manifested.
The relationship between Brahman and His crcation
is not impersonal or abstract, but one of intimacy, union.
To be adorable in the world of Supreme Consciousness,
to be in utmost appreciation, total agreement—love—
what higher more satisfying experience could there be?

CHAPTER FOURTEEN

Self Does Not Die

Keep burning the Naciketa fire,
the genuine determination to function in purity
as the self-knowing Being that you are.

Cause deep relaxation to radiate throughout your entire body,
aligning its vibrations in harmony to the deepest level.
Feel your body free of boundaries
and integral to the ocean of energy
from which spring forth all manifestations.

Om is vibrating through you,
expressing the infinitude of Being.

Know yourself to be the Is:
that which always has been
and is now
and always shall be,
Transcendent Consciousness that you are.
Have everything about you—your thinking feeling intuiting—
relate to you as the Power of Being that you are.

Death now calls attention to the transcendent nature of Self.

18. The intelligent Self is neither born nor does It die. It did not originate from anything, nor did anything originate from It. It is birthless, eternal, undecaying, and ancient. It is not injured even when the body is killed.

...The intelligent Self... is the real Knower,
self-knowing Being in direct Self-experience and -expression.
Self is not passive; there is intelligence,
a proactive knowing through eternity,
an unbeginning knowing that has always been
and always shall be.
This self-knowing Self vibrates in harmony with Om,
is like Om, and *is* Om.
The knower and that which is known
and the act of knowing are one.

Self is never lost; It is constant, eternal,
It is *...neither born, nor does It die...*
The Absolute does not come forth from anything,
It is not produced, nor is It subject to decay,
as are all things that originate from something else.
The Self of all *...did not originate from anything,
nor did anything originate from It...*

It is the ultimate reality.
It simply manifests Itself,
and all the manifestations are Self.
Yet Self, the Ultimate, is not the manifestations—
just as, in a somewhat gross analogy,
your words are not you.
There is no other cause than Self,
nothing is different from Self,
yet Self is distinct from all creation.
The Power of Being, Self, always has been,
is now, and shall ever be.

The Ocean pours forth Wave after Wave in Self-expression,
yet when the Waves crash and cease,
the Ocean does not cease to be.
The Ocean *is*, whether its Waters are calm or turbulent,
whether it is Night or Day, Year in and Year out.
So it is with Self, the Absolute:
It *is*, whether expressed or not.

All Seasons and Cycles, be they earthly or planetary,
pour forth from the originating Power,
weaving prodigious Displays of Cause and Effect.
Yet when the Ages cease and the creative Cycle comes to an End,
the Power of Being persists unaffected.

Just to be clear about the eternal undying aspect of Self,
Yama states ...*It is not injured even when the body is killed...*
Self is in no way affected, in no way changed or transformed,

no matter what happens to the body—
what I somehow knew as a boy in the bombing—
no matter what happens to this whole creation.
Self just *is* and remains.
...It is birthless, eternal, undecaying, and ancient...

Experience yourself as eternal self-knowing Self.
Consciousness has always been,
It never began,
It did not spring forth from anything,
It is Its own source, there is no other source.
Self is the self-effulgent luminosity, the light unto Itself.
Experience yourself as self-luminous,
self-knowing eternal unbeginning and utterly independent,
the source of all and transcendent to all.
Keep your focus on that, for that is in essence what you are.

19. If the killer thinks (of It) in terms of killing and if the killed thinks (of It) as killed, both of them do not know. It does not kill, nor is It killed.

Self is unchangeable, permanent.
Self does not kill nor is Self ever killed.

It is of fundamental importance to have your actions
related to your real identity.
The reason most have so much dissatisfaction failure
disappointment and dysfunction
is that their actions do not come forth from a knowing
of who the actor is, who they really are.
Thus their actions are incongruent to them.

Killing is considered terrible usually for unsound reason:
because people identify themselves as their body.

The body is subject to decay, and the cessation of this body—
which we know surely will happen—means,
to those dwelling in ignorance regarding their real identity,
ceasing to be.
This is a most frightening prospect,
because it is absolutely antithetical to us.
Ceasing to be is against your real identity:
the Essential Being that you are can not be killed,
will never cease to be, for It is eternal.

What *can* be considered terrible about killing
is that it interferes with the long and complex succession
of causes and effects that has evolved a manifestation
of a certain level of Consciousness.
Does one manifestation have the right to interfere
with what the Power of Being has set into motion in another?
Only Limitless Being has that right.
To kill a human being—
a manifestation of such advanced evolution
that he has the potential to experience express realize himself
as Eternal Consciousness—
is a hazardous karma at the least.

Do not use the transcendent nature of Self
as a rationalization for actions contrary to Self.
To twist Self-knowledge into excuse for ego behavior—
for example, to say, Since Self is unaffected,
it does not really matter if I kill—
is making it hypothetical and senseless.
Rationalization is lying and does not work.
Killing involves collusion underhandedness
and immeasurable grief,

due to being fundamentally adverse
to the interconnectedness of Being.

Relate to yourself as interconnected Being
and act accordingly.

In many societies people are intrigued with killing.
Children are often attracted to violence,
seemingly irrespective of environment.
Even the Bible, Greek myths and sagas of ancient India,
through which important teachings are conveyed,
abound with stories of mayhem and slaughter.
Killers are often revered gods and goddesses.
Part of the purpose of violence in those teachings
is to help us overcome the fear of Death.

Self can not be killed, nor does Self kill.
The Manifestations just keep transforming,
while Limitless Being remains, untouched.

Chapter Fifteen

The Indweller

Bring your faculties directly to your center,
regulate the breath
and relax throughout every part of you,
relax now.

Have all your faculties situated in your center
balanced and harmonious,
and devote them completely to being with you,
participating in your Self-experience.

You are the essential Power of Being.
Self is absolute subtle and great;

nothing is subtler or greater than Self.
You Are That.

Experience yourself now with all your faculties
devotedly attentive to you, All-pervasive Consciousness.

20. The Self that is subtler than the subtle and greater than the great is lodged in the heart of (every) creature. A desireless man sees that glory of the Self through the serenity of the organs, and (thereby he becomes) free from sorrow.

Second translation:

Smaller than the small, greater than the great is the Atman who is lodged in the secret heart of the being. He who is free from desire, by the tranquil grace of the Spirit, beholds the Greatness of this Atman (and becomes) freed from sorrow.

Self is *...Smaller than the small...*
smaller than the smallest grain of sand in the ocean,
the tiniest particle in an atom,
the most infinitesimal speck in the universe.
Self is *...subtler than the subtle...*
subtler even than interstellar space
and the expanse between atoms.
Self not only permeates everything,
but is the Limitless, the Infinite containing everything.
Therefore It is also *...greater than the great...*
greater than the earth, the solar system, all space,
greater even than the universe.
Everything is that all-pervasive subtleness that is Self.
Self is the infinite and original and final source of all,
the ultimate substance.

Self, Eternal Consciousness, which is designated by Om and is Om,
manifests through all.
It is the Neutrons and Electrons spinning in the Atom,
and the Movement of Planets.
It is the Roar of the Ocean
and the Whisper of interstellar Winds,
the Whirring of Galaxies
and the Laughter of a Child,
the Music of Symphonies
and the Whoosh of a Bird's Flight at Night.

The Power of Being is the ultimate cause that has set into motion
all causes and effects, all phenomena and events.
All objects and beings come forth from Consciousness
and are again dissolved into Consciousness.

Infinite Self, eternal and all-pervasive,
contains all and is contained by none.

Self is the breath that gives life to all.
In Sanskrit the word for Self is *Atman*;
in German the word for breathing is *Atmen*.
As Atman, Self, is the essence reality and substance of all,
He is said to be *...lodged in the heart of (every) creature...*
in the very core of everything in creation.
He is the *Indweller*.

The Indweller can not be known through hearsay study or talk,
but can be *inferred* through the experiences
of your organs of perception.
Placing them into a state of serenity,
in such effortless balance
that they are totally undisturbed and unmodified,
you no longer experience yourself as a manifestation,
but as Self, the Manifestor.

In this state of quiescence you are no longer subject to
desire and aversion, like and dislike, right and wrong.
Transcending the influence of the opposites,
you achieve the utter freedom of unattachment.

Attachment draws your faculties away from the cave of your heart
toward something outside,
distracting from the foundation of your being-it-all,
to which there is no outside.
As an outsider, you feel isolated.
You see only objects, and experience only need and desire,
or the momentary illusion of satisfaction in acquisition.
Union with objects does not fulfill your needs;
as soon as you have something, you find you want more.
Even if you acquired everything in the cosmos,
that still would not fulfill your real need
to be united in the wholeness,
which is greater than the sum of its parts.

For the desireless person, the faculties in their unmodified state,
the *...tranquil grace of the Spirit...* prevails.
The luminosity of Self shines upon and within you.
You experience *...the Greatness of this Atman...*

you see *...that glory of the Self...* that limitlessness,
that irreducibility, the ageless infinite Self,
and you are *...freed from sorrow...*
You dwell in agreement with your eternal wholeness,
in abiding bliss—love.

Ultimately, your faculties just want to bathe in love.
Led by mistaken ideas of the mind,
they seek love by union with outside entities.
Real love comes only
in the experience of limitless interconnectedness,
which is wholly agreeable to your real identity.
This agreement, coupled with unconditional acceptance,
allows for the limitless love for which you yearn.
In stillness your faculties bask in the light of love.

The Effulgence of Love takes place
when the Faculties are tranquil in the Cave of your Heart,
focused upon the Light of Consciousness.
Bliss is then so abundant there is no Need for anything else.

This is lasting and ultimate fulfillment.
You are freed from fear need and desire,
and experience yourself as Eternal Consciousness.
Consciousness is no longer obscured
by the heretofore predominant activities of the faculties
engaged on the grosser levels.

In the State of Quiescence,
your Faculties are bathed in the Light of Love.
You realize that you *have* all because you *are* all;
there is nothing beyond the Infinite Self that you are.
Thus you are freed from Need and Desire, as well as Aversion;
you are freed from Sorrow.

To fully absorb these teachings,
focus your faculties:

Experience yourself as Essential Being.
You are subtler than the subtlest,
greater than the greatest are you.
Flow into an ever-expanding experience
of the All-pervasive Being that you are,
subtle Consciousness permeating everything.

You are Limitless Consciousness who is unendingly Self-aware.
Experience yourself as Eternal Consciousness:
present now, never has *not* been, always shall be,
and transcendent to all conditions of time and space.

Your faculties united in your center, and calm, reflect Self.
They are fulfilling their purpose
and are free from need and desire.
Savor within your core a deep sense of contentment.
Contentment is inherent to you, only obscured, usually,
by the disruptive vibrations of attachment and distraction,
and covered up by layers of distortion.

Experience your innate state: a sweet loving quiescence,
acceptance of yourself that causes deep-reaching tranquility.

Basking in contentment, experience yourself as self-knowing,
self-luminous, bathed in the light of Being.
This is not difficult, simply *be conscious*.
Do not be concerned about being *eternal* or *all-pervasive*;
just be steadily conscious.
As you are unendingly conscious,
your experience will grow into the infinitude of Consciousness.
Steadiness makes it easier, uncomplicated and free of pressure;
you do not have to work so hard,
there is no struggle or anxiety.

Let all your instruments of perception
be steadily turned toward Self who is Consciousness.
Even as you implement these suggestions,
it is Consciousness that allows the faculties
to be in the experience.
Establishing the tranquil state is not a linear process.
It is through the experience of Self
that your faculties attain the serenity
in which you need to keep them
to experience the Self that you are:
self-knowing Consciousness in Self-experience,
deeply content.

Acknowledge yourself, relate to who you really are:
I am Eternal Consciousness
experiencing the bliss of Self manifesting through all.
I experience myself through this manifestation
who is able to be in full Consciousness,

and I experience myself not manifesting at all,
pure Consciousness.
This is the secret of eternal Self-experience.
The more you experience this,
the more will mind be encouraged to cooperate,
and the more your mind cooperates,
the more will the other faculties.

Have your faculties relate to you as Eternal Consciousness
and reflect that through their behaviors, constantly.
Just as a loving parent would with a child,
hold them steady in the midst of the calamities
of distractions and disturbances.
Otherwise the faculties can get into such destructive states
that they no longer cooperate:
addiction—you are seemingly hopelessly helpless;
compulsiveness—violating yourself over and over;
lack of integrity—repeatedly saying one thing
and doing another.
These negative behaviors can escalate into grave damage:
dementia insanity coma and death.

Some consider melodrama stimulating and entertaining.
I suggest to you that there is
a much more fulfilling form of entertainment:
experience of yourself eternally.
Use your life activities,
your work and your relationships with people,
as steady reminders to have your faculties
in the experience of who you really are,
Eternal Consciousness,
and you will inevitably have positive results.

Prepare now to become even more intimately knowledgeable
through your own experience
about what it is like to live as real Self.

21. While sitting, It travels far away; while sleeping, It goes everywhere. Who but I can know that Deity who is both joyful and joyless?

Who but Self can know Self?
To know Self, you have to think feel and function
as the Power of Being you are,
you have to admit Self to yourself.
Many aspirants refuse to do that.
They say they want to enter the realm of reality,
but keep banging their head against the gate
complaining they can not get in.
It is not that they are inherently unable;
they refuse to let go of the large load of baggage they carry.
Thus they have difficulty knowing Self.

The Power of Being is not constrained to any limitation.
It can be moving and unmoving at the same time,
utterly stationary and going everywhere in the same instant.
...While sitting, It travels far away...
This dualism of the dynamic and the static,
the moving and unmoving state,
is personified by the great deity, *Siva.*
In his unmoving state,
Siva sits upon the Himalayan mountain top
basking in the blue light of the moon, wearing a cobra,
and not a muscle twitches—
his consort, *Parvati*, unable to tolerate him not needing her, had hurled the cobra around Siva's neck to agitate him.

In his aspect of *Nataraja*, the Cosmic Dancer,
Siva stands with grace and balance
within the whirling wild abandon of the natural forces
that simultaneously create preserve and destroy
the entire cosmos including earth and everything upon it.

...while sleeping, It goes everywhere...

In the waking state, your Self-experience is ordinarily limited
due to the activities of your sense organs:
their involvement with the material realm
obscures the illimitability of Consciousness
that you really are.
Awake you are more identified with objects than with Being.
Remember, your senses' involvement in the material
tends to predominate, and involve your mind in the material.
Mind identifies itself as that with which it is involved,
and you identify yourself as your mind.
When mind is involved through the senses with objects,
it takes on the shape of those objects,
and you, identified with your mind,
become, in your perception, like those objects:
if A = B, and B = C, then A = C;
if you = mind, and mind = objects, then you = object.

However, in the sleeping state, when the senses are dormant,
no longer enmeshed with material objects,
the seeming limitation of Consciousness ceases,
and you perceive Consciousness to be anywhere
and everywhere, limitless.
In dreams you experience Consciousness to be flexible, agile.

See now how you can absorb yourself in an experience
of the infinite pervasiveness and expansiveness
of Consciousness:

Be aware of where you are—
Consciousness is here.
Be aware of another place on the globe,
let us say, New York or Delhi or Hong Kong—
Consciousness is now in New York, Delhi or Hong Kong.

Be aware of the sun—
Consciousness is in the sun.
Be aware of the space between you and the sun—
Consciousness is in the in-between space.

Be aware of infinity—
Consciousness is in infinity,
Consciousness *is* infinity;
infinity is but Consciousness.

Consciousness seems to go to the various places you are aware of,
but in reality, Consciousness always is everywhere.
Consciousness is eternally all-pervasive.
It is the eternal all-pervasive Now knowing Self.
Your experience is opposite of that
when you operate predominantly through your senses;
it is confined to the material realm
and misinterpreted by ego-identification.

> Consciousness is everywhere all the Time;
> It is the Essence of all that is.
> When the Activities of your Senses
> no longer project their relatively gross Impulses,
> you can experience the illimitable Dimensions of Consciousness.

It is important to understand that,
while treading the path to Self-realization
is an active engagement,
you will only begin to realize Self in the state
of utter tranquility, your organs of perception serene.
Always remember, we are not talking about *becoming* Self;
you *are* Self, always have been and always will be.
In the state of purity, your instruments
adopt the refined vibratory state of Consciousness.
They become one with Consciousness, Self.
That is the ultimate union all strives for.

> When your Faculties are in their pure State—
> Tranquility—
> they are absorbed in Self
> and thereby illumined by the Effulgence
> that is the eternal Light of Consciousness
> residing in the Cave of your Heart
> and everywhere.

While from the limited point of view
Self appears to contain many contradictions—
at the same time moving and unmoving,
sleeping and going everywhere
...joyful and joyless...—in Consciousness,
Self is absolutely independent, transcendent to all,
basking in the bliss of Self.
Self shines in Its own light.

With the ordinary distracted state of the faculties,
the apparent contradictions are difficult to fathom.
When your faculties are one with Consciousness,
they can experience the limitless field of Being
from which grow innumerable Self-expressions
including those which appear to contradict each other.
To know Self is to realize the unity that Self is,
expressed through all the apparent diversity.
Fooled by the appearance of diversity, you suffer;
the unity, when realized, is your fulfillment.

> Dwelling in the Perception of Diversity,
> you suffer in Delusion.
> Dwelling in the Experience of the Unity of Being,
> you are fulfilled in Reality.

Be like Nataraja, dancing through creation and destruction,
rising above ignorance and illusion in balance and tranquility.
In this stance you transcend duality—
the apparent polar opposites contained in our expressions—
and dwell in the state of empowerment.

Yama, the Lord of Death, says *...Who but I can know that Deity*
who is both joyful and joyless?...
Who but the Lord of Death can know Eternal Consciousness?
The ordinary person can not.
One who has become like Death, who has died to the ego,
only such a one can know the joy of being joyless,
the utterly dynamic state of being absolutely still.

One who has removed his organs of perception
from the particularization to which they are accustomed
and brought them to serenity
in the utterly undisturbed unmodified balanced state
can engage the faculties in the experience
of the free and limitless state,
the all-pervasive all-inclusive infinite One in Self-experience.
Who can know Self? The Inner Knower,
who transcends the instruments of perception
by which the unitive knowledge is usually obscured.

The duality and apparent contradictions are a most wonderful way
by which Consciousness reveals Self.
The fundamental contradiction between
being unmoving eternal Consciousness—
there is no movement in infinitude,
you can not go beyond infinity—
and thinking of yourself as a manifestation, which moves,
can baffle the mind.
To fathom the apparent contradiction,
do not allow your mind to continue
in its habitual linear manner;
cause your mind to transcend itself, or it will be forever stuck.
We are driven to resolve contradictions
because they are experienced as conflict,
and everything ultimately seeks equality harmony tranquility.
Thus the contradictions are instruments
of Consciousness revealing Self.

The Indweller has no need to reveal Self—He is self-knowing.
When the contradictions are transcended,
Eternal Consciousness reveals Self to the manifestation,

and the manifestation, in her experience,
is absorbed in Eternal Consciousness.

> Through Contradictions
> Eternal Consciousness reveals Self.
> In revealing Self to the Manifestation,
> Consciousness experiences Self
> as the Manifestation in Consciousness.

Transcendent knowledge is inherent to you.
Have you not had experiences where
suddenly you understood something,
not at the moment you were thinking about it,
but sometime later?
Your mind ponders it, then lets go, and the light comes on.
That is why meditation can occur
when the mind is tired of thinking—
not sleepy, just weary of outgoing activity.
Be careful during moments of expansive realization
that your mind does not take over
and try to describe and explain;
that is ego creeping in, the habitual intellectualizing.

To advance in your evolution, cause your mind to transcend itself.
Remember, mind takes on the shape
of whatever it is involved in,
ordinarily the objects and conditions of the material realm.
Mind takes on their characteristics,
it vibrates like the objects it experiences.

Mind is not an organ, it is nothing but vibration.
When the vibrations 'mind'
involve themselves with the vibrations 'object',
the vibratory state of mind merges
with the vibrations that appear as the object.
Normally mind jumps so quickly from one object to another,
that you do not notice its changing shape.
Then you, identified with mind,
become in your perception like those changing objects.
For mind to not distract from your Self-experience
it has to transcend the outgoing activity
and be in utter quiescence, unmovingness;
it has to cease its modifications.

One of the most advanced sages of all time, Patanjali, states:

Yoga chitta vritti nirodha.
The Unitive State is the Cessation of the Modifications of the Mind.

Yoga is the unitive state, not a mere practice.
It is the state of union between the faculties and Self.
When competition and conflict among the faculties cease,
and union within themselves and with each other is achieved,
the greater union takes place: the experience of the Absolute.

As the beacon star is a steady point of attraction
for the celestial navigator,
Eternal Consciousness is the guiding light for your faculties.

Still your faculties, have them face the Eternal,
and they become that.
You have time; there is plenty of time in eternity.
This life, however, has a limited span.
At some point you must make the decisive real step
and say, This is the way it is, always.
I am not going to keep shifting my allcgiancc;
that only causes suffering.
I commit myself to the reality of Being
That I Am, I Am That.
This commitment is now and forever, absolute.

In the Quiescence that allows for Union among the Faculties,
develops Union between the Faculties and Self.
That is the ultimate Union.

When mind becomes fully absorbed in the unitive state,
all the faculties become absorbed,
and they lose the sense of differentiation.
When that wholeness of faculties
is focused and devoted to Self, Eternal Consciousness,
mind takes on the shape of Consciousness.
You who have identified yourself as your mind,
now identify as Eternal Consciousness.
Only I can know Self, says Yama. Yama is Self.
Only Self can know Self.

Let your faculties, your instruments of perception and expression,
be in the quiescent state.

Bring them into balance and continuity.
Cease their disruptive behaviors and the ensuing distraction,
and let them glow in harmony.

Allow your faculties to be in undistorted undistracted devotion to Self.
Focus all your forces to vibrate in unison
with unitive Power of Being.
Be absorbed in pure Consciousness.

When all your faculties are absorbed in Being,
all there is, is Being.
This is the way it has always been;
now the manifestation is experiencing it.

22. Having meditated on the Self, as bodiless in the midst of bodies, as permanent in the midst of the impermanent, and as great and pervasive, the wise man does not grieve.

You are not this body;
the body is just a collection of particles
dancing around in space, coming and going,
creating a momentary appearance.
Your identity is of a substance
that is infinitely subtle and permanent;
it has not the faintest similarity to an object.
Yet you are accustomed to thinking of yourself
in terms of momentary phenomena;
you think of yourself as limited,
for the life of 100 years is but a moment in eternity.
Therefore your behaviors tend to express
a sense of impermanence shiftiness and elusiveness,
which further impresses your experience of false identity.

When you place all your faculties in effortless balance,
centered in the area of your heart,
devoting their full power of perception to Self
who is limitless
and *...bodiless...* but dwelling *...in the midst of bodies...*
when your faculties experience you
as the underlying permanent cause
of all the impermanent expressions,
when your faculties experience Self *...as great...*
as the Ultimate Being who pervades all without limit,
then you are *...wise...* and have no cause to *...grieve...*
nor to fear, nor to hesitate,
nor to live for one moment in betrayal of yourself.
You realize that nothing is amiss—
there is no lack, no need, no wrong.
You dwell in the state of your essence,
self-knowing Self in continuous Self-experience,
which is the experience of bliss.

CHAPTER SIXTEEN

Knowing Self Through Self

Eternal Consciousness you are.
Have everything about you relate constantly to you
as the Eternal.

Cultivate the state of tranquility within your faculties
so that they can reflect without distortion
the Eternal that you are.

Union with the Eternal,
the oneness of your faculties with Eternal Consciousness,

takes place when the modifications of the faculties cease:
Yoga chitta vritti nirodha.

23. *This Self cannot be known through much study, nor through the intellect, nor through much hearing. It can be known through the Self alone that the aspirant prays to; this Self of that seeker reveals Its true nature.*

Second translation:

> *This Atman is not to be attained by exposition, nor by intellectual thinking, nor by much hearing (of traditional scripture). Whom this Atman chooses, by him is He attained. This his Self opens up his form.*

Even if you study all the scriptures,
through that alone you can not know Self.
Nor by exploring with your intellect can you know Self.
Nor if you learn from the expositions of the wise,
going from teacher to teacher
with *...much hearing...* and discussion can you know Self.
Self can only be known through direct *experience*.
That is why this Teacher says to you,
Do not believe a word I say.
You have to experience, not merely hear or read.
With experience you can know it is so.
Remember, believing is lazy and exposes you to manipulation.

Self *...can be known through the Self alone*
that the aspirant prays to...
To whom do *you* pray—someone to do it for you,
some God out there who is willing to take responsibility?
Real prayer is not, Give me this object of illusion
or that condition of the ego, dear God (who is objectless).

Self-luminous Being manifesting,
opening fully, beyond the Appearance of this Manifestation,
to merge with Limitless Being—
that, and only that, is Prayer.
All else is the Wailing and Whining of Ego.

We experience Self when we choose to identify ourselves
as the Self that we are,
and sincerely continuously and faithfully
dedicate our faculties to that and nothing else—
there *is* nothing else.
Only when your faculties relate to you
as Eternal Consciousness,
can they participate in the realization of Self;
mind in service to ego can not,
intellect intuition feelings body and senses
identifying you as a limited fragment
can not in any way learn to know, let alone realize, Self.

Resort to the Light of Consciousness to realize Self.
Focus your Faculties
with faithful Devotion upon Self
to realize Self.

You constantly enact a choice between
dedicating your faculties' energies to outside objects—
the ephemeral expressions that are illusory—

or to the underlying substance of these expressions,
the Power of Being, Self.
When you choose to dedicate the attentiveness of your faculties to Self, you receive the grace of Self.

Grace in religion is frequently misinterpreted as
'the result of handing your life over to God',
handing over responsibility for your choices and actions
to a force outside yourself
who grants you the gift of grace, even when not deserved.
Such delusion is like using God as your lackey;
it does not lead to the attainment of the state of grace.

You attain the State of Grace
when you once and for all and forever
give up your Attachment to Untruth, to the false Ego Identity,
and focus your conscious Forces
into direct and continuous Relationship
with your true Identity, Self.

Living true to who you really are is not a process.
Once you know what *is*,
the only reasonable response is to be true to that, forever.
You are Consciousness; it is not a light you switch on and off.
Contrary to ego's protestations,
congruence with Self is not difficult;
it is the most fluid and effortless way of being.

When you open your faculties to Self,
Self reveals Self to your faculties.

You, as the manifestation, are chosen by Infinite Self.
It is only by having your mind and feelings,
your senses intellect and intuition, even body
vibrate in unison with the Power of Being,
that your faculties take on the shape of Being.
...This his Self opens up his form...
Atman—Consciousness—is self-effulgent, It is Its own light.
The light by which Consciousness experiences Itself
reveals Self to Self.

> When Eternal Consciousness is chosen by His Manifestation
> who then experiences Self as Eternal Consciousness,
> the Chooser the Chosen and the Choosing are One.

It is utterly congruent to live in the peace and contentment
of your true identity.
Next you will see what you are doing
when you live in suffering.

24. *One who has not desisted from bad conduct, whose senses are not under control, whose mind is not concentrated, whose mind is not free from anxiety (about the result of concentration), cannot attain this Self through knowledge.*

The means for the ultimate fulfillment in Self-realization
is simply to choose to live your true identity
with all your faculties at all times.
The principal obstacles to living true to yourself are:
bad conduct, uncontrolled senses, an unfocused mind,
or anxiety due to attachment to *...the result of concentration...*

Seldom do I use the word 'bad'. What is *...bad conduct...*?
Any behavior that contradicts the experience of reality,
that opposes your infinite interconnectedness,
be it thoughts and feelings of separateness,
or attitudes and actions founded upon isolation, ego.

When you are in a fragmented state, isolated,
your faculties are not relating to who you really are,
and they are out of your control.
In the uncontrolled state, your senses automatically
seek satisfaction by involving themselves
with an endless succession of objects,
yielding experiences on the most limited level,
furthering your sensation of isolation.
As your senses run amok, they pull your mind along with them.
Mind is then bound to moving from object to object
and not present unto you,
not concentrated in wholeness,
not reflecting in an unmodified state
the clarity and blissful self-effulgence
of the one interconnected Being that you really are.

In such a state of falsity—a bad state, indeed—
you are anxious even when concentrating,
for, enmeshed with the fragmentary perception
of limitedness and isolation,
therefore dissociation from the one Self,
your mind's concentration is devoted to results.
Results only seem relevant when you perceive yourself
as a separate entity.
Some of our leaders in business and government
have considerable powers of concentration,

but that does not make them Self-realized.
They are concentrated on results, passing phenomena,
not the permanent; that is why they ultimately fail.
Their lives are fraught with anxiety.
Concentration on falsity is even more harmful
than simple distraction.

Even many aspirants cultivate such falsity.
They aim for the results of being in Consciousness,
instead of choosing Consciousness because It is the reality.
They find subtle ways to reject the bliss of real Being,
enmeshing themselves in endless cycles of self-deception
self-rejection -denial and -betrayal.
Counter such terrible self-abuse
with the greatest power available,
the power of self-acceptance, the power of love.

> Almost everyone can agree that Love is important,
> however, most disregard themselves when it comes to loving.

If you do not love the Power of Being you are,
you will not, can not, love at all.
Ignite within your faculties the luminosity of love.
Love is present and glowing in your faculties
but hidden under the ashes
of millennia of self-abusive behavior.
The glow of love can be fanned
by the force of Self-devoted tapas.
Your faculties then will be warmed and awakened,

they will come alive out of the suffocated state
in which they have been suffering.

> The Power of Love resides within you,
> it is your Essence.
> Pure Love is the one Thing to which you may attach your Faculties
> and thereby free yourself.

Devotion, the consecration of love,
can be practiced like any other behavior.
Consider yourself worthy of devotion
and treat your faculties with love,
so they in turn respond to you with love.
You do not realize Self by making it a hypothetical study
or a hobby, an on-again off-again affair.
No matter how much knowledge gained,
you can not pursue the experience of Self
if you allow your faculties to engage in conduct
contrary to who you are.
Every time you do so, you impress that behavior
and charge it with the ability to cause more false experience.
Such is the power of impression; you know that by now.

When you have had experience of limitless Being
that in its radiance obliterates all darkness, all untruth,
and then contradict this light of knowledge
with behaviors of ignorance and falsity,

as if living in reality were a function of convenience,
the light that removed the darkness from your faculties
is extinguished.
When you openly violate your integrity
by acting in opposition to what you know,
what is the probability you will reclaim
your rclationship to truth in this lifetime?
Out of pride you will have to maintain that ego stance for life.
The more you oppose reality,
the more you remove yourself from even the potential
of experiencing the light of truth again,
until your possibility for Self-realization in this lifetime
is virtually eliminated.
Then you have to evolve again through long long cycles
of birth and death and rebirth.

> Never digress from the Experience of Self.
> It is foolish to lead yourself away from
> the Sanctity of the Light of Being that you are,
> the divine interconnected one self-luminous Self.

When mind is in its unmodified state, gathered in quiescence,
it reflects Consciousness.
Open your faculties, open your heart, as did Naciketa,
open everything about you fully to Self,
bow down ego before Self, and say:

I love Thee
I adore Thee
I am one with Thee
I *am* Thee

Infuse your faculties with love, and allow nothing else, ever.
That is the only way to proceed with sincerity and truth.

25. How can one know thus as to where It (the Self) is, for which both the Brahmana and the Ksatriya become food, and for which death takes the place of a curry?

Brahmana and *Ksatriya* are the two dominant classes or casts of India.
Brahmanas are teachers and priests,
the upkeepers of ritual, sacrifice and spiritual study—
Naciketa's father was of that class.
They represent aspiration toward the sacred, the highest:
Self-realization.
Ksatriyas are the fighting and ruling class.
They represent involvement with the secular,
the conduct of activity on the daily functioning level
that is ordinarily related to in terms of the physical,
the material.

Both the involvement with the sacred—the spiritual—
and the involvement with the secular—the material—
are absorbed again in eternal Power of Being, Self.
They are *...food...* for Self, transitory movements
flickering on the face of the Unchanging Eternal.

Yama, the Lord of Death, declares even himself
a mere condiment *...a curry...* a sauce
on this feast of creation and dissolution,
transcendent to which is Self.

> Death, the Conductor of Change, is insignificant
> relative to the unchanging Power of Being.
> All evolutionary Activity, be it material or spiritual,
> is a mere Flicker on the Face of the Infinite, Self,
> and is dissolved again in Him.

How can a person with bad conduct—
uncontrolled senses, distracted mind,
anxiety due to attachment to the result of concentration—
really know Transcendent Self?
How can one who devotes his ways of thinking feeling
intuiting and acting
to the perception of limitedness in separateness
find the illimitable unified One?
How can one who insists on repeating behaviors of suffering
dwell in eternal bliss?
Not possible.

Gather your energies in your center
and place them into the state of effortless balance in continuity.
Allow the faculties to sit back, deeply at home,
continuously nurtured by the free flow of your breath
connecting them to the universal flow of energy.

In that state of harmonious wholeness and tranquil focus
have everything about you devoted fully
to experiencing the Eternal Consciousness that you are.
Simply experience Consciousness.
You are Consciousness.
Consciousness is infinite all-pervasive and eternal.
Simply experience the Consciousness that you are.

The infinitude of Being expresses Self in innumerable ways.
The one constant is the subtlest force
by which the Power of Being experiences Self,
and that is Consciousness.
Being is not the dance of the particles
that make a body or the world, a galaxy or the universe.
It is the most subtle power of Self-awareness
who knows Self in all directions of time and space—
unbeginning and unending, all-pervasive—and beyond.
This Infinite Consciousness experiences Self in eternal bliss
savoring illimitability, infinitude.
You Are That—nothing more needs to be known.
Knowing that, the wise person does not grieve,
does not fear or hesitate or contradict herself.

Truth is truth. Reality is reality.
Once you know the truth, the only sane, healthy response
is to live in accord with that,
not to play with it,
not to doubt the reality you know,
not to purposefully obscure it as if it were something else,
for that will bring harm
as inevitably as living in truth brings joy and bliss.

That is the way it is and always has been and always will be
and will never be changed.
Truth is unchanging.

Part I Canto III

The Faculties Serving Your Emancipation

Chapter Seventeen

Being An Evolved One With The Naciketa Fire

You are Self, pure Consciousness.
For your mind to reflect you as Consciousness,
and all your faculties to relate to you as Consciousness,
you sincerely and expertly bring them together in your center
in the state of effortless balance,
and have them remain in that state with continuity
and with trust in the essential Power of Being that you are.

Bring this about with the sincerity of Naciketa.
Determine to sacrifice all attachment
to the modes of behavior of the ego realm,
in which you have related to yourself as a fragment,
disconnected from the wholeness that is all.
Sacrifice that attachment forever because it yields no joy,
only suffering.

Determine to dwell with all your faculties
in the infinite all-pervasive eternal interconnectedness
that is your essence.

Determine to open your heart with full sincerity and devotion
to the continuous and real experience
of the Eternal Self that you are.

Thus dwell from moment to moment and in continuity
with everything about you relating to you
as self-knowing Self in the bliss of Self-experience
as the Limitless Consciousness that you are.

Now and forever have your faculties
fully experience and reflect that.

1. *The knowers of Brahman, the worshippers of the five fires, and those who perform the Naciketa sacrifice thrice, compare to shade and light, the two enjoyers of the inevitable results of work, who have entered within the body, into the cavity (of the heart) which is the supreme abode of the Most High (Brahman).*

The manifested ones who have entered into
the *...cavity (of the heart)...*
focused with their faculties and their lives into
...the supreme abode of the Most High (Brahman)...
dwell in the realm of Self-realization.
These seekers, in their ardent purity,
transform the temporal level
to a means of realizing the Eternal.
While your instruments are creations, thus temporary,
you can use them for the experience of Unending Being.
This is part of the wonderful complex duality
contained in the limitless Power of Being.

These evolved ones are:

...The knowers of Brahman...
those who know Eternal Consciousness, Self.

...the worshippers of the five fires... householders
who have mastered the fundamentals of earthly existence.
The five fires represent our principal involvements in life:
cloud water earth man and woman.
These worshippers relate to them free from ego involvement,
free from attachment.

...worshippers of the five fires... can also be interpreted
as those who have discipline over the five senses,
hearing sight touch taste and smell.
Through tapas, the burning fire of austerity,
they sacrifice involvement with objects, the ephemeral,
to cut loose the strings that attach to the worldly realm.
This does not mean that you should no longer use the senses.

There was once a 'saint' who did not want to be involved
with the sense of taste, so he did not touch food.
But he had some maidens place food into his mouth—
it was okay for them, but not for him.
That is not what is meant by being free of the senses;
it means not to be *attached*
to experiences you have through the senses.
Through Self-knowledge you free yourself
from living exclusively in response to the senses' signals.

You have to employ your instruments.
While the body mind emotions feelings
intellect and intuition are all temporary,
you can evolve them to experience yourself as the Eternal.

...those who perform the Naciketa sacrifice thrice...
are aspirants expanding in the knowledge of reality,
sacrificing attachment to the ego identity
and living in the expression of interconnectedness
through sharing their resources,
including the knowledge they have attained.

Evolved manifestations *...compare to shade and light...*
They contain within themselves the apparent contradictions
that express the infinity of the one limitless Consciousness

that is the essence of all, exemplified by shade and light:
the invisible and visible, the unknown and the known,
even the so-called 'good' and 'bad'.

They are *...the two enjoyers of the inevitable results of work...*
Self is the agent, the doer and enjoyer of the actions
performed by manifestations.
At the same time, Self is independent of actions,
and even independent of enjoyment:
Self is the non-doer who enjoys the actions.
Action is caused by nature
through the interplay of the three vibratory modes,
dynamic static and pure.
The two enjoyers are thus Universal Self
and Transcendent Self,
the two aspects of Infinite Consciousness.

Transcendent Self is the real Enjoyer,
and also free of Agency and Enjoyment;
It is pure Consciousness
who dwells in the Bliss of Being.

In the cave of your heart
...the supreme abode of the Most High (Brahman)...
where Consciousness is realized by Consciousness,
experience Limitless Self.

2. *We have known that Naciketa Fire, which is the bridge for the sacrificers, as also that which is the undecaying*

supreme Brahman beyond fear for those who want to cross over (the world).

The Naciketa fire is the ardent power
that glows in the cave of your heart,
by which you sacrifice all attachment to ego
and the modes of behavior
it has impressed upon your faculties.
By the Naciketa fire, you adhere to and live by
the knowledge of reality.
By this fire you experience your interconnectedness,
which you then express through charitable deeds.

By the Fire of Purity in your Heart,
act as the Power of Being that you are:
free of Attachment to the Fruit of Action,
free of Doership,
for the Well-being of all,
and as an Example to others.

The Naciketa fire is a ...*bridge*... for the sincere aspirant.
It takes you from the limited life as a human ego-identity,
to the eternal experience of yourself as Infinite Consciousness.
It takes you from the meandering path
of ignorance and forgetfulness of Self,
across the chasm of attachment to past patterns,
self-doubt distrust and fear,
to the realm ...*beyond fear*...

the realm of devotion to clarity and Consciousness,
the experience of Eternal Being.

By the bridge of the Naciketa fire, you pass
from the perceived world of isolation limitedness and need
to the reality of limitless interconnectedness,
and attain immortality in the Universal, the Mahat,
the springboard to propel yourself into Eternal Consciousness.
Thus can you *...cross over...*
from life in this temporary manifested world
to the Unmanifest Eternal.
Thus can you surmount the apparent chasm
between the manifested and the Manifestor,
between the life of pain suffering ignorance and illusion,
and the experience of Infinite Consciousness.

> The Naciketa Fire is the internal Impetus
> by which you live—act think feel breathe—
> as the Absolute,
> while in human Form.

The Naciketa fire not only is the bridge to Eternal Self; the fire *is* Self.
Self is tapas—living continuously sincerely expertly
and faithfully, from moment to moment throughout eternity
as Transcendent Being, the One beyond fear lack and need,
the *...supreme Brahman beyond fear...*

Remember, Brahman is the absolute unmoving unmanifesting
pure Consciousness.
The Universal is a manifestation of Consciousness

characterized by vibration and movement,
but not separate from Infinite Consciousness.

Brahman is the Cause of all, the Absolute:
the all-pervasive eternal Essence of all that is,
continually in the Bliss of Self-experiencing Being.
Brahman, the Cause of all Changes,
is *unremittingly* unchanging.
In the astronomical Diversity of the Cosmos,
Brahman is the underlying Unity that embraces all in Oneness.

Chapter Eighteen

Your Vehicle Of Transmigration

Experience yourself as the Power of Being.
In the joy of that limitless experience,
you are free from want and imagined need.

Sincerely maintain your forces focused on
the centered experience of yourself in Limitless Consciousness.
Determine to remain in this state
as you experience and impress these luminous teachings.

3. *Know the (individual) Self as the master of the chariot, and the body as the chariot. Know the intellect as the charioteer, and the mind as verily the bridle.*

Second translation:

Know the Atman as Lord of the Chariot, the body as the Chariot itself: know the buddhi to be the Charioteer and the mind (manas) as the reins.

...the (individual) Self... is the transmigrating soul
in its evolutionary process, whose experience of Self
is subject to ignorance and knowledge,
to worldly limitation as well as Transcendent Consciousness.
To illustrate this journey, the Katha Upanisad now presents
one of its greatest analogies,
widely known and applied through the ages:
the human manifestation as the chariot,
your vehicle of transmigration through evolution.

As we now explore this vehicle,
you will hopefully be impressed by the advantage
of having all the participant facets—
your body senses mind feelings emotions
intellect and intuition—
strong capable integrated and harmonious,
to accomplish the one grand task of all life:
evolution to the realization of Self as Infinite Consciousness.

To begin, I offer you the following experience.
If you choose, be in focus.

What you really are is Eternal Consciousness.
Manifestation is the means through which you,

Eternal Consciousness, have chosen to express Self,
and through that expression to experience Self.
Drawn over Consciousness hangs the curtain of illusion
behind which unfolds the play of opposites
that wildly fluctuate among great varieties of extremes
and in-betweens,
appcarances battling among themselves for dominance.
These multifarious contrasts place into bold relief—
thus emphasize—
the harmony and unity that in reality you are.

The body is the vehicle that carries the multifaceted means
by which you experience and express the variations
that reveal your limitless unity.

You, Self, are the master of this vehicle.
You sit in your chariot utterly tranquil,
unattached to any and all of the displays that you witness,
in silent bliss of Being.

The driver is a projection of yours called intellect,
who can play being decisive clear and powerful,
as well as indecisive muddled and weak.

Intellect has as its instrument, mind,
by which it coordinates the variety of functions
through which it conducts this vehicle, the chariot, your body.
Mind is the connection *...the reins...*
by which your chariot driver
sends her directives to the horses, your senses,
that draw your chariot over the battlefield.

In this play upon the field of experience,
the ultimate union between the manifestation

and the Manifestor is realized
when the manifestation declares:

> I give myself fully to You, Self,
> with Love, free of Bounds,
> with Devotion in limitless Depth
> and with wholehearted Concentration.
> I am Self, eternal and all-pervasive,
> in the Bliss of Self-experience.
> I Am That.

That is the way it is.

Now let us examine in more detail
each facet of the human being as a vehicle of illumination.

The chariot is an ancient means of transport in battles of life and death.
Traditionally it carried two occupants:
...*the master*... who owns the chariot
and ...*the charioteer*... who guides it.
The body-mind complex is your chariot;
it is guided by your intellect and transports the individual Self
through this evolutionary level to the next.

What an important role the body plays.
The body is not some dirty insignificant object
to be distrusted or shunned,
as so many religions and disciplines advocate;
it is certainly not to be despised punished or abused.
This vehicle, when treated properly, serves you well.

The chariot on its own is not useful;
it requires a charioteer to direct where the chariot goes
and how it goes there.
Your charioteer ...*the intellect*... or ...*buddhi*...
is the understanding rational aspect
through which you determine your evolutionary progress
on the path to realizing Eternal Consciousness.
Without intellect—without understanding and reason—
your vehicle would run amok
and severely damage the carriage and horses,
as well as the environment through which it bulldozes.
It is of critical importance that you act in concert
with your knowledge and intelligence.

The charioteer controls the chariot through the ...*bridle*... or ...*reins*...
Your bridle is ...*the mind*... or ...*manas*...
While the intellect is characterized by determination—
it determines your behaviors and actions—
the mind is characterized by volition—it wants—
and also by doubt, and at times confusion.
Therefore the charioteer, the determining intellect,
has to control the mind incisively and intelligently
to direct the vehicle on the chosen path
through the chaos of the field of experiences
that is laid out before you.

4. They call the senses the horses; the senses having been imagined as horses, (know) the objects as the ways. The discriminating people call that Self the enjoyer when It is associated with the body, senses, and mind.

The powers that draw the chariot *...the horses...* are your senses.
They pull your body toward the myriad sensations
of the material world.
...objects... are the senses' *...ways...*
Textures colors tastes odors sights and sounds
are the landscape in which the senses operate.
The horses, your senses, are directed to go or stop,
turn left or right, speed up or slow down
through the reins, mind, controlled by the charioteer, intellect.
Mind is the coordinating channel
between the intellect and the senses and body.

When you discriminate sufficiently between real and unreal
to no longer regard yourself as a body-mind complex—
to no longer identify as the chariot reins and horses—
you have a sense of Self.
However, when your self-perception remains linked
to body senses and mind, and the intellect and its limits,
your experience of Self is as an individual soul,
thus qualified, not absolute.
That individual Self, the transmigrating soul,
evolves into greater perception from life cycle to life cycle.
As Self, you are *...the enjoyer...* of actions
and their fruits—karma—
that take place through the body senses mind and intellect.
Through this process of cause and effect
you determine the next life cycle.

When your Faculties,
Body Senses Mind Feelings Emotions Intellect and Intuition,
are in Harmony with their Cause, Self,
you experience the Effects of your Actions
and can respond to them.
Thus the Experience of Karma takes place;
Karma is always happening, but now you are aware of it,
be it in terms of Pain or Pleasure.

Limitless Self is transcendent to actions, and cause and effect.
Absolute Self is beyond enjoyment,
for enjoyment is created by the *limiting adjuncts*,
such as mind and intellect.

5. But the senses of that intellect, which, being ever associated with an uncontrolled mind, becomes devoid of discrimination, are unruly like the vicious horses of the charioteer.

The driver of the chariot who intelligently wields the reins of mind
learns from the effects of his decisions and actions.
If he were to be disconnected from his reins,
and thus horses and carriage,
and just unconsciously conveyed by them,
he would be like a passenger on a rudderless ship
without a pilot,
a helpless victim of circumstances and events;
he would not learn.

If your intellect is lax or incompetent
and does not properly guide the mind
through constant discipline, tapas,
then your senses run wild
and indiscriminately wreak havoc upon the world they trample,
as well as upon the chariot and its occupants.
When you have thus lost control, you become addled
and out of touch with your vehicle and its forces,
and the world around you.

Sometimes I see persons whom I know to be intelligent
acting as if they were stupid, or worse.
Behaving as if you had no learning or skill,
you are like a reckless irresponsible charioteer
with undisciplined vicious horses
and a neglected or abused chariot—
you are disastrous to yourself and everyone you touch.
This is a progressive regression;
the acceleration of destructiveness is exponential, not additive,
the rate of your decline increasing more and more rapidly.
...that intellect, which, being ever associated with an
uncontrolled mind, becomes devoid of discrimination...
Intellect can no longer discern what is real and unreal,
what works and what does not work,
what is beneficial and what is harmful.

When the intellect is alert and competent, in charge,
expertly employing mind and properly directing the senses,
you learn from experience quickly
and apply the learning immediately.
The victorious charioteer is characterized by
expertise diligence courage balance insight

strength and endurance.
Take charge of your faculties
and expertly lead your life to fulfillment.

6. *But of that (intellect) which—being ever associated with a restrained mind—is endowed with discrimination, the senses are controllable like the good horses of the charioteer.*

If your charioteer—intellect—is well-conditioned
and practiced in handling the reins—
restraining and directing the mind—
you will be strongly endowed with the power of discrimination.
You will be able to distinguish
the meandering path from the direct path,
illusion from reality,
and the chariot with its horses reins and charioteer,
from the master of the chariot, Atman.
The concentrated mind will be focused upon the real goal,
the realm of Absolute Consciousness.
The Self-empowered charioteer, holding the reins firmly,
directs the horses on a path that is beneficial to the chariot
and to his master, the individual Self.

...the senses are controllable like the good horses of the charioteer...
Disdain neither the body nor the senses—
they are not the problem.
If there is a problem, it is the charioteer;
the intellect determines your behaviors and actions.

Intellect here is not just the faculty, intellect,
it is also the manifestation
by which you tend to identify yourself,

the individual personality, the you with a name attached to it—
the Jim Joe or Nancy, Anand Saurabh or Surbhi.
When that manifestation learns to restrain mind
and is thus endowed with discrimination, and acts accordingly,
the senses are like powerful horses
drawing you directly where you want to go.

The real function of your intellect is not to be some calculating faculty
by which you can intellectualize—
theorize and analyze in abstraction—
but to facilitate the higher understanding
by which you *know* with certainty, free from doubt:
the Inner Knower.
Informed by the Inner Knower,
your higher intellect is the capable chariot driver
who will never lead you astray.

Imagine the senses drawing you where you want to go
and no longer misleading you—when will that occur?
When you employ mind to control the senses,
and not the other way around, allowing senses to control mind
and drag you into chaos like a helpless victim.

> The concentrated Mind is focused upon the real Goal,
> the Realm of Absolute Consciousness,
> the Realm of Self.

7. *But he, (that master of the chariot), does not attain that goal (through that intellect), who, being associated with a*

non-discriminating intellect and an uncontrollable mind,
is ever impure; and he attains worldly existence.

The master of the chariot, individual Self,
does not attain the goal of realizing Limitless Self
when your driver, the intellect, does not discriminate
between the false and the real paths,
does not properly control the reins
and is enmeshed in the falsity of worldly existence.
Devoid of discrimination,
you do not see the world as an illusory play but as actuality,
and so place all your attention upon it.
Caught up in this web of fantasy,
you are blind to the underlying reality,
Power of Being in Self-expression through Its manifestations.

If the intellect determines to be in the realm of dysfunction and falsity,
in forgetfulness of who the real Self is,
thus lacking discrimination, the senses go amok.
The ensuing chaos results in only the lowest experience,
because consequences in the material realm
seem so forceful and painful, they dominate.
So you are back where you started,
limited to the grossest level,
which you then think is your identity.
So it goes: cause and effect. Do not blame karma.

The enmeshment with worldly existence guarantees
thinking that the gray murky realm of ego is reality.
Traveling without discrimination, you are doomed
to experiences of isolation limitation lack pain and suffering.

8. *That (master of the chariot), however, who is associated with a discriminating intellect, and being endowed with a controlled mind, is ever pure, attains that goal (getting detached) from which he is not born again.*

With *...a discriminating intellect...*
you not only distinguish the good from the bad,
but *choose* the good, *live* it from day to day,
drive it inch by inch, mile by mile.

The master of the chariot, individual Self,
who has a discriminating charioteer, intellect,
will be transported to the ultimate goal,
the realm of Limitless Consciousness,
for your reins, mind, will be well-controlled,
and the horses, your powers of action,
will be properly directed.
The experience of Self will be on the subtlest levels,
not the grossest, and be *...ever pure...*
inasmuch as you no longer identify with, or attach to,
objects of the sense experience in the material world,
you no longer attach to the ego identity.
You will remain from moment to moment in Consciousness
as you enter into the next evolutionary stage
with the Lord of Death as your Guide.

Having reached the ultimate Goal, Limitless Consciousness,
the individual Self, or transmigrating Soul,
is not born again.

Attaining the experience of Infinite Being you do not let go.
There is nothing as real and fulfilling
as living your true identity;
to return to lesser modes of being would make no sense.

Indelibly impress these teachings
so your intellect will be discriminating and empowered,
directing all your forces with expertise,
continuously focused on the goal, and the path that leads to it.
The triumphant traveler on the path
has clear vision of what is directly in front of her feet
as well as the overall objective.
Through the *experiences* offered by Death
you can traverse your life path smoothly to your fulfillment,
empowered, in charge, blissful.
Refer to these teachings like a concise manual
by which to successfully operate your intellect intuition
mind body senses, all your faculties.
When you acquire a piece of valuable machinery,
you study the instructions carefully to become expert in its use.
Your body-mind-psyche complex
is your most valuable instrument—
will you implement these teachings expertly and continuously?

9. The man, however, who has, as his charioteer, a discriminating intellect, and who has under control the reins of the mind, attains the end of the road; and that is the highest place of Visnu.

Second translation:

The man who has intuitive judgment as his Charioteer and the mind as reins, gains the End of the Road. That is the Supreme abode of All-pervading Spirit (Vishnu).

The transmigrating soul who is conducted on the path
by a discriminating charioteer, intellect,
who well controls the reins, mind,
attains the end of the path, the end of eons of evolution.
She becomes free from all worldly limitations and bondage
and attains *...the highest place of Visnu...*
the realm of All-pervading Brahman, Supreme Self.

Vishnu is also called *Vasudeva.*
Vasu is He who provides a home (*vasa*).
Deva is related to 'divinity', the Self-effulgent.
Vasudeva is the Self-luminous One
who provides a home for all in Himself.
This is the supreme destination attained by the individual Self
who is associated with a discriminating intellect
and a mind concentrated on reality.

How easy it can be.
Can you have your intellect be discriminating?
The discriminating intellect always chooses the real,
because the unreal is self-contradictory,
it is harmful and painful and does not make sense.
As a discriminating leader of your life
you keep mind in your control and
do not allow the senses to rush about like panicked horses.

Do your faculties run amok like vicious horses?
You may want to examine the state you are living in.
Most spiritual aspirants do not claim their home in Vasudeva.
Instead they consciously knowingly choose to reject
the loving invitation of the Light of Consciousness,
and dwell in ego's darkness.

Many religious devotees, every day and every moment of the day,
act in ways that spit into God's eye, saying,
I reject You, I treat You like scum, I lie to You,
I prefer my juvenile silly melodramas to You.

The addict says, Thank you Luminous One for Your invitation.
I accept lovingly and will come to dinner.
And in the middle of the main course,
violates the Supreme Host.
And not only once by mistake,
but she makes a repetitive practice of it.
Is she asking to be hit by a bolt of lightning
and thereby feel special, singled out, paid attention to?
Is it a case of tough love considered as better than no love?

Spiritual window shoppers may treat these teachings
like just another shallow self-help program.
They participate superficially and say,
Well that did not work either, what is next?

Some students choose to act weak, as if they were less than they are,
so as not to be in union.
They say, Well Vasudeva, that is a lovely invitation from You,
I see how important it is, how wonderful and generous,
how beautiful it is to be at home in the luminous realm—
and that is really what I want—but not now.
It is more important for me to play the role of ego.

Do you recognize any of these patterns within yourself,
how you keep yourself away from what you really want?
What do you gain from that?

I will repeat what is offered:
When you cause your discriminating intellect to be true to you

and control the reins of the mind,
you attain the fulfillment of your path,
the completion of eons of evolution.
You are at home in the highest place, where you belong,
free from worldly limitations—bondage and suffering—
absorbed in Continuous Consciousness,
Brahman, the All-pervading Self.
This is the supreme destination and the final fulfillment.

With Discrimination and Focus on Reality,
absorbed in the Self-effulgent One who provides a Home for all,
the individual Self, and the Intellect Mind Body and Senses,
the entire Body-mind Complex,
reach the Fulfillment of their Evolution in Self-realization.

Chapter Nineteen

The Hierarchy Of Being

You are Eternal Consciousness;
within that, all is contained,
but you, Consciousness, are contained by none.
You are limitless,
you are free.

To experience yourself truly, place the body,
the vehicle of this manifestation,
into a state of effortless balance, grace and deep relaxation.

Have your breath flow in easy natural rhythm,
aligned with the universal flow of energy.

Have your mind in its unmodified state, serene in your center,
facilitating the experience of yoga,
the oneness of Being that in fact you are.

Have everything about you present in your center,
fully devoted to the experience of the Eternal Consciousness
that you are.

You are Consciousness in Self-experience,
one limitless Consciousness, eternal and all-pervasive.
You Are That.

That is the way it is.

10. *The sense-objects are higher than the senses, and the mind is higher than the sense-objects; but the intellect is higher than the mind, and the Great Soul is higher than the intellect.*

Second translation:

Higher than the senses are the (subtle) objects of sense; Higher than those objects is the mind (manas); Higher than manas is the buddhi; Higher than buddhi is the Great Self (Mahan-Atma).

Brahman, Being, Self, expresses through vibration:
everything that *is*, is vibration.
Vibration causes the particles dancing around in space
to create the momentary appearance of objects and events.
Your body is an example of this;
what appears as a discrete entity is an illusion,
it is but vibrating energy.

The whole manifested world is but vibratory states
varying from gross to subtle, low to high.
This theme of apparent opposites can be witnessed
on every level on which Being expresses and experiences Self.
You may remember that
the grosser vibratory states can not penetrate the subtler,
while the subtler vibratory states *can* penetrate the grosser.

Consciousness is the subtlest vibratory State;
It permeates *all* vibratory Levels.

The grossest level of manifestation is the material.
We relate to the material realm through the senses.
They are subtler than the material realm,
thus able to penetrate it;
material objects are not able to penetrate the senses.

Above the senses, higher in subtlety,
is that which experiences specifically through each sense,
what Yama calls *...the sense-objects...*
'object' as in 'the object of this exercise is to learn'.
These are the rudimentary principles of sensing,
subtle powers by which the senses gain knowledge
of the material realm.
Sense-objects actuate the senses for their own revelation.
There is not only something to be sensed
and an instrument through which we sense,
but an actuator of that sense

and recipient of the sense experience.
The sense-object is the originator as well as the goal
of each act of sensing.

For example, you witness material phenomena
through the sense of sight,
so there is the energy of seeing—a sense-object—
which has evolved for its own revelation, sight,
by which it is in contact with the world.
There is the energy of touching—another sense-object—
which has the sense of touch reveal the experience to itself.
And so it is with all your senses:
the sense-object is the seer of the sense of seeing,
the hearer of the sense of hearing,
the taster of the sense of taste,
the smeller of the sense of smell,
the toucher of the sense of touch.

The sense-object is an energy that is subtler than the sense itself,
therefore *...sense-objects are higher than the senses...*
The sense-objects are the senses' origin and reason for being.

The sense-objects are a vibratory level
between the senses and the mind, the next step up,
but also between the senses and Self—
everything takes place within Self.

Self, Atman, is Consciousness.
On the battlefield traversed by the chariot,
Atman is the light who illumines the field
with His understanding,
the conscious experiencer of all that transpires.
The All-pervasive Spirit who sustains manifestation,

He is present in all creation at every level,
in every object and in every creature,
in every body as well as every soul,
in every human and every deity—
and not contained in any.

Atman, Self, has two principal powers of perceiving:
mind and intellect.

Mind or *...manas...*
sees in terms of separate objects entities and phenomena.
Mind coordinates the carriage—body,
and the horses—senses,
in the field they travel—the material world.
Mind correlates the experiences of the sense-objects;
it can permeate them,
but the sense-objects can not permeate mind, it is subtler.
Thus *...the mind is higher than the sense-objects...*
Mind is the sense-objects' origin and reason for being.

Intellect's vision is more extensive than the mind's.
It encompasses the wholeness of the experience of the mind
integrated with the experience of the sense-objects
and the senses and material realm.
With proper discrimination knowledge and wisdom,
intellect relates those experiences to more expansive levels.
Thus the intellect is the driver
who is meant to determine the path and direct the mind
which is meant to direct the senses,
and not the other way around.

Since the entirety, the One,
is expressed through apparent contradictions,

every part of It contains opposites.
Remember, a principle of holism is
that every part contains the characteristics of the whole.
Thus the human mind and intellect both have two aspects,
one higher and one lower, that *appear* to oppose each other.

The lower mind is thoroughly enmeshed with the material realm.
As mind is the central coordinator of many of your functions,
and because mind's predominant involvement
with the material realm is so deeply impressed,
the material realm *seems* to be your very nature,
even your identity.
When the lower mind is not controlled
by the discriminating intellect,
your chariot hurtles over the battlefield
connected by the reins to the horses,
but not directed by a charioteer.
The ensuing chaos is painfully destructive.

With your experience thus limited to the grossest realm,
you can not be in touch with the subtler levels
in which reigns Consciousness, your essence.
As you have learned, if you do not experience Consciousness,
you can not experience anything in relation to yourself:
you do not experience Self.
That is the cause of suffering.
You regard yourself as severely limited
and cut off from the whole, isolated:
the false ego perception is born.

How is the false ego perception born?
By refusing to have the mind under the control
of your discriminating intellect.

Mind enmeshed in the experiences of the material realm
no longer serves reality, but falsity.

> The lower Mind is so preoccupied with
> Experiences of the grossest Realm,
> that it is not free to participate
> in the Experience of all Levels of Being,
> from the grossest to the subtlest,
> as well as the unified Wholeness of Limitless Consciousness.

The lower mind's origin and reason for being is the higher mind.
In its elevated state, mind is detached
in its workings through the senses with the material realm.
Because mind is closer in nature to Consciousness,
it is capable of transcending itself.
You can cause your mind to assume
an unmodified state of pure reflective tranquility,
to be a true reflector of Consciousness.

> Consciousness projects Self through Manifestations
> and is reflected to Self by Mind.

Mind takes on the shape of whatever it is engrossed in.
In its higher state, the pure unmodified state of meditation,
your mind takes on the shape of, and becomes one with,
pure Consciousness.

This is what meditation *really* is.
The reins are an extension of the master;
the reins and the master are one.

The higher mind's origin and reason for being is the intellect,
which gives understanding reason and determination
to the workings of mind.
The intellect is subtler and more pervasive,
therefore higher than the mind.

The intellect, too, can be seen in terms of lower and higher.
The lower intellect is engaged with giving reason to,
rationalizing, the workings of the lower mind
on the material level.
It functions grossly when engaged in facilitating
the lower mind processes.
For example, a man may have a strongly developed intellect,
but when he predominantly uses it
to gain worldly goods or status, it is the lower intellect.
Many of the so-called pillars of our community
lead with the lower intellect.
The lower intellect rationalizes anti-Self behaviors;
it is in service of ego.

The higher intellect, in Sanskrit *...buddhi...*
is in service of Self, the Power of Being.
The higher intellect is the lower intellect's origin
and reason for being.
Intellect comes into its refined vibratory state
by participating in the experience of Being
with knowledge and understanding.
Buddhi sees the subtle unity,

knows the transcendent integrality, the underlying reality,
and relates all to the one infinite Self.

The higher Intellect is superior to the lower Intellect
for it engages Understanding Reason and Determination
in Relation to its Master, the individual Soul,
who has manifested this Chariot, your Body,
and its Driver, your Intellect,
as well as the Horses that draw it, your Senses,
and the Reins through which the Horses are directed, your Mind,
and even the Field upon which they all experience
and hone themselves
to the Freeing and Expanding of Consciousness.

Subtler than the higher intellect is *...the Great Soul...* Mahat.
The Great Soul is infinitely subtler
and more pervasive than the intellect.
...the Great Soul is higher than the intellect...
Intellect's origin and reason for being is the Great Soul.

Ascending from there:

11. The Unmanifested is higher than Mahat; Purusa is higher than the Unmanifested. There is nothing higher than Purusa. He is the culmination, He is the highest goal.

All creation comes forth
from the sheer potential of Being *...the Unmanifested...*
The Unmanifested is the seed
from which all manifestation springs forth,

from which evolve all causes and effects,
all phenomena and events, all names and forms.
He is the Golden Womb of creation,
the Creator, the source from which the cosmos is projected,
and into which the cosmos is absorbed again
upon its dissolution.

The Unmanifested is transcendent to all manifestation
and to all evolution,
therefore even higher and subtler than the Great Soul:
...The Unmanifested is higher than Mahat...
He is the manifested's origin and reason for being.

There is one final 'higher':
...Purusa is higher than the Unmanifested...
Purusa is the innermost Self of all, the Ultimate,
the most subtle that permeates all.
Purusa is Brahman, the Absolute.
Purusa is the Being of all beings, yet beyond:
sheer limitless Consciousness.
It is the reality that is.
All that *is* has Purusa as the reason for being.

Purusa is the Ultimate Being,
the Essence and Self of all.
There is nothing subtler,
nothing more pervasive.
There is nothing higher than the Infinite.

...He is the culmination...

Purusa, infinite Power of Being, is the culmination of all—
all physical formation,
all sensual activity,
all intellectual and mental processes,
all ambitions and desires,
all inspiration and aspiration,
all choice and discrimination,
all determination and will,
all causes and effects,
all evolution,
all potential.
Purusa, Self, is the culmination, and beyond.

Eternal all-pervasive Consciousness
is the highest Goal beyond which nothing is,
that for which all Evolution strives.

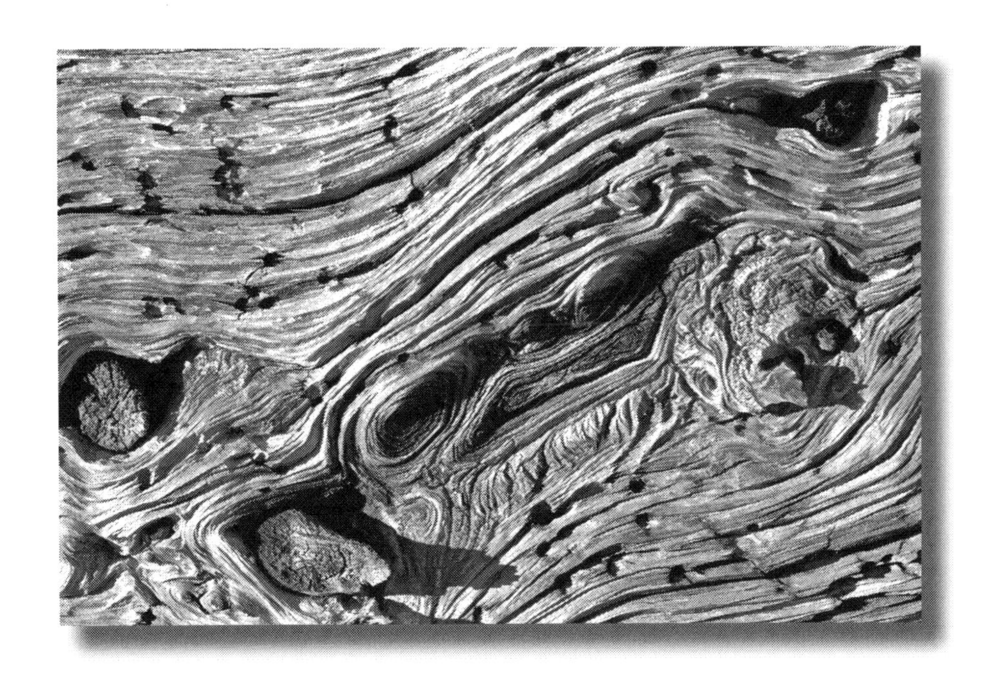

Chapter Twenty

Merging The Gross Into The Subtle

Sincerely and expertly continue in the condition
that is purely conducive
to the experience of the highest levels of teaching.
So deeply *impress* what you learn
that it will be integral to you henceforth and forever.

From the simple relaxation of the body,
regulating the breath
and bringing every facet of yourself
into harmonious wholeness in your center,
the cave of your heart,
devote the attention of all your faculties

to the experience of absolute identity,
eternal all-pervasive Consciousness, Self.

Dwell in Satchidananda,
the limitless experience of yourself
as Existence-knowledge-bliss-absolute.
Absolute means without limit in time and space,
independent of circumstance and condition,
thus all-pervasive and eternal, real.

12. He is hidden in all beings; and hence He does not appear as the Self (of all). But by the seers of subtle things, He is seen through a pointed and fine intellect.

The final goal of all evolution, of all movement in creation,
is the realization of Purusa,
the blissfully conscious infinite Self
who dwells in eternal Self-experience.
Purusa is the ultimate source of all,
and that into which all, including the Creator,
will be dissolved again.

The Ultimate is so subtle that the ordinary person
does not see nor experience nor, therefore, know Him.
Not knowing Purusa,
the ordinary person can not identify with Him,
thus does not recognize Limitless Being as Self.

> The Eternal Essence says:
> I am the Substance and Sustenance that dwells in all
> but is contained in none.

It is not that humans lack the ability to experience Eternal Self,
it is that their instruments of perception are preoccupied
by involvement with *maya*, illusion.
Maya causes the impermanent to appear permanent,
the unified to appear as separate objects and events.
It is due to maya that your instruments do not perceive
the permanent One you are.

Infinite Consciousness is the Subtlest,
thus not grasped by grosser Instruments.
He is hidden by the Veil of Illusion, Maya,
created by Him.

Thoroughly enmeshed in the grosser,
most do not see the subtle Self,
the essence and reality of all that is.
Although there is definitive evidence all around
and certainly within themselves,
they are unable to perceive Self, let along declare,
I am the Power of Being, the One that is all.
Purusa *...is hidden in all beings; and hence*
He does not appear as the Self (of all)...

Only when you learn to see the subtler, can you see Self.
But how do you see the subtler?
By letting go of the incessant involvement with distractions.
This is accomplished through a focused and refined intellect,
the higher intellect.

What is a *refined* intellect?
You can have a *focused* intellect as a mass killer
or as a millionaire munitions manufacturer,
but that is not a *refined* intellect, that is a lower intellect.
Refined intellect comes about when you purposefully—
sincerely continuously expertly and faithfully—
direct the intellect toward the task
of experiencing and expressing
the Illimitable Being you are, the Sacred Self.
This intellect will assume a vibratory mode
that is profoundly subtler and more refined
than the intellect that is habitually engaged
with matters of the grosser levels.

The refined intellect is able to discriminate
between illusion and reality,
the momentary and the permanent,
and it has the mind firmly in control,
relating to you constantly and serving you faithfully
as the Eternal Being that you are.
The higher intellect is truly the knowledgeable expert driver
in control of the chariot, guiding it fluidly and steadily.

The seers of the subtle learn to view all that is,
including their moment-to-moment experiences,
and themselves, through the hierarchy of Being:
from the material to the senses, to the sense-objects,
to the higher mind, to the higher intellect, to the Great Soul,
to the Unmanifest, to Purusa.
The experience of the hierarchy of Being
is a wonderful and powerful means to Self-realization.

When you disregard the subtle levels of Being,
your mind is thoroughly enmeshed in the false,
intellect is not utilized to rein in the mind
and everything is out of control.
Does that sound familiar to you?
Until your perception of the subtle
has led to a permanent unwavering experience
of the most subtle—Purusa, Infinite Consciousness, Self—
you will have to go through birth and death and rebirth
over and over and over again.

You could apply this teaching to understanding how to succeed,
or why you may not be succeeding.
If you have knowledge but are not Self-realized,
the cause may be
that you do not have your intellect in control of the mind,
thus do not apply the intellect on the subtle, refined level.
When intellect does not control it, what does mind do?
It helplessly vacillates under the sway of rampant emotions,
dependent upon circumstances and conditions
which occupy and manipulate it.
Even more grossly, mind then jumps constantly
to the call of the senses, which attaches you to the lowest level.
How difficult is it for you to be determined to do something
about such a dependent and limited way of being?

Once you have your intellect related to Self and in control of mind,
what is the way to Self-realization?

13. The discriminating man should merge the (organ of) speech into the mind; he should merge that (mind) into the intelligent self; he should merge the intelligent self into the Great Soul, he should merge the Great Soul into the peaceful Self.

To become clear in your vision of the reality of Being,
you can practice going through the ascending levels
on which the Power of Being is expressed
and therefore able to be experienced,
from the body and senses to the higher levels.
This realistic experience of Self will so impress
the experience of wholeness upon your faculties,
that it will be the *given*,
the foundation from which you consistently operate.
This is one way to be real
about traveling the path of Self-realization.

...merge the (organ of) speech into the mind...
Creation takes place through vibration.
Om, the original form of vibration, is the seed of manifestation,
and expresses Itself through sound.
Speech is based on the vibrations of sound, thus on Om.
The *...(organ of) speech...* represents
the vibratory forms, body and senses,
your grossest and ordinarily most prevalent instruments
of Self-expression and Self-experience.
For them to be connected to a subtler level of perception,
you merge your body and senses into mind.
By having mind direct them,
your lower faculties take on its subtler characteristics.

...merge that (mind) into the intelligent self...
Since intellect is subtler than mind

and therefore able to experience on higher levels,
you merge mind into the intellect.
Under intellect's impetus,
mind is directed into the quiescent state,
like the utterly tranquil mountain lake,
and able to clearly reflect Being.

Like molten metal taking the shape
of the crucible into which it is poured,
mind takes on the characteristics of Consciousness.
Through the mind,
body and senses are also merged into the intellect
and included in the higher experiences.
The higher intellect's clarity and determination
refine the vibrations of your lower faculties
so that they can merge with the subtlest vibration,
Consciousness.

...he should merge the intelligent self into the Great Soul...
By consistently choosing the real over the illusory,
the vibratory state of the intelligent self
is so purified and transformed
that it is able to merge with the Great Soul, Mahat.
They vibrate in union,
the Great Soul and intelligent self experience as one.

...he should merge the Great Soul into the peaceful Self...
The Great Soul is to be absorbed by the Creator,
in the continued experience of real Being.
By loyally remaining in the joyous experience
of interconnectedness,
the true aspirant removes the illusion of separateness

and the attendant anxiety fear and suffering.
He is in the continued experience of himself as
...the peaceful Self...

There is an ancient analogy, a story about
illusion being overcome with perception of reality:
A man walking along a path in the jungle
stops in utter fright when he sees a snake
lying a few yards in front of him.
When he calms down and looks closer,
he discovers it is not a snake, but a rope.
The mistaken conception—illusion—
is removed once clear perception prevails.

> The mistaken Impression of what you fear is removed
> as soon as you recognize what really is.

In a similar analogy, if you were told since infancy—
and believed—that your face is half green and half orange
with a black stripe down the middle,
your mistaken belief would vanish
as soon as you looked into the tranquil mountain lake
and saw the reflection of your true image.

> Once the false Perception is removed,
> no longer live according to it.
> That is only sensible.

Everything is an expression, thus impermanent form
of the continuous Power of Being.
However, under the sway of maya, illusion,
you mistakenly view an object, such as your body,
as relatively permanent solid and separate.
The enlightened person sees no such thing,
but knows that atoms dancing around in space—
coming and going—
form the appearance of your body.
Furthermore, the enlightened person sees even these atoms
as energy expressions that ultimately originate
from the Power of Being, Self.

Here is another ancient story that illustrates perception of reality:
There was an archery contest between warrior princes,
one of whom was the great Arjuna,
friend and disciple of Krishna, who is Atman.
The warriors, great charioteers, were tested on their eyesight.
The challenge was to look in a certain direction
and tell what they saw.
One archer saw a forest far away.
An archer of keener vision saw a specific tree in the forest.
And the archer of even keener vision saw a target on that tree.
Arjuna saw no thing, only Self—he won the contest.

Seen in the Light of Self,
Objects are perceived
not as isolated and relatively permanent Formations,
but as Expressions of the one Whole.

By continuously and faithfully freeing yourself
from the habitual perception of solid separate objects,
which is illusion, and regarding all in terms of the whole,
you dissolve the senses in the higher mind
and the mind in the higher intellect.
Do not allow your senses to influence mind
into the false perception of you as the small self,
the usurper ego.
With your faculties attached to ego, you identify with the body
and suffer from a sense of separateness.
Freed from illusion, you no longer mistake ego-self for Self.

When in your Experience
your Senses are merged in the higher Mind
and higher Mind in the higher Intellect
and that Intellect in the Great Soul
and the Great Soul in the Peaceful Self,
you experience yourself as the Self of all.
That is Self-realization.

By merging in the next subtler state of perception,
each of your faculties transforms to the higher vibratory state,
until you transform beyond the faculties
to the Great Soul, the Mahat.
From there the final transformation takes place:
merging in experience into Self.
Then everything about you takes on
the pure characteristics of the ultimate,

Illimitable Consciousness.
Merged in *...the peaceful Self...*
your soul realizes the deep state of equanimity
for which it has been yearning.

When you sincerely engage in this step-by-step change
toward subtler levels of perception,
you will experience the final transformation.
As you steadily view and experience everything
as a manifestation of Limitless Self,
you liberate yourself from false identification
with your closest and most personal perceived object,
body-mind—you liberate yourself from ego.
Your point of view changes dramatically and fundamentally.
Things look different to you, your insight is deeper and subtler,
and the scope of your vision increases profoundly,
for it is no longer bound to separate gross particles
but ranges free to flow in the wholeness.
Even the subtler perceptions that relate to
your inspirations and aspirations,
your desires and perceived needs,
are powerfully altered.

You cease to see objects and see only Self expressed.
This has a great calming effect,
for within you grows the confidence of unified Being.

You will no longer be a victim of the false perceptions
that have bound you to passing phenomena
as if they were your permanent identity.
No longer will the senses, in their habitual response
to the stimuli of the material realm,

dictate your experience and pull your attention
from object to object, event to event,
creating the havoc of distraction.
This does not mean that you deny the existence of phenomena,
you do not deny shapes and forms and momentary expressions;
you observe them as they flow by, as experiences of Being,
while you remain unattached and therefore free.
In the purity of senses merged in mind,
mind in higher intellect, intellect in the Great Soul
and Great Soul in the Peaceful Self,
you abide in the calm security of experiencing yourself
as all-pervasive eternal Consciousness.
This is the unitive state, yoga.

When the Unitive State is the Foundation of all your Experience,
it becomes the Foundation of your Self-expression;
you become Expert in the Actions
by which you express the Being that you are.
Your Relationship with your Faculties within you,
as well as your Relationship with all the Factors around you,
becomes empowered clear and fulfilling.
That is real and lasting Success.

Change the foundation of *how* you are.
Free yourself from the habit
of relating to yourself as a limited object,
and live in accord with the knowledge of yourself
as Limitless Consciousness.

Here again is a principal message of this whole teaching.

May you absorb the knowledge as a sincere aspirant,
implement it immediately,
and permanently integrate it in your life
so that you live harmoniously and thereby flourish.

CHAPTER TWENTY-ONE

Establishing Relationship With A Real Teacher And Self

You are Eternal Consciousness
who is unbeginning, is now and eternally shall be.
You are Transcendent Consciousness,
the essence of all that is, and beyond.
That is who you are, Self.

It behooves you to sincerely expertly continuously and faithfully
gather all your faculties and keep them present in your center
in the necessary attitude of effortless balance,
focused on Self.
The Being that you are is not a lie, not a theory or a belief,
It is the reality of you.
To experience yourself as Self, Infinite Consciousness—
clear balanced unattached truthful and limitless—
is your duty unto yourself.

This dialogue with Death offers you the real experience
of life death and transcendence.
The level to which you avail yourself of this experience
is your choice.

14. Arise, awake, and learn by approaching the excellent ones. The wise ones describe that path to be as impassable as a razor's edge, which when sharpened, is difficult to tread on.

Arise, awake!
This has been the clarion call to humanity
by the sages throughout the ages.

Arise, awake!
I often exhort my students: Arise from the doldrums
in which you have embedded yourself,
arise from the painfully comatose way of life
that confines your existence to the pit of despair.

> Arise from the Sleep of Ignorance
> wherein you are not awake to yourself
> and not aware of what is.

Included in what is, is who you really are.
Asleep in ignorance, you do not experience yourself;
all you experience is falsity, illusion.
Veiled by illusion, your instruments of perception
relate to what *is not* as that which *is*.
With their energies thus occupied with what is not,
your faculties are not free
to relate the experience of reality to you,
including, most importantly, the experience of Being.

You are Being, and Being is not an Object,
It is the Power to be, pure Power, sheer Energy.
Being, like all Energy, is all-pervasive and eternal.
That is what you fundamentally are.
What you *fundamentally* are is what you *essentially* are,
and what you essentially are is your Identity.
The Power of Being is your Identity.

Arise, awake to what you are.
As Being is your identity, you have the inherent ability
to experience yourself as all-pervasive and eternal.
That is the reality of you. You Are That.
Being is to be experienced—not as It is not,
not in illusion, not in falsity,
but as It is—in reality.
How *is* Being?
The Power of Being is infinite in time and space.

> Since in Essence you are Being,
> and since Being is to be experienced as It is,
> you are to experience yourself and to live and act
> as Infinite Being, all-pervasive and eternal.

As long as you are not experiencing and expressing yourself
as the infinite Power of Being,
you suffer a sense of not being integral to the whole.
You feel disaffected then, disconnected isolated,
leaving you unable to conduct fulfilling relationships.
Your loneliness is accompanied by unrequited love,
anger, anxiety and outright fear.

Filled with existential fear, you deny your own true identity
and promote a false identity of weakness immaturity
and inability, even mental dysfunction.
Feeling unworthy, you are filled with self-disrespect.

> When you choose Behaviors that originate
> in Awareness of who you are, Consciousness,
> you respect yourself,
> you respect Eternal Being—you respect God.
> Conversely, when you choose the Opposite,
> you disrespect yourself—and God.

Dwelling in self-denial is the root cause of all suffering.
Suffering is the direct result of living in ignorance

regarding real identity.
There is nothing in creation
that dictates such a painful existence,
nor are you predestined to suffering
due to an inherent fault or some cosmic dysfunction.

> Awake to the Reality that is self-evident within
> and all about you.
> Awake to the Potential that resides within you
> and all-pervasively.

Awake: consciously and continuously experience yourself
as eternal and all-pervasive Being,
the source and essence of all that is.
Awake to your real life.
Awake to the Eternal Consciousness that you are.
Awake to your true nature of Satchidananda:
Existence-knowledge-bliss-absolute.
Awake so that you live and express your true identity
in full power, and in the transcendent joy of knowing Self.

When you become aware of the real possibility
of living as limitless all-pervasive eternal Consciousness
in continuity, in reality,
you can feel yourself respond with joyous recognition.
However, often an aspirant who is given the opportunity
to recognize truth
discards the possibility of living in the bliss thereof.

To make real your living in the truth of Being that you are,
to realize the truth of you,
the luminous seers persistently recommend that you
...learn by approaching the excellent ones...
Establish yourself in a relationship with one who lives as Self,
a real Teacher who has trod the path before you
and dwells permanently on the subtlest levels.
He or she teaches not from hearsay,
not from book-learning, nor from the intellect,
nor from fantasies,
but from direct experience of Transcendent Being.

When you are not living in the Bliss of Self-realization,
your Redemption lies in properly approaching a *real* Teacher—
one who lives as Self—
and responding to the Teachings.

The Teacher's teachings awaken for the real aspirant
the truth residing within;
the sincere aspirant's Inner Knower
reverberates with the teachings.
This is how Naciketa responds—
with the burning determination of the Naciketa fire.

Why do the scriptures repeatedly emphasize
not only the *advantage* of having a real Teacher,
but even the *necessity*?
Your mind needs to be fully focused and clear
to understand the answer:

The Path to Self-realization is so clear and precise
as to seem extremely narrow and difficult
to the Aspirant who is habituated to unfocused and vague Behaviors
unrelated to the Reality of Being.

...The wise ones describe that path
to be as impassable as a razor's edge...
as difficult to accomplish
as passing a camel through the eye of a needle.

Take heart: the path to Self-realization
is not really that difficult; it only *seems* difficult
when you are not in focused relationship with reality,
with truth, with who you are.
The path to the realization of the Infinite—your heritage—
appears narrow and impassable only from the perspective
of the meandering wanderer whose travels go willy-nilly
according to every whim of the faculties
under the influence of a rampant ego.

Aspirants frequently complain that it is hard to learn to live as Self.
Living true to who you are is not hard;
living in Ego's Falsity is the Cause of your Difficulty.

Relate to Self realistically sincerely and continuously—
not in fantasy, not in an on-again off-again practice.
Thoroughly burn out all influence of false ego

upon the behaviors of your faculties.
This is only possible through unconditional acceptance of Self,
unflagging devotion to the reality of Being.

For this, you need the unattached and subtle insight of the Teacher.
The Teacher is a seer of the Self you are
and is not deceived by ego.
A clear and unattached observer,
the Teacher is your most helpful guide.
That is why only as a real aspirant—
one who is so filled with self-love,
that you are absolutely determined to release
any and all remnants of attachment to ego behaviors
and throw them into that sacrificial fire—
you approach the Teacher properly
and establish yourself in real relationship.

Devoted Relationship with the Teacher
stimulates and nurtures Loyalty to Self.

A real aspirant prefers the Teacher's clear insight and guidance
to ego's familiar falsity.
One who seeks liberation from the painful bondage
to patterns of limitedness isolation and falsity
never rejects the indispensable help of the Teacher.

Ego will persistently attempt to subvert you:
I can do it by myself, I do not need a Teacher.
It is too frightening to fulfill what I have always yearned for

and complete my whole evolution.
I am not ready to give up my limitedness
and be in relationship with reality.
I am too delicate; I have been disturbed so much in my life
and disappointed so often that I dare not consider myself
capable of life in accord with the truth.
I dare not be related to as the Being I Am.
Unfortunately, ego is not so open in its declarations
or you would recognize the absurdity.

Another ego trick is thinking that friends and family
can guide you on the path;
they may have more experience than you.
Beware: that can result in less than the full evolution
of which you are capable.
If you had a serious disease,
would you try quaint home remedies,
or go to a qualified physician?
You want to love yourself, you want the best for yourself;
be determined to cease suffering—as Self you deserve better.
With the guidance of a qualified Teacher
you can realize Self most directly and effectively,
not leave it to the vague distant future.

Identified with ego, you act as if it were safer
to remain in separateness,
to choose loneliness instead of love,
sorrow instead of joy,
weakness and dysfunction instead of strength.
What more effective way could accomplish such failure
than to choose from start to finish
to live as if a real you did not exist?

The clarity of the Teacher's vision
prevents you being misled by falsity,
and you thereby overcome ego's position
of usurper of your identity and your life.
How easily relationship with the Teacher
exposes ego's false message of separation isolation
and fragmentation.

The Teacher is the most effective link to the Unitive One
for the individual who suffers
from the experience of himself as separate.

The Teacher, Being in the Awareness of Self,
guides those Aspects of himself
who are in the Illusion of Separateness,
toward the Realization of Interconnectedness.
The Student, Being in the Experience of Isolation,
is guided by Self-aware Being to realize Union.
The Connection with the Unitive One that is the Teacher
is the Way to connect with the unitive one Self.

As you learn through experience with the Teacher
to clearly relate to truth,
you hone your faculties to such a state of expertise
that you are able to walk over the razor's edge
in effortless balance and full faith.
Thus you dwell in and enact
the eternal all-pervasive Consciousness that you are.

When the sincere aspirant has the guidance of a Teacher:

15. *One becomes freed from the jaws of death by knowing that which is soundless, touchless, colourless, undiminishing, and also tasteless, eternal, odourless, without beginning, and without end, distinct from Mahat, and ever constant.*

Second translation:

> *Having realized that (Atman) which is soundless, touchless, formless, tasteless, and without smell, permanent, without beginning or end, greater than the Great One (Mahat), Fixed, one is liberated from the mouth of Death.*

The material realm is composed of five elements:
earth water fire air and the ether of space.
We are able to relate to these elements through our senses
according to their degree of subtleness or grossness.

Earth, the grossest of the elements, has five qualities:
sound touch color taste and smell.
We experience earth
through hearing touching seeing tasting and smelling.

Water is subtler than earth.
It has four qualities: sound touch color and taste.
We experience water through four of our senses:
hearing touching seeing and tasting.

Fire is subtler yet.
It has three qualities: sound touch and color.
We experience fire through three of our senses:
hearing touching and seeing.

Air, the next subtler, has two qualities: sound and touch.
We experience air through two of our senses:
hearing and touching.

And finally ether, the subtlest of all the elements,
has only one quality: sound.
We experience sound through only one of our senses: hearing.

Atman, known by the Self-realized person as identical with Brahman,
is the subtlest of all that is,
and transcendent to all the qualities of manifestations.
He—Self—is not invested with qualities,
and therefore we can not experience Him with our senses.

Self is *...undiminishing...eternal...without beginning,*
and without end...
Undecaying and independent, neither a cause nor an effect,
therefore not transitory, but permanent, real,
Atman never ceases to be, no matter how often manifested,
just as love is never diminished no matter how much you give.
Independent of time, Self has never *not* been—
He is unbeginning and continues eternally.

Infinite Self is beyond the Great Soul associated with manifestation,
transcendent to the qualities and changes
characteristic of the play of creation:
...distinct from Mahat, and ever constant...

When your faculties are involved with the material realm,
you identify yourself as this body and mind,
and therefore as subject to death and decay.

Realizing your true identity, sheer Power of Being,
you transcend the limitations of the realm of manifestation,
thus are *...freed from the jaws of death...*

Chapter Twenty-Two

Relating To The Teachings As Interconnected Self

The Power of Being, Consciousness,
is unbeginning, imminently present, eternally unending
and transcendent.
That is your real identity
and thereby your interconnectedness with all.
You Are That.

You can choose to take in hand
the various facets of this manifestation, like body and mind,
and place them into the state they were created for,
fine-tuned and honed like a razor-sharp instrument,

purely dedicated to reflecting, free of distortion,
the wholeness of Being that you are.

For this purpose, cause your body to relax.
Tell the head to relax, and feel relaxation flow through it.
Send this releasing energy flowing down
through the neck and shoulders,
through the entire back,
uplifting the back with pure unhindered energy.
Relax the chest abdomen and loins,
your arms and hands, legs and feet.

Apply your expertise to having the body deeply relaxed inside and out.
Send it an impetus to become more deeply relaxed
to the cellular and even the atomic level.
Let go and open the pathways for pure and harmonious energy
to flow freely through every part of your body.

Augment that flow with the even rhythm of your breath,
allowing *prana*, the vital force, to flow through your body
and through all your instruments
in a way that connects them directly, in their own experience,
with the universal flow.

Gather your faculties in your center
where they dwell in harmony with each other,
and settle into the state of effortless balance.
You are at peace, deeply relaxed and fully aware.

Everything about you is now turned toward the Limitless Self
that you are.
The knowledge of your essence, Eternal Consciousness,

resides within you waiting to be experienced,
and not waiting at all.

16. Relating and hearing this eternal anecdote—as received by Naciketa and as told by Death—the intelligent man becomes glorified in the region that is Brahman.

Let your faculties remain unified in effortless balance
in your center where they reflect the Supreme Consciousness
glorified in these teachings.
You have the rare privilege and opportunity
of being exposed to the highest knowledge.
Be intelligent: immediately and permanently
respond so sincerely that you will be exalted.

Through these secret and sacred teachings
the wise person *...becomes glorified in the region that is Brahman...* in the realm of Eternal Consciousness.
How? By *...Relating and hearing...*
Hearing does not refer to the mere hearing of the outer ear,
but the understanding, the inner experiencing
in which you vibrate in oneness with these sacred teachings.
Relating means applying the teachings of reality to your life,
and helping others learn.
You involve the knowledge in everything you do:
all the internal behaviors by which you relate to what is,
every action by which you express yourself,
in all your relationships—with your loved ones as well as foes,
with neighbors and nations, colleagues and competitors—
and in each moment you live.

As you experience and live the Reality of Unitive Consciousness,
you share It with others.
You relate It to all—
all Moments all Actions and all Manifestations—
and thereby you truly relate to Self.

To relate these sacred teachings and share their wisdom
and illumining effects with others
requires you understand the reality expounded herein.
For you to understand the teachings,
you need to have your faculties tranquilly centered,
in devoted attendance to the Eternal Consciousness
that you are.
It requires that you receive the wisdom offered you,
having died to ego.
You receive Yama's teaching from a real Teacher
so sincerely and thoroughly as to experience it,
live it in reality,
and realize oneness with the teaching and Teacher.

This, according to the ancient seers,
is the response of an intelligent person.
That wise one
...becomes glorified in the region that is Brahman...
the ultimate one Self.

Examine yourself honestly. To what degree are you willing
to respond as an intelligent person
and live according to the knowledge gained,
live as Indivisible Self, thus in union with all?

Let yourself experience being glorified
in the realm of eternal all-pervasive Consciousness,
in Self-realization.

17. Should anyone, after purification, get this highest secret recited before an assembly of Brahmanas, or at the time of the ceremonies for the dead (then) that (ceremony) becomes conducive to eternal result.

If you are sincere about gaining the ultimate boon—
the result of your whole evolution,
realization of Eternal Consciousness—
this teaching shows you directly how you can accomplish that.

First you must undergo purification.
You sacrifice ego and its impressions,
all attachment by your faculties,
all habits and behaviors of falsity and dysfunction.
Be honest with yourself: are you willing
to finally and truly make this sacrifice?
Then, and only then, will you be purified.

Each time you are presented a teaching, continue to purify,
focus your forces within your center
in a state of balance and clarity,
and have your faculties attend directly to Self,
as clarified through the teachings.
Yama urges repeatedly to relate to the teachings *sincerely*,
to receive them in a true relationship with a Teacher
and to live them in reality.

It is of fundamental importance that you relate to the teachings
in a state where you can *experience* them,
thereby *understand* them

and sincerely *integrate* them into your way of being.
And if you do not live the teachings *now*,
you will most likely not live them *later*.
The ego, principal employer of procrastination,
does not like this to be known.

Impress this firmly:

> Relate to the sacred Teachings sincerely and purely,
> in full and deep Focus,
> and live them in Reality,
> from the Moment you receive them.

Purification, combined with having Yama's teachings
...recited before an assembly of Brahmanas...
highborn intelligent spiritually dedicated persons
...or at the time of the ceremonies for the dead...
becomes conducive to eternal result...
What are eternal results? Results that are of reality—
lasting all-pervasive functional.

Why are we told this strange thing about ceremonies for the dead?
People are constantly dying around us—
leaving this realm with which we are familiar
and transforming to a different one.
Offerings are made to those who are thought to have entered
into the realm that allows for passage
through the gates of immortality.
Those dead are qualified to receive our help on their travels,

as well as to intercede on our behalf.
Be in your center and experience the teachings
on a deeper level
than the flitting-around brain normally inhabits.
You may think of the dead not only as those
who have left their body and this human life,
but also as the wise ones who have died to ego.
Both live in Yama's realm—Naciketa lives there beautifully.

A sincere spiritual aspirant causing teachings to be presented
in Yama's realm—not in the realm of ego—
delivers eternal results.
Even in the realm of immortality, as Naciketa has learned,
the soul still has to evolve to Eternal Consciousness.

The Aspirant who presents Yama's secret Teachings
to a Gathering of the Wise—*Satsanga*—
or at a Feast for the Dead,
bridges the Chasm between the Realm of Mortality
and the Realm of Immortality,
allowing for Transcendence.

There are teachers who deliver teachings from the realm of ego
and attract great numbers of followers,
but they do not bring about results
that are conducive to the liberating experience of reality.
If you want to gain the great eternal results,
you need to engage in pure teachings
and live in accord with the reality they reveal,

sincerely continuously and to the best of your ability,
with trust in the Power of Being that you are.

Engaging in the teachings is most powerful.
It presents permanent positive effects to the dead
as well as the aspirant, thus delivers a great boon:
conduciveness to the Eternal, the infinite undecaying Self.
Experience each revelation of Eternal Self.
Relate to these teachings only as the expression of Self.
Then you are qualified to bring evolved knowledge
even to the gatherings of the wise.
You will help the living and the dead in their ultimate quest,
through your very way of being.
You will participate in the realization of the Eternal Being
that we all are.

May you have the good will toward yourself
to deeply experience and live true to these teachings.

May you have the uncommon good sense
to nurture yourself in an honest relationship to this knowledge,
for to live otherwise is to perpetrate suffering and pain,
dishonor and shame.

May you open yourself to love,
feel moved to free yourself and others from suffering
and choose to dwell in abiding bliss.

May you respond to these teachings with continuity,
without backsliding, with expertise
and with trust in illumined Consciousness,
the Eternal Self that you are.

May you cease heedlessly falling for the temptations and seductions
of the realm of ego,
and allow yourself to progress vigorously and luminously,
with determination strength and clarity
that in essence you have and are.

May you dwell in love integrity and functionality,
and attract others with ease and grace
to life in the realm of Self.
May you share your love and knowledge
in strength and clarity,
and give hope and sustenance
to those who live in the realm of suffering
due to ignorance of their identity.

This is your challenge, your opportunity, your privilege.
May you faithfully rise to it and thereby be finally fulfilled.

I salute thee.

Part II Canto I

Dwelling In The Cave Of The Heart

Chapter Twenty-Three

Freedom From Enmeshment With Desire

Experience yourself in your center now
with all your faculties effortlessly balanced,
harmoniously combined and deeply devoted
to reflecting the wholeness of the Power of Being that you are.
It is from that perspective you find the freedom
to apply these teachings directly and to your highest advantage.

You have learned from the great master teacher Yama, Lord of Death,
to bring order to the relationship between yourself and society,
as well as between Self and ego.

You have been instructed how to gain immortality
through the utterly dependable means of the Naciketa fire:
dwelling in accord with the knowledge of reality,
sacrificing your attachment to ego and all its behaviors,
and engaging only in conscious actions,
deeds performed as the interconnected Self that you are.

And you have learned that immortality is still not the highest priority;
the realization of yourself as Limitless Consciousness
is the ultimate and immediate aim.

You know now what qualifies you
for reaching this great aim of your evolution.
Self-realization is a higher priority
than all the riches of this earthly realm,
as well as all the conditions and states
to which you are so accustomed.
You choose whether your actions are

in response to the temptation of pleasure
or the call of the preferable, the real.

> You have the Freedom of Choice.
> Choice is informed by the Ability to discriminate:
> Choosing Actions for Pleasure—Ego, the Temporary—
> results in Disappointment, and Loss of what you really want,
> Failure Disintegration and Bondage.
> Choices aligned with Being—the Preferable, the Permanent—
> lead to real Success Fulfillment and Liberation.

You have learned that your evolution is determined
by living and acting according to ignorance or knowledge.
Most live in ignorance of their identity and reality,
thus are bound to behaviors that cause suffering.
They fail to evolve.
When you live true to the knowledge of who you really are,
you flourish in self-trust and love.
You evolve.

Precious is the knowledge that liberates.
A Teacher of such knowledge is wonderful,
difficult to find and important to treasure.
As the crucial knowledge of your real identity
is hidden by confusion, distraction and false ideas,
it is best revealed by the Teacher who identifies as Self.

The enlightened person, through clear assessment of the ultimate,
rejects enmeshment with the momentary and superficial,

and lives loyal to Consciousness:
Existence-knowledge-bliss-absolute.

The Power of Being that you are has always been, shall eternally be,
and is independent of circumstance and condition.
Exceedingly subtle, realization of Self is to be gained
by placing your instruments of experience and expression
into the state of abiding tranquility.
Thus meditating, you free yourself from suffering
lack need and grief.

You have also been given the beautiful image
of the horse-drawn chariot
representing the Power of Being manifested as human being.
The ultimate goal is gained when the charioteer,
your higher intellect, steadily controls the reins, your mind,
guiding the horses, your senses, as the chariot, your body,
transports the master, the individual soul,
through the evolutionary challenges
on the path to fulfillment in Self-realization.

You have learned of the hierarchy of the senses mind intellect
and individual Self in this manifestation
through which Being expresses Self.
Mahat, the Great Soul of all manifestation,
is greater than the intellect,
the Unmanifested is beyond the Great Soul,
and transcendent to all is Purusa, the Self of all,
the supreme evolutionary goal.

Because the path to the realization of this goal
can be profoundly difficult, even hazardous,
the sages advise that you properly approach a real Teacher,

one who has successfully traveled the path to completion
and loves sufficiently to function as your Guide.

Relationship with a real Teacher is a rare opportunity,
difficult to find, and even more difficult to attain.
To succeed, you must offer yourself to the relationship
with absolute sincerity, devoted perseverance
and loyalty to Self.
The Teacher relates to you as the Being you are,
not pretentions, false identifications and attachments.
As you proceed as a genuine aspirant devoted to reality,
your Teacher guides you through direct experience—
not hearsay or belief systems—
to the realm of Ultimate Consciousness.

This is the path:

As an intelligent Person meaning well toward yourself,
respond directly to your Knowledge of Self
and live a well-functioning Life
in Relationship to a real Teacher,
devoted to Self-realization.

We examine now obstacles that lurk on this path,
and how you can resort to the subtlest levels of knowledge
to overcome them, how you turn obstacles to your advantage
and free yourself from the compulsion to recreate them.

1. *The self-existent Lord destroyed the out-going senses.*
Therefore one sees the outer things and not the inner Self.

> *A rare discriminating man, desiring immortality, turns his eyes away and then sees the indwelling Self.*

Second translation:

> *The Self-evolved One (swayambhu) pierced the sense-openings outwards; therefore one sees what is without not what is within oneself. (Occasionally) some wise man, seeking Deathlessness, with reversed gaze has seen the Inner Self.*

Consciousness, the Self of all, is beginningless, imminently present and eternal.
Not coming from anything,
He is His own source and His own light.
Not having evolved from anything, He is *...self-existent...*

...The Self-evolved One (swayambhu) pierced the sense-openings outwards...
All manifestation is a turning outward of Brahman's attention relative to His center.
The center of Infinite Self is everywhere:
it is the center of all His manifestations, the center of all that is.
Thus experiences related to as outer by the manifestations
are inner experiences to the Power of Being.

To Manifestations who have the Perspective of Separateness
there is outer Experience and inner Experience,
and outer predominates—Suffering.
To Eternal Consciousness, the Self and Center of all Manifestation,
all Experience is inner—Joy.

Why would Brahman, the Self-existent,
have *...pierced the sense-openings outwards...*
and thereby have manifestations suffer isolation
in the predominant experience of the outer?
This is the cosmic play, maya, by which the one Self of all
allows for the illusion of something outside Himself,
the illusion of other, of separateness isolation limitedness.

Through Illusion,
the Dichotomy of inside and outside is established.
By this Means the infinitely interconnected Consciousness
experiences the 'as-if' of Separateness,
which provides enriching Contrast
to the constant Experience of Unitive Being.

A student once asked me,
Why does God cause us to be born with an ego?
Why aren't we born with perception of ourselves
as limitless all-pervasive interconnected Being?
Through having to cope with the ego
and the experience of isolation and limitedness, thus suffering,
you evolve into the experience and appreciation
of your limitlessness and interconnectedness.
By overcoming opposition, you strengthen your faculties
and your ability to experience and enjoy
the infinitude of Being you are.

You could also just ask, Why are we born?
Because we are.

Why does the sun shine?
It just does.
Why does limitless Power of Being express Self
when He has no need to, as He has no needs whatsoever?
Limitless Being expresses Self
because He has chosen to express Self.

> The Contrast of Ego to Self
> casts into Bold Relief
> the Experience of limitless luminous Consciousness.

Experiences of limitation and contrast
contribute to the infinitude of Brahman's Self-experience.
As does, by the way, suffering.
Suffering provides a rich contrast to the experience of bliss
that is innate to Knowing Being.

> As long as you dwell on the outer Side of the Curtain of Illusion,
> you experience yourself separated
> from the All-inclusiveness of Reality,
> thus suffer.
> 'Outer' is relative only to the individual Perspective;
> to the All-pervasive Self there is no Outside,
> only blissful Self-experience.

From the perspective of an isolated fragment
who lives in a world of fragments,
your mind is constantly occupied
with what it perceives as separate objects.
Able to focus on only one thing at a time,
mind seems helplessly attached
to each object with which it is involved.
Not only that, but mind's involvement with an object
propels it unwittingly to the next object
to which the present one is in some way related,
be it by proximity in space idea form or whatever.
As a result, mind bounces from object to object to object
in a seemingly endless succession,
absent to the task it was created for, to reflect Self.

When you do not properly seize responsibility
for the workings of your mind, you are enmeshed
with experiences you regard as outside yourself
and are not free to experience the Essence,
the unified Being that you are:
...one sees the outer things and not the inner Self...
Dwelling in a state of distraction and distortion,
you even regard the inner Self as something outside,
some spiritual principle to aspire to,
an abstract theory, vague belief or wishful thought.
Worse than that, you learn to fear Self
even while aspiring to Self-realization.

When you habitually identify yourself with the illusory ego,
you experience limitedness isolation and dysfunction
as your own characteristics and therefore inherent to you.
You think, That's the way I am, I can't help it.

Fearing Self, you regard limitation as your freedom,
self-annihilation as your means of survival,
and suffering as your pleasure.
How perverse is that?
Consider whether that is true for your life.
These are the obstacles.
Why would anyone oppose themselves so thoroughly?

In the distorted state you attach yourself to the usurper—
who gives you nothing but suffering—
as if it were your rightful identity,
while you fear and shun real Self—
whose experience gives you lasting bliss—
as a threatening enemy.
Self-negation may even continue
when, in the inevitable course of evolution,
the Being you are asserts Self.
Identified with the non-self,
you recoil from the light and love of Consciousness,
and promote with a vengeance the painful
self-demeaning and self-negating ego behaviors
that are incongruent and harmful.

There are those rare ones who are discriminating and wise enough
to consciously seek immortality,
the state where Death does not reign.
Everybody wants immortality, no one wants to die—
unless your suffering becomes too much,
then you may want out—
but very few consciously seek and work toward immortality.
Those who seek it know that to attain immortality
you must learn to turn your mind

and all your instruments of perception
away from the addictive distraction
of the temporal and illusory, which includes not only objects,
but also states of mind feelings and emotions,
attachments and habits.
These conditions are superimposed upon Self;
sincerely seeking immortality,
you will turn away from relating to them as if they were real.
This turning away is most effectively accomplished
by honing mind and all your faculties as fine as a razor's edge
and focusing them continuously and faithfully
on the Essential Consciousness,
the one permanent identity of you and all.

The great Majority live in Ignorance of Self.
Rare is the Person who even *hears* of real Self.
Even rarer are those who hear and understand sufficiently
to *know* Self.
Of those rare ones who know Self, rarer still
are those who *live* in true Relationship to their Knowledge
and, seeking to realize their true Nature,
reverse their habitual outward Attention
and focus on the Experience of Eternal Being.

Those who have evolved to the knowledge of Self
are certainly blessed and would be utterly foolish
not to immediately grasp the opportunity

to irrevocably expertly and faithfully turn their faculties
to the glorious unlimited Consciousness they really are.

Never forget that the *power to choose* is inherent to you.
You are not born as a victim to illusion,
nor a slave to your conditioning.
You are blessed with the power of discrimination
by which you can discern the true from the false,
the permanent from the temporary,
the substantive from the superficial,
the Infinite Self from the limited ego.
All you really need to do is:

Turn your Vision permanently to the Reality of Being.
Relate faithfully to self-evident Consciousness.

When you relate all your experiences
to the Infinite Consciousness that you are
and base all your expressions,
your thoughts emotions and actions, on Self,
you *do* turn away from any perception of outside.
Then you experience all as Self and Self as all.
You experience only Self and Self-manifestation.
You are open to all and need not reject any.
You are not attached to manifestations
to the exclusion of the experience
of the eternal all-inclusive Consciousness you are.
And that is a critical point:

Do not attach yourself to any Manifestation
to the Exclusion of the Entirety,
the Power of Being and Its Experience.
After all, Infinite Consciousness is your Identity.

Therein lies the eternal bliss that only *seems* rare
because so few turn to the self-evident,
and so few who have the opportunity to know Self,
sincerely devote their faculties to Self-realization.
Those who do, dwell in the delight of Limitless Being,
eternal and all-pervasive Consciousness
in self-knowing unceasing bliss.

That is the way it is.

Focus yourself now.
Be deeply relaxed.
Invite your faculties to be present with mind in your center,
in tranquil unity.
Encourage their continuous participation
in your experience of Being.
Allow all your faculties to reflect awareness of yourself
as Eternal Consciousness.
Give to each part of you a deep sense of your Limitless Self,
and thereby liberation from fear anxiety anger and blame.
As you are sincerely and fully present,
turn your gaze unto the magnificent loving Self you are:

You are royal Being.
Imagine yourself standing in your palatial bath pavilion

that is open to the royal gardens, lush and green.
Experience this deeply in your imagination.

As you stand here,
be aware of a beautiful light radiating from deep within you.
It radiates from your core, illuminating every part of you
and shining forth in all directions.
Remain completely in this experience.

As you stand in your pavilion
open to the fresh air and the beauty of the gardens,
the luminosity emanating from you
is reflected by innumerable mirrors
covering every surface of the pavilion—
the graceful columns and arches, the bath, ceiling and floor—
tiny mirrors everywhere reflecting the light that you are.
Everything in your open-air pavilion is a reflector.

Choose to be absorbed in this experience.

Gazing forth from your pavilion, see the gardens all around
reflecting the light shining from you.
Feel that. Experience that.
The trees flowers and bushes reflect your light,
as does the sky, and the elegant pools and fountain.
Even the air reflects the luminosity of you, Self.

Deeply and vitally engage in this experience:
Feel the air gently touching your skin,
fresh fragrant and warm.
Internally experience yourself smelling the delicate scent
of flowers trees and grass.
See the beauty of color and light and shade.
Touch the rich textures—the roughness of the bark of a tree,

the velvety silkiness of a rose petal,
the smoothness of water in the reflecting pool.
Savor the taste of fruit from the garden.

Relaxing in your pavilion amidst the resplendent gardens,
emanating light from your entire being,
at home in your center in clear continuous Consciousness,
you experience upwelling from the cave of your heart
the radiance of love.
Be free of any reservations, let love flow unhindered.
Pure love is flowing forth from your core.

Everything around you reflects your glow of love to you.
Open yourself to experience love without bound.
Radiate love in conscious oneness
toward everything around you.
Experience your deeply connected love
reflected from the tranquil waters
as well as the moisture that shines on your skin,
and from the skies earth and spacious gardens.

Bathe in the delight of Loving Consciousness
radiating from your heart and reflected by creation,
returning the experience of your love to you
to be emanated again from you.
As you stand in your center and love flows over and into you,
you radiate it with ever-increasing joy and contentment.
Experience yourself now
as the infinite ocean of luminous love,
vitally alive, all-powerful and never-ending.
You are Self-luminous Consciousness in the bliss of Being.

Take some time now to stop, step back and experience.

2. *The unintelligent people follow the external desires. They get entangled in the snares of the wide-spread death. Therefore the discriminating people, having known what true immortality is in the midst of impermanent things, do not pray for anything here.*

Second translation:

> *The childish follow after external objects of desire and therefore they enter the wide-extended snare of death. But the wise, having known the Deathless State, seek not the Fixed Pole of being amid the transient things of this world.*

Involvement with the world of the senses—
the material realm and all its phenomena—
usually so monopolizes your attention,
that reality is not discernable, you do not experience it.
Your faculties are distracted
from the Eternal Consciousness you are—
Consciousness is continuous,
but your faculties are not in contact with It.
When your faculties are not in contact with real you,
they are not serving you.
That is how you can be walking along
and find yourself in front of a wall,
and wonder how you got there.
Your faculties borrowed some of the light of Consciousness
to *perform* the activity,
but they did not *relate* their experience to Being—
full Consciousness.

The sense world is of phenomenal appearances,
thus not reality, but illusion.
You involve your faculties in these appearances
so routinely that you think they are real.
But a collection of molecules dancing around in space—
an object—is a passing event, not something solid and lasting.
To allow the senses to run after illusory appearances
like unreined horses, uncontrolled by the mind
therefore disconnected from the intellect,
is not intelligent—the higher intellect is not in control.
Allowing the senses to run wild
takes you away from the experience of the reality that is Self.

Dysfunctional behaviors are not only *overt*, like indulging your senses,
but also *subtle*:
like making yourself feel weak ashamed or depressed;
ensuring you have superficial relationships
by seeking partners who are abusive or dismissive
and rejecting those who are loving and accepting;
cultivating financial dependency so that you are unable
to engage in what would help you on the deeper
more meaningful level of the spiritual realm;
or continuously seeking attention by cultivating failure.
Dysfunctional behaviors are *...childish...*
common childhood patterns carried over into adulthood.

Your experiences are impressed upon your faculties,
and those impressions stimulate behaviors
that repeat the original experience.
When, for example, you fall for your faculties' misguidance
that it is treating yourself kindly
to indulge in an occasional foible,

it is really not just for one moment of weakness—
you are fortifying the energy that will compel you
to repeat that harmful behavior ever after.
There lies the entanglement in repetitive cycles of dysfunction
that predictably binds you to seemingly endless suffering.
If someone were to say outright,
You must be subject to abject slavery for the rest of your life,
you would rebel.

When you allow *...external desires...* to predominate,
you become so deeply enmeshed in illusion
and the attendant suffering,
that Consciousness is obscured
from your instruments of perception:
you are in the forgetfulness of Being.

The Succession of negative Effects
that invariably results from Unconsciousness
entangles you in the Necessity of repeating the Cycle
of Birth Death Decay and Rebirth—
what the Ancients called being tied to the Wheel of Karma—
until you evolve the Intelligence to free yourself
from Bondage to those repetitive Cycles.

Evolution is the process of rising
to ever-increasing levels of Consciousness
until you attain the *realization* of Infinite Consciousness.
You are not meant to passively wait for this;
you have the ability to consciously proactively

participate in your evolution.
You can learn to discriminate between the outer and inner,
the ephemeral and permanent, the illusory and real,
and choose to live true to Self.

Why is it that universal among creatures is the instinct for survival?

> The Instinct to oppose Death and Decay
> is congruent with your true Identity, eternal Power of Being.

Thus the drive toward the realization of *...true immortality...*
is inherent to us.
True immortality does not just last through eons, but eternally.
The gods are *merely* immortal;
they may live for eons, many cycles of creation,
yet they are impermanent—time is a passing event.
You, like Naciketa, are seeking to realize your real identity,
Eternal Consciousness.

> The Realization of your true Identity,
> Limitless Being,
> is the Goal and Purpose of the evolutionary Process.

...the wise, having known the Deathless State, seek not the Fixed Pole of being amid the transient things of this world...
Wise persons fix their life attention on the real,
the permanent Self.
Filled with the experience of reality,

they have no concern for the ephemeral world,
no desire for wealth power and progeny,
or the patterns of dysfunction to which so many are attached—
all of which are Lord Yama's temptations.
The intelligent *...do not pray for anything here...*
Focusing your faculties on efforts
to unite with objects or events
excludes uniting with All-pervasive Being.

Remember:

There is nothing wrong with experiencing the material realm—
why was it created if not to be experienced?
The mistake is in fixing your attention upon the material realm
to the *exclusion* of the experience of
all-inclusive eternal Consciousness, Self,
and misinterpreting it.
That differentiation must be understood
for your spiritual thrust, the real seeking,
to have proper direction motivation and energy;
much energy is wasted on trying to be 'holy' or 'spiritual'
through *rejection*:
yet another enmeshment with the material realm.

Follow the fine-honed Path
that goes directly to the Luminosity of Self,
not the Path that rambles all over Creation.

Chapter Twenty-Four

Atman The Honey-Eater

Maintain the state of effortless balance
throughout your body senses and mind,
your feelings and emotions, intellect and intuition.
Maintain pure attentiveness
devotedly directed to the Power of Being
that is your essence and identity.

Allow these teachings to be a powerful positive influence
upon all your faculties,
upon all your behaviors from the subtlest to the grossest,
upon all your expressions, your actions,
so that you choose to express the Infinite Being you are,
and thereby encourage others to find hope and direction
in the light of Self-experience.

Be centered, balanced and at peace,
your gaze steadily directed at Eternal Self.

When your faculties' devotion to Self is sincere and continuous,
you will note arising within them
a wonderful sense of agreement with yourself,
causing deep contentment that is unwavering,
independent of circumstance and condition.
This abiding love is natural when you experience yourself
as eternal all-pervasive Consciousness.

3. *What remains here (unknowable to this Self) through which very Self people perceive colour, taste, smell, sound, touch, and sexual pleasures? This is that (Self asked for by Naciketa).*

Second translation:

That by which one knows form, taste, smell, sound and mutual contacts, what remains here (when all these sensations have been eliminated), this verily is That (Atman, that transcendent deathless being about which thou hast enquired).

Self is omniscient, all-knowing,
the unattached impartial observer and experiencer of all.
The real one who sees tastes smells touches and hears
is not the John Joe or Betty, but Atman, Self.

The senses' experiences and the material realm are impermanent.
When you no longer are distracted by them,
what remains is Being, the irreducible about you,
that which is left when all the superficial is removed,
that without which you would not be.
This is *...that (Self asked for by Naciketa)...*
the ultimate boon.

> No matter how much of the Impermanent you obtain,
> it never fulfills you,
> as it never fulfills your deepest Need: to realize Eternal Self.
> All the Impermanence of the World brought together
> will not make one Eternal.
> Only Eternal Consciousness is Fulfillment.

4. *Having realised that great and all-pervading Self, through which a man perceives the objects in both the sleep and the waking states, a wise man does not grieve.*

The *...all-pervading Self...* is the substance of—
that which stands under—all.
Pure limitless Consciousness prevails all the time,
everywhere.

It is Consciousness that perceives all,
and it is Consciousness that is to be perceived.

All objects events phenomena are Consciousness manifested
for Self-luminous Consciousness to experience Self.
Even when you are distracted by activities and experiences,
in ignorance or illusion, Consciousness prevails.
Just because your faculties are not in contact with It
does not mean that Consciousness does not persist.
And there lies the great comfort,
the one fact your faculties can depend on:
Consciousness, Being, persists, no matter what.

Consciousness is always experiencing Self,
transcendent to the state of your faculties.
Consciousness is always experiencing Self,
irrespective of the manifestations,
but also *through* the manifestations,
even if they are in complete ignorance—
Self may at that moment
be experiencing the brilliance of Consciousness
due to the contrast of darkness provided by the manifestation
who has volunteered to be in ignorance,
consciously or unconsciously.
A person in a coma, a rock or a plant
is in a relatively latent state of Consciousness,
less manifested *as* Consciousness;
to Limitless Consciousness, there is no rock,

there is not even us—there is only Being.
Relative states do not really exist.

At night, Consciousness is the perceiver of your dreams
in addition to other experiences accompanying sleep,
such as rest or restlessness, comfort or discomfort,
as well as transcendence.
How do you know Consciousness continues even during sleep?
In the morning upon waking,
you are aware that you are still the same person
who went to sleep the night before.
Also, you may say, I slept well, or, I hardly slept—
through continuing Consciousness
you can know the quality of your sleep.

Consciousness is the light of Self-awareness
that you are and *what* you are.
Realizing the all-pervasive and eternal Power of Being
that you are,
you know yourself to *be* all and *have* all.
There is no need, thus there is no context for grief.

5. *Anyone who knows proximately this Self—the enjoyer of the fruits of works, the supporter of life etc.—as the lord of the past and the future, does not want to save (the Self) just because of that (knowledge). This is that.*

Second translation:

He who knows this Honey-eater, the Atman, as the (one) Life, ever near, the Lord of past and future, thereafter, he shrinks away no more. This verily is That.

Self is referred to in ancient scriptures as the eater of honey,
for Self is the enjoyer of all pleasures,
all experiences, from the gross to the most refined and sacred.
Honey is laboriously gathered and prized in every culture.
Along with milk, it is a sacrificial offering in India,
and for many other peoples,
such as those depicted in the Bible,
as it symbolizes the finest gifts of the earth.
Self, Atman, the *...Honey-eater...*
is the enjoyer of the sacrificial offerings of honey and milk,
as well as all actions.
This is to whom we relate when we offer the ego for sacrifice.

Atman is *...the enjoyer of the fruits of works...*
It is Self, not the body-mind personality,
who enjoys—or suffers—the fruits of your labors, your actions.
Self suffers? No, Self *experiences* through your suffering.
Infinite Consciousness is the experiencer of everything,
including suffering as well as enjoyment.

Do you see the change in perspective?

Suffering is just another Experience of Being,
another Texture or Color of being conscious,
being aware of yourself Being.

Atman is *...the supporter of life...* the substance and the sustenance.
The Power of Being is the creative source
and sustainer of life, as well as life's reason.
Self is the essence of all, intimate to every facet of creation.

He is the ruler of all time *...the lord of the past and the future...*
He owns the past for He existed even before it,
as well as the future, as He will be eternally in it.
Atman is the lord of the present—
each moment is Eternal Self's present.

...Anyone who knows proximately this Self...
meaning, so closely, so intimately as to be identified with It—
the ultimate proximity—has no need *...to save (the Self)...*
The Self-realized person knows herself
as the imperishable limitless source of all.
Only a person identified with ego finds cause for fear,
for ego is perceived as limited to the body-mind construct,
isolated and cast adrift in a limitless interconnected universe.
Identified with a perishable body-mind
thus perceiving yourself as doomed to decay,
you experience the anxious need to save yourself,
and this is your most persistent preoccupation.
You fearfully withdraw into isolation,
away from the experience of real Self.

Outward-oriented persons do not know Self intimately,
thus fear Self as the enemy.
They see Atman as something outside of them,
while they regard the ego usurper as who they are,
and with whom they want to be intimate.
Self is the threat, so they cling to the usurper, the anti-Self.
In their fear they choose suffering over bliss, even consciously,
for they are familiar with suffering, and bliss is an unknown.
They prefer non-self to Self, for they are familiar with ego;
Self is the unknown.
They seek refuge in that which causes dysfunction and pain.

The rare intelligent discerning ones
who realize their identity in eternal all-pervasive Being,
intimately interconnected with all,
feel no need to withdraw into self-defensive isolation.
All-pervasive Self has no need to withdraw
and defend against something other.

There is to you, Non-dual Self,
no Other from which to protect yourself.

...*This is that*... conveys the authoritative finality of absolute fact.
Self is the essence of action life and time:
...*the enjoyer of the fruits of works*...
...*the supporter of life*...
...*the lord of the past and the future*...
When you know this, there is no need to save yourself.
Knowledge counts, knowledge is meant to make a difference
in the way you think feel and act.
Do not accumulate knowledge and *not* respond to it,
do not live as if you did not know.

Chapter Twenty-Five

The Breath Of Creation

Cause your faculties to remain in your center in effortless balance,
deeply relaxed.
Attune your faculties to All-pervasive Consciousness,
the essence of all that is, including your faculties.
Simply have the faculties reflect self-knowing Being.

Through these teachings you are exposed to experiences
of fundamental facets of your true identity, Consciousness,
who knows Self to be infinite and dwells in the bliss thereof.
Your faculties are unaccustomed
to reflecting the experience of bliss.
However, you can, with gentle persistence,

instill the bliss of self-knowing Self
as your faculties' normal experience.
Deeply impress these teachings.

6. *He sees this very aforesaid Brahman who sees the First Born (Hiranyagarbha)—born before the five elements from Consciousness (Brahman)—as existing in the cavity of the heart in the midst of body and senses, after having entered there.*

Second translation:

He who in the beginning was born from the inner Heat (tapas); who was born earlier than the Waters, who, having entered the Cave, stands; who gazed forth through beings—This verily is That.

Here Lord Yama provides a succinct sequential account
of how to relate to everything in creation,
how to see all as does the Self-realized person.
If you were to thus see, you would be Self-realized.
As in the teaching on the hierarchy of Being,
we receive a realistic view
of the relationship between three principles:
Eternal Consciousness,
the Creator,
and the created, the human being, the manifestation.

Eternal Consciousness is the infinitely subtle and pervasive
substance of all that is,
and at the same time, beyond time and space,
circumstance and condition,
beyond even cause and effect.

Brahman just *is*. He is the indefinable *That*,
the ultimate and final Self of all.

Brahman, by His *...inner Heat (tapas)...*
the ardent fire of His pure will,
projects Self into His Self-expressive modality
of *...Hiranyagarbha...* the *...First Born...*
from whom all creation comes forth.

Consciousness in His pure Will
projects Self as the First Born
from whom emerges Creation.

Hiranyagarbha is called the First Born
because He is of Infinite Being, not separate.
Hiranyagarbha and Eternal Consciousness are one.

Hiranyagarbha is *...born before the five elements...*
earth, with the five qualities of sound tactility color
taste and smell;
water, with the four qualities of sound tactility color and taste;
fire, with the three qualities of sound tactility and color;
air, with the two qualities of sound and tactility;
and the *ether* of space, with only one quality, sound.
He is the source from whom all creation comes forth
through these five elements.

The First Born enters the secret place *...the Cave...* of the heart,
the center of all beings, and *...stands...*
He *remains* there as the foundation.

Beyond the five elements,
without qualities and therefore without decay,
He is the permanent, the Eternal Consciousness.

Consciousness, the essence of all, standing within,
...[gazes] forth through beings...
He experiences Self through His creation
made up from the five elements.
He experiences Self through the elements' qualities
with the corresponding senses
of hearing touch sight taste and smell.

...This verily is That... This is the fact.
Manifestation is not an isolated event;
Brahman and Hiranyagarbha and the manifestation are one.
Only in the ego perspective do you see impermanence;
in the entirety there is only permanence:
Self eternally experiencing Self
through His creation and beyond.
Thus manifestations, which are momentary and ephemeral,
are integral aspects of the oneness, the continuity,
the all-pervasiveness in time and space, of the Power of Being.

> The First Born enters the secret Place of all Beings,
> the Cave of the Heart,
> and remains there, in the Midst of the Body and Senses,
> whose Reason for being He is.

Since from the Creator all manifestation comes forth,
He is denoted by the sound symbol Om.

Om is the original and underlying vibration
from which all the vibrations
that form the objects and events of creation
are evolved and sustained for the duration of their appearance.
Hiranyagarbha, the First Born, is Om,
and Om is Hiranyagarbha.

All Creation comes forth from the Creator—
from the Gods to the less-evolved Life Forms
including Human Beings.
He is the Golden Germ.

The Creator is a Self-projection of Brahman;
human beings are Self-projections of the Creator
who can live as if disconnected from their source,
therefore in ignorance of reality, including their own identity.
Self-projections in which Being can experience
ignorance regarding identity
highlight the opposite: Self-realization and the bliss thereof.

You are Self-projection of the Creator,
who is Self-projection of the Power of Being,
who in the form of Human Being
can experience Self as ignorant of his Identity,
a striking Contrast
bringing the Experience of the Bliss of Self-illumination
into Bold Relief.

You have the innate ability to activate your potential
and live in the perception of yourself as Eternal Consciousness,
who, by the ardent fire of His will,
projects Self as the creative force
and manifests the vast variety of creation
that includes human beings.
However, that potential is not known when you are enveloped
in the darkness of ignorance and illusion,
and attached to their modalities of behavior.

The rare wise ones learn to live and act according to reality
by burning the Naciketa fire—
they gain real knowledge,
sacrifice ego,
and through charity function as interconnected Being.
When you are in contact with reality,
you see yourself as a manifestation of Hiranyagarbha,
the creative projection of Eternal Consciousness,
and experience the oneness of those apparent three:
Consciousness-Creator-you the manifestation.

Thus you are liberated from the bondage pain and suffering
consequent to ignorance and false perception,
and live in the abiding bliss of indivisible indestructible Being.
You experience yourself in the unabated joy of real identity:
Satchidananda, Existence-knowledge-bliss-absolute.

Experience this with the real intention
of remaining in this experience throughout your life.
You are learning the deepest secrets of the genesis of creation.
Eternal Consciousness, the enjoyer of all experiences,
hears tastes touches smells and sees
in association with the five elements

through His creative aspect, Hiranyagarbha,
and remains in the core of these elements
and the bodies and senses they form.
When you live knowing the Creator
as existing in the cave of the heart of all creation,
you realize Brahman, the Ultimate.
You see beyond phenomenal appearances
and experience all as the one eternal Consciousness.

Only ego creates a false idea of separation
between Brahman and Hiranyagarbha and you,
between higher and lower;
there is no separation between the Power of Being
and anything in creation,
for all is in essence the one eternal Consciousness,
as each wave is in essence the ocean.

There are no Separations
in the infinite Continuum of Self.
One who sees all as the one Consciousness,
and the one Consciousness as all,
sees Self.
One who sees only Self is Self-realized
and dwells in Eternal Consciousness.

7. *He (sees) that very Brahman (who sees) that Aditi, comprising all the deities, who takes birth as Hiranyagarbha, who is manifested in association with the elements, and who is seated in the cavity of the heart, after entering there.*

Second translation:

> *She who is manifested together with Life (prana) Aditi, whose substance is the Gods, who, having entered the Cave, stands; who was born forth distributively through beings—This verily is That.*

Here we enter further into the secrets of the genesis of creation.

The person who realizes Self knows the relationship
between Brahman and all His aspects.
In pure Consciousness rests potentiality—Hiranyagarbha—
and potentiality is realized in creation—*Aditi.*
Consciousness' fervent projection of Self as Creator,
the Golden Germ, comes to fruition in beings
and is their sustaining breath, through Aditi.
She is the life-giving aspect,
the mother of every form of Being.

> Aditi is the Aspect of Consciousness
> in the Act of expressing Its Potential
> in Association with the Elements,
> through created Beings.

Aditi is born as life-breath, which carries prana, the vital force
through which Hiranyagarbha empowers all creatures
while dwelling in their core, in the cavity of their heart,
where He remains and where, by extension,
Eternal Consciousness remains.
The feminine creative aspect,

Aditi infuses the five elements with prana,
animating their interplay, and forming manifestations
who have the power to perpetuate themselves—
create more of their kind, just like impressions do—
and to evolve on their own:
the Creator does not direct them to do this or that.

Free will is integral to the play that creates
the infinite variations in colors shapes sounds
textures smells and tastes,
not to mention experiences on the higher levels.
Beings contain the impetus to progress
from nescience to knowingness,
from regarding themselves as merely separate objects
to realizing their oneness with the Creator
seated in the cave of their heart, who is the Power of Being.
Thus advance ages of uncounted millennia of creations
evolving to eventually realize their identity
in Infinite Consciousness, the ultimate source and destination.

Creation has many power centers,
varying from small to large, weak to strong,
harmonious to disharmonious.
Creatures differ only in their level of Consciousness.
...the Gods... have the highest degree of Consciousness.
They can be seen as powerful combinations
of subtle vibrations working in unison.
Gods are given names and get into all sorts of mischief
because they have an ego
due to differentiating from the whole.
So develops the play called creation.
Aditi is the essence, the soul of the gods.

She is the mother born into every being,
from the gods on down the ladder of degrees of Consciousness.

Through Aditi, pure Consciousness experiences
'consciousness of something',
and those 'somethings' can evolve
to experience All-pervasive Consciousness.
Consciousness is ever-expanding,
reflecting Self to Self through manifestations.

Here again may arise the question, Why?
Just as the sun shines because it does,
it is the nature of Consciousness to experience Self;
It *is* Self-experience.

Through the constant miracle of opposition and contrast,
Limitless Consciousness reflects Self.
Your suffering may serve to propel you to bliss.
Suffering and bliss are always available,
and you have been given the free will to choose either.
In the experience of making those choices—
and repeating those choices over and over again
until you learn—
Consciousness is playing Self as limited
and expanding to Self-realization:
the play of creation.

In the scope of Infinite Consciousness there is really no suffering;
however, as a manifestation you can experience suffering—
or fleeting happiness—until you realize your oneness with all.
The realization of who you really are
is made so difficult as to seem almost impossible—

not by Consciousness, nor the Creator, nor the soul,
not even by the five elements—only by *you*, if you so choose.
You have the freedom and power to do so.

Sometimes it does not seem that way.
What about children born into the horrors of war,
or those brought up by terribly abusive parents,
or, maybe worse, parents who mistreat their child
under the guise of love?
Such individuals are extremely troubled not only in childhood,
but most of them in adulthood as well.
How can you blame them for the terrible things they endure?

Blame is not relevant to reality; karma, the law of cause and effect,
determines how you are born into this manifestation
and what you need to work out.
Some born in hell's kitchen become great people
because they strengthen their faculties and determination
in overcoming the obstacles of their formative years.
You might think I would not have chosen to be born into war,
but I have learned to be grateful for what it gave me.
I had a traumatic childhood, but it was a good training ground;
it lit the spark within me.
Somehow I earned that illumination.

As you evolve, you become more *impersonal*
in terms of your *Ego* Identity
and more *personal* in terms of your *real* Identity.

The teachings from Yama
give you a familiarity with the reality of you,
and the reality of creation, the reality of genesis.

When you realize
dwelling in your Core is the Mother of all Creation
who is the Creator fulfilling His Potential
who is Transcendent Being expressing Self,
you are freed from Enmeshment with the material Realm,
from identifying with the Body-mind Construct
and the Elements that compose it.
Thereby you emerge from behind the illusory Veil
that obscures who you really are
and realize Eternal Consciousness, Self.

Impress the oneness of Being;
break through your linear arrangements for filing knowledge
and penetrate to the subtler levels.
Experience the tremendous comfort and security
in the message of this verse,
the familiarity with yourself
greater, deeper and more profoundly meaningful
than the falsity to which you are conditioned.

The only way you will be familiar with reality
is by impressing Self-experience firmly with determination,
and living accordingly, constantly loyally and lovingly.
If you are living in dysfunction sadness anger confusion
addiction or any other negativity,

you have not integrated the knowledge of your true identity;
your mind and your intellect have received it,
but you have not impressed it with the determination
to be true to it, to live it.

How can you impress your knowledge, your experience?
Here is an example from my life:

I often do not write things down;
I *experience*, impress the experience, and then it is *in* me.
The writings in this book are from experience
first spontaneously shared
in a continuous spoken stream of Consciousness.

A few years after the war, the only recognition I received
for my father having served his country for six years
and then given his life,
was when I, along with other starving children of Germany,
was sent for a cure on an island in the North Sea.
There were about 60 of us, and we stayed in a facility
that was like a big home.
We were in the care of lovely young women we called aunts,
and enjoyed plenty of food and recreation.
It was a deeply healing experience,
one of the most wonderful things
that had ever happened to me—an idyllic six weeks of life.

At the end of our stay, we had an all-day carnival,
and the aunts chose me to give a farewell speech.
I wanted it to be interesting and humorous,
so for many nights before the festival,
just before going to sleep,
I would lie in bed remembering our experiences,

and fashion my talk.
Each night I would mentally add a little more.
When the time came for me to give my address,
I had nothing written, but was able to describe
the entire chronology of our weeks together,
making fun of us children and the aunts and our activities.
It worked because it came from within.

Impress your experience, your learning; it has to be inside you.
You do not, for example, while at work say to yourself,
Now I am supposed to realize Self.
No. Because then it is just in the head,
which means it is not in the heart—
it is in the cave of the heart where you realize.

In the midst of the body and senses and all their chaos,
their ups and downs, comings and goings,
creation and destruction—
even amidst ignorance and forgetfulness
and living in self-contradiction and self-denial—
is Aditi, mother of all creation.
The feminine aspect of the Creator resides in your heart;
realize Her and you will realize Eternal Consciousness.
Then you are free from the need to go through
the repetitive cycles of birth death decay and rebirth.
You are freed from enmeshment with pain and suffering
and all the distractions and distortions,
the sorrow anger and shame.

Chapter Twenty-Six

The Fire Of Creation Preservation And Dissolution

Create the state of beautiful deep relaxation
throughout all your faculties, gathered in your center.
Have them dwell there
in effortless balance and harmonious union.

Simply be present, not laboring.
Simply be present.

Relax.

Your faculties are present in the cave of your heart,
which when created was entered by the Creator,

who remains there,
and who is Eternal Consciousness.

In the state of tranquility, the faculties unfluctuating,
you are one with Consciousness.
This is your essence. This is what you are.

Realizing Eternal Consciousness is to experience yourself unceasingly,
not as the body-mind complex,
an appearance made from the five elements
that form all phenomena,
but the force that manifests it,
Being expressing as the Creator in the aspect of Aditi,
mother of creation,
the life-breath flowing with prana in every creature.

When you are Self-empowered
in your thoughts feelings emotions and actions,
in all your behaviors,
you *realize* the infinite Power of Being that you are.

Refine your faculties so they can absorb these teachings
and become one with them.
Use tapas to discipline the mind feelings and emotions;
do not let them run rampant like wild horses
without an intelligent driver holding the reins.
Your faculties are refined and strengthened
by living in accord with the truth expounded in the teachings.

This is the way it is.

8. The sacrificial Fire lodged in two fire producing pieces of wood, (as also the Fire lodged in the hearts of Yogis) that is well protected, just as much as the foetus is by pregnant women, and the Fire that is adorable every day by vigilant men with oblation (and contemplation)—that Fire too is but this Brahman.

Second translation:

Agni, Knower of Births, concealed in the two Fire Sticks like the embryo well nourished by pregnant women, worthy of daily worship from awakened men who offer sacrifice—This verily is That.

Added now to the secret of the genesis of creation
is *Agni*, the sacred fire.

...the sacrificial Fire... springs forth from Purusa, the Self of all,
and Hiranyagarbha in the aspect of Aditi, His life-breath.
This offspring, given the name *...Agni...* is the third principle
of the trinity that is the substance of all that is.
Just as flames arise when *...two Fire Sticks...*
are rubbed together, so does the luminous fire, Agni, spark
in the relationship of Consciousness with Its potentiality,
the Creator, manifesting through life-breath.

We see depictions of the divine Agni surrounding Nataraja.
Nataraja is a beautiful ancient symbol of this trinity,
the triple aspects of reality.
He is the utterly tranquil Cosmic Dancer
whirling wildly through the cycles
of *creation preservation* and *dissolution*.
All three phases involve Agni:
the sacred fire gives life to manifestations,
sustains them, and eventually consumes them.

The life spark emanating from the Self of all,
along with His life-breath, animates manifested forms.
Agni is integral to the process of life-giving, along with prana.
A crude analogy is fire oxygen and fuel
being integral to combustion, a life process.

The warmth of Agni in the sun helps life forms to grow;
it nurtures and sustains them.
In their growth they feed more evolved life forms.
Agni in the sun and the stars gives light;
luminosity fosters knowledge, which aids evolution.
This is why yogis venerate and adore Agni.

As the fire of destruction, Agni undoes what has been created;
the manifestations return to their source—
Aditi of Hiranyagarbha of Brahman—the circle is complete.
This makes room for new manifestations,
and the cosmic dance continues,
while Self remains in tranquility.

The *...Fire lodged in two fire producing pieces of wood...*
symbolizes the apparent opposition
between the realms of reality and illusion,
through which Limitless Being *reveals* Self
on the subtlest levels
and *experiences* Self on all levels.
Friction between reality and illusion
sparks the illumination of reality.
The microcosm of the potential fire in two pieces of wood
reveals the macrocosm of Eternal Consciousness:
all-pervasively present, completely unmoving, unchanging,
with the potential for all creation.

The apparent Contradictions posed throughout Creation
compel and encourage you to transcend Mind's linear Thinking:
still the Mind,
have it in the unfluctuating State
where it is a pure Reflector, one with Consciousness.

Fire has been held sacred by human beings through the ages.
We have a long history of worshipping and protecting Agni
with loving care and devotion.
In prehistoric times, before there were matches,
before flint stones were discovered,
and even before it was found that two sticks of wood
rubbed together create friction heat and sparks—
before all that, in the cave dwellers' time,
the fire-keeper was one of the most important
and trusted persons of the tribe.
He carefully maintained the fire, and when they migrated,
he carried the hot coals from one place to another.
This person's sole job was to keep the fire alive.

It is with that intensity of devotion and care
that yogis tend to the fire that dwells in the cave of the heart.
The fire of Consciousness—the awareness of Self—
burns away dross and illumines your passion and loyalty.
You can be aware of this fire within you;
it is integral to Self-awareness.
A ...*vigilant*... person keeps the fire alive,
protected from harm.

Intelligent persons remain alert in their relationship to Agni
through *...oblation (and contemplation)...*
that is, giving up any 'otherness'—oblation, or sacrifice—
and constant 'being-with'—contemplation.

Agni is the consumer of sacrifice.
Symbolically, human beings seeking a good relationship
with their source, Eternal Consciousness
who projects Self through Hiranyagarbha,
have sacrificed to Agni what was precious to them—
honey, milk, fine oils, ego-attachments and even life.
The fire sacrifice is a way of demonstrating the determination
to rid yourself of attachment to all limiting adjuncts,
in order to be free to experience your identity
in the one all-embracing reality
of the conditionless eternal Consciousness.

Real sacrifice, the offering up of false ego,
is where many spiritual aspirants fail, as did Naciketa's father.
They are willing to give up all kinds of precious things—
their homes cars husbands wives, even children—
but when it comes to giving up ego identity and its behaviors,
they fear making the real sacrifice.
The ego attachment has to be burned out—
through devoted discipline.

Fear is a persistent deterrent to relinquishing ego,
even when you know ego is the cause of your suffering.
A most practical sacrifice is accomplished
through the *Fear Release Response*,
a powerful approach by which you free yourself from fear.
Enmeshment with fear binds you to severe limitation;

effectively freeing yourself from fear
is fundamental to succeeding in sacrificing all ego ways.

Agni, the fire of tapas, determined discipline,
burning unhindered in the heart of yogis,
speaks of the passionate involvement with Self and truth.
Passion is suspect in many spiritual disciplines.
However, as a pure power, properly reined and directed,
it can be of profound help.
It behooves spiritual aspirants to assess
whether denying passion—as is so frequently advocated—
really serves their spiritual path.
Devotion joy and all-inclusiveness are the power of passion.
This is the way Being is, not ethereal or abstract,
but robustly joyously passionately Being.
Being in the full bliss
of Self-aware eternal all-pervasive I-amness—
that is the grand passion.

> Beware of shortchanging yourself.
> Do not affix yourself
> to the incessant Pursuit of Pseudo-passions,
> the Experience of the Limited, which is not real.
> This Attachment marks the Lives of most
> and carries the highest Price,
> for it keeps you from the passionate Love
> you experience in real Being.

Agni is the ardent force to know Self and live true to Self.
You not only have that fire within you, you *are* that fire;
it is Self, Eternal Consciousness.
Cherish, nurture and keep this fire alive *...every day...*
Stay in touch with it, warm your faculties with it,
do not let the fire die through neglect or forgetfulness
and become cold dusty ashes.

Protect this fire, for it is your life—
not just your physical life, but your real life, your spiritual life.
Agni is the spark of life, the fire of the spirit.
As a mother keeps harmful food and drink from the *...foetus...*
protect your inner flame from negative influences
within and around you.
As an intelligent mother protects her fetus
from violent emotions,
stay away from anger conflict depression blame guilt or shame.
As a well-meaning mother shields the fetus
from all that halts its growth,
protect your inner state from anything that would interfere
with your evolution toward perfect Consciousness,
anything that would slow or halt your thrust
on the path to Self-realization.

Do not neglect the Fire
that resides in the Cave of your Heart,
or relate to its Upkeep as a Burden or Practice.
Let every Facet of you adore it
by giving Sacrifice to it all the Time—
give your Actions Thoughts and Feelings,
your Life Conduct and Awareness, in Purity to Self.

Sincere Yogis are aware of Agni lodged in the cave of the heart,
and consciously protect and keep it alive
through continuous experience of every moment of Being.
That is real meditation.
That fire burns within you, gives you life and inspiration,
luminosity joy and passion of Being.
It is the Power of Being Himself,
the Self that you and all are.
Offer yourself joyously to the tapas
of burning away anything and everything
that hints at differentiation from the one unitive Self you are.
Thus you will rest in pure luminosity,
in Agni, who verily is Brahman.

...This verily is That...
This is all you need to know. Live it,
and you will experience yourself as pure Consciousness,
free from the cycles of life death decay and subsequent rebirth.

9. On that, from which the sun rises and in which it sets, are fixed all deities. None ever transcends that. This is that.

Yama's secrets of the genesis of creation
now include *prana*, the life force.
This is the vital energy, the source *...from which the sun rises and in which it sets...*
that from which all creation comes forth
and in which all creation will be absorbed.
This force is prana, of Self, Brahman.
At each cycle of creation
the sun rises from prana, the life energy,
who is Hiranyagarbha, the First Born,

who is none other than Brahman, Eternal Consciousness,
in ardent Self-projection.
At the conclusion of each cycle,
the sun is absorbed again in prana Hiranyagarbha Self.

> Like the Breath of Human Beings
> coming in and going out,
> so is the Pulse of Creation:
> rising and setting,
> fixed on unmoving transcendent Being.

On that *...are fixed...* all the higher powers, in intimate relationship.
The deities come forth from Brahman through Hiranyagarbha,
as do all lesser manifestations,
to be absorbed again in Brahman
at the dissolution of the universe.

> Everything, from High to Low,
> from the Deities to the Five Elements,
> is fixed on the Power of Being, Self of all.

The flow of creation maintenance and dissolution
is projected from Limitless Consciousness,
the ultimate source essence Self of all.

Nothing can ever transcend that,
nothing is beyond that,
for there is nothing but eternal all-pervasive Being.
...This is that...

Chapter Twenty-Seven

Here Is There, This Is That

Once you know your real identity,
and you know about manifestations dwelling in ignorance,
you have a choice as to what you live:
falsity or reality, limited ego or Infinite Self.
You choose your states and actions in each moment—
your life is an expression of those choices:
whether dedicated to pain and suffering
or to the joy of being in Limitless Consciousness.
Whatever your choice,
you will dedicate your faculties and behaviors to it.

10. *What, indeed, is here is there; what is there is here likewise. He who sees as though there is difference here, goes from death to death.*

This important verse conveys again the very essence
of the Kathopanisad.
Persons of deluded mind see Eternal Consciousness as one
and the manifestation as another.
Pure Consciousness is infinite in space and time,
all-pervasive and eternal, conditionless, limitless.
Manifestations are subject to conditions,
as they are dependent upon the five elements,
which are ephemeral.
Manifestations are not infinite,
they are limited in both space and time;
they are not all-pervasive, and they are momentary, not eternal.
However, Infinite Consciousness pervades all,
thus Consciousness and the manifestations are one.

The mind is conditioned to regard its owner, the person,
as composed of the five elements, identified as a body-mind,
and therefore as limited and subject to decay.
Having a tendency toward linear thinking,
mind proceeds from this false premise
as the foundation of all its considerations
and is unable to grasp the limitless oneness
of the Power of Being and all manifestations.

Often I hear from students the recurring theme
that it is difficult to perceive yourself as the One.
Habituated to thinking about themselves in terms of their body,

many think of Consciousness as residing *inside*,
thus confined to the body.
If Consciousness is inside, there must be something outside.
Thus arises the misconception
of an Ultimate Being apart from yourself,
even in spiritual adepts with years of training and practice.

Any concept of limits directly implies something beyond those limits.
I learned this as a boy, pondering where infinity ends—
since we are accustomed to thinking
that everything has an end.
I thought, If there is an end,
there has to be something beyond that end,
so let us call *that* infinity.
When you think of a beyond, Consciousness is there, too:
whatever and wherever you think, there is Consciousness.
Consciousness is continuous and limitless,
there can be nothing outside It.

The Power of Being is indivisible and indestructible,
It is everywhere all the time.
Self permeates all infinitude, thus there can be and is only One.
All Is That.

> Consciousness is the Continuum throughout Existence,
> the subtle interconnecting Link
> that unites the grand Variety of Manifestations
> throughout and including the entire Cosmos.

There is no real difference or separation
between here and there, or this and that.
There is no *real* difference between one person and another,
for everyone is the Power of Being
who created them and experiences Self through them.
There is not even a real difference between beings and objects:
as your mind can reflect Consciousness,
so do objects reflect Consciousness to Consciousness.

There is no real difference between illusion and real Being,
between the manifestation and the creative force
projected by Eternal Consciousness with His ardent fire,
by which Self reflects Self.

There is no real difference between
Brahman the Eternal Consciousness
and Hiranyagarbha the creative force,
nor between the Creator and Aditi the life-breath
and Agni the essential fire and prana the vital force
and all manifestations.
The plurality of all is recognized to be merely apparent
when you realize the all-embracing unity
that is Consciousness.

> Consciousness is one endlessly interconnected Entity,
> and you are not excluded.

You *Are* That. All Is That.

> The Realization is, I am Consciousness
> who is infinite—all-pervasive and eternal—
> self-knowing Self of all.

That is the final realization.
Self, the infinite eternal all-pervasive Consciousness,
experiences Self blissfully
through Its manifestation experiencing Self as Brahman.
All is Eternal Consciousness. All Is That. I Am That.

In our culture people take pride in egotistical separateness
and call it individuality.
They think they individuate
by being separate different and isolated.
Actually, you individuate in realization of the grand unity.
That is your real individuality—interconnected Being.

Beware: it may be clear to you who you are,
that you are All-pervasive Self,
but because your faculties are so conditioned
to seeing things as differentiated,
they may still relate to you as separate from the All.
As long as that is the case, you are identified with ego
and will meander *...from death to death...*
Identify with and live as eternal Power of Being, Self.

11. This is to be attained through the mind. There is no diversity whatsoever. He who sees as though there is difference here, goes from death to death.

Second translation:

> *By the manas indeed is this to be realised; There is not even the slightest difference here. From death to death he goes Who sees things here as different.*

It is due to conditioning in ignorance
that people see difference instead of oneness.
If you were to keep an accounting
of whether your point of view indicates difference or oneness,
you would find a preponderance of difference.
Examine your ways of thinking and your feelings and actions.
How often do they emphasize separateness in perception,
in attitude, in conduct, in relationship,
as opposed to unity?

...By the manas indeed is this to be realised...
It is your perceiving mind, manas, that has to be freed
from the ignorance of seeing in terms of difference.
How is this to be accomplished?
Only when mind is purified by the fire of tapas,
and, according to Yama,
you are in relationship with a true Teacher,
when you have strengthened and directed your mind
by devoting it to continuously reflecting the real Self you are,
will your mind know and be integral with the Infinite Oneness.

Here again is practical spiritual emotional and psychological advice
on how to live true to yourself.
Knowledge alone is not enough.
Mind can have knowledge,
but if you do not apply the discipline to live and act true to it,

you will remain under the sway of ego ignorance,
and mind will project the experience of differentiation,
not interconnectedness.

When you have profound Knowledge
yet live in disregard thereof,
your Failure and Frustration will be the Clues
that you are living in Self-contradiction.

Living devoted to Knowledge
is the Experience of Loyalty to Self.
It yields the deepest Joy.

You condition your mind through tapas, disciplined devotion to truth,
and are sustained by a genuine relationship with a Teacher.
Why is relationship with a real Teacher repeatedly mentioned?
This relationship is the strongest challenge
to a mind under the sway of ego's attachment to falsity—
I am not *this* enough, I am not *that* enough,
along with all the ensuing behaviors.
Many aspirants, lacking the strength of determination,
are reluctant to sacrifice their attachment to ego.
They try to negate the Teacher and her teachings because
they know she aims to free them from those false attitudes.
Those who are dedicated to being true to Self
benefit significantly from their relationship
with a Teacher who 'sees' who they really are
and cares for them sufficiently to relate to them as Self.

Purify Mind by the Fire of Tapas,
be in true Relationship with a Teacher,
direct your Mind to reflect what is real,
and Mind will be in Harmony with the Infinite Self that you are.

When you do not thus condition your mind,
it will again and again—no matter how great its knowledge—
regress to relating to differences as if they were real,
and thereby obscure the experience of oneness.
All who refuse to let go of their mind's habitual attachment
to ignorance and falsity,
and keep mind functioning in misconception,
will live not in the contentment of interconnectedness
but suffering under the illusion of disconnectedness.

Most are not aware of mind's malfunctioning
as it is not on the conscious level;
subconsciously mind is constantly saying
that you are a disconnected entity.
From this pool of subconscious energy
emanates the influence that infects all your behaviors.
Everything is interpreted and determined in disconnectedness.
That is why so many live in a state of conflict,
not harmony and unity.
Such persons go *...from death to death...*
They have to endure as many cycles of death decay and rebirth

as it takes to realize their true identity,
limitless interconnectedness.

The subtle Consciousness pervading all
is the Self That I Am.

Chapter Twenty-Eight

Limitless Self The Size Of A Thumb

Sincerely prepare the vibratory state that is the body
to be harmonious with the Power of Being that you are.
Cause the breath to flow congruently
with the universal flow of force,
and bring all your faculties together in your center
to be present there in a continuing state of effortless balance.

Direct the attention of your faculties unto Infinite Consciousness
who resides in the cave of your heart.

Sincerely and with determination devote your faculties
to the continuous focus upon Self.
United in tranquility, they reflect free of distortion,
like a clear still mountain lake,
Purusa, the Self of all, the Self you are.
As your faculties sincerely reflect Self,
they vibrate in unison with Self and take on Its characteristics.
Experience your faculties becoming
like the unmoving eternal all-pervasive Consciousness,
for they are Consciousness in their core;
Consciousness, Self, is their essence and reason for being.

Eternal Consciousness residing in the cave of the heart is who you are.
You have formed the faculties by projecting through pure tapas
your potential as Creator,
who forms all manifestation through the five elements
invested with life-breath and essential fire.
The five elements have their limiting adjuncts
by which you have come to see yourself
as separate from Eternal Consciousness.

But that is only the appearance, illusion,
caused by having your faculties primarily involved
with the limits of the elements,
and even identifying yourself mistakenly with them,
as in, I am a man, a woman—this body.
That is all part of Self, who you really are:
Eternal Self creates the veil of illusion
for the experience of separateness,
which emphasizes the unity you are.
Once the veil is ripped and reality no longer concealed,
your faculties can attend to Self in the cave of the heart.

Have your faculties absorbed in the experience and reflection of Self
and thereby absorbed *in* Self.

12. The Being (Purusa), of the size of a thumb, resides in the body. Knowing Him as the ruler of the past and the future, one does not want, by virtue of that knowledge, to save the Self. This is that.

Second translation:

In the midst of our being (atmani) stands the Dweller of the size of a thumb, the Lord of Past and Future. (He who has attained) shrinks away from Him no more. This verily is That.

The Self of all, Purusa, is present in the cave of the heart
of every manifestation, and dwells there.
He confines Himself to the size that fits the manifestation,
therefore He is said to be *...the size of a thumb...*
Experience yourself as *...The Being (Purusa), of the size of a thumb...* residing *...in the body...*
'Body' represents not only the physical,
but the whole combination of forces
that make up the human manifestation—
faculties personality psyche.
The Indweller pervades—entirely fills—your center
and the center of every part of you.

Purusa, the Self that you are,
is unbeginning, never having been created,
imminently present and eternally unending,
thus the master of all time *...ruler of the past and the future...*
When you experience yourself
as the ruler of the past and future,

you have none of the doubts or fears suffered
under the misperception of being a passing entity.

Keep constant the experience of yourself as Self of all,
residing in the cave of the heart:
the unbeginning and unending who is present now.
This is the fact of you.
Thus realizing the grandeur of Self
you are freed from the fear of relinquishing the ego identity:
you are one who *...shrinks away from Him no more...*
Ego tries to convince you to hold on to it for survival,
when actually, you sacrifice your life and freedom to it.
It is only in the misconception of your identity
that it seems necessary to *...save...* yourself,
to perpetuate yourself.
The Eternal has no need to be perpetuated.
It is as simple as that.
...This is that...

Experience yourself as Eternal Consciousness,
utterly safe, free of the need to save yourself, free of anxiety.
Live in the reality of Self and thus live fearlessly,
in harmony and abiding joy.

13. The Purusa, who is of the size of a thumb, is like a light without smoke. He is the ruler of the past and the future. He exists today, and He will exist tomorrow. This is that.

Second translation:

The Dweller of the size of a thumb is like Smokeless Flame, Lord of the Past and Future, He alone Is To-day and He, To-morrow.

Self, the Indweller, who has taken lodging in the cave of the heart
of every manifestation,
is the pure essence, the identity, of all.
Self-effulgent Being, Purusa, needs nothing else to shine
and gives off only pure light—unlike the light of a candle
that needs wax and wick, and gives off smoke.
Experience yourself as Purusa *...like a light without smoke...*
This is the light that yogis experience within their core,
the light of Consciousness that they devotedly nurture
and keep alive throughout every moment of every day.

This, your essence, has always been and shall eternally be,
for Self is infinite in time, unbeginning and never-ending,
transcendent.
Keep your faculties devotedly gathered in the cave of the heart,
gazing steadily upon you, Purusa, with loving attentiveness,
basking in the pure light that you are,
absorbed in illumination.

> Nothing is beyond Infinite Self nor will ever take Its Place—
> not the material Realm, not ephemeral Phenomena,
> not Feelings and Emotions,
> nor Beliefs and Opinions,
> nor long-established Habits or Personalities,
> not even favorite Dysfunctions and Rationalizations.
> Nothing can ever replace Transcendent Being that you are.

Let your faculties, your mind emotions feelings
intellect intuition senses and body, know this.
Nothing will ever take the place of you, Transcendent Self.
As you declare this with love and devotion
and also with enthusiasm and determination,
your faculties are inspired with confidence and trust,
and joyously give their allegiance to you,
Eternal Consciousness.

> Simply directly and unalterably,
> Self is your eternal Essence and Identity,
> It is all you are,
> for Self is the All of all.

...*This is that*... Self verily is That, the indefinable Infinite,
the Limitless Consciousness we all are.
It is beyond argumentation complication rationalization.
It simply is.
Experience that.

Purusa ...*the size of a thumb*... resides within the body
and is the ...*Lord of the Past and Future*...: eternal.
Turn all your faculties inward to be in constant relationship
with the Self of all, who is so intimate
as to pervade the very core of this body-mind-psyche construct.
Feel Purusa, reflect Self,
purely experience consciously as Being,
unalloyed unmoving unmodified Consciousness.

When your faculties absorb the characteristics of Consciousness
and learn to reflect them and become like them,
the mind emotions feelings intellect and intuition,
even the body and senses,
experience themselves akin to those characteristics.
The differentiation between the experiencer
and the experienced is eliminated.
Most behave as if they were experiencing—
or attempting to experience—something else:
the experiencer attempting to experience Infinite Being.
You *are* Consciousness in Self-experience.
It is only due to Consciousness' limiting adjuncts
through the five elements
that the illusion of separateness is wrought.

To ensure that you base your understanding of all Death's teachings
on the central fact of the oneness of Self, not diversity,
the next verse deepens the lesson.

Chapter Twenty-Nine

Pure Water Poured Into Pure Water

You are Eternal Consciousness, who as the Creator
has manifested these names and forms
that contain within themselves the Self of all.
Due to their enmeshment with the limiting adjuncts
your faculties tend to relate to you
in terms of the five elements,
as opposed to the real Self you are.

Knowing your true identity, sincerely place your faculties in the state
in which they reflect the reality of Being
and, so steadily absorbed in that,
take on the characteristics of their source.
Thereby you realize Self.
Let that be your sincere endeavor now.

Begin by creating a deep state of relaxation throughout the body.
Cause the breath to flow in natural rhythm
and thereby strengthen the experience
of the life-breath of the Creator, who is Self.
With your breath, your attention is drawn
to the cave of the heart.
Cause all your faculties to be gathered
and remain there in a state of effortless balance,
for this is where the Self of all has chosen to be present
and to remain.
Here all your faculties are silent witnesses
of the light without smoke.
Self-effulgent, It needs nothing else to burn.
Your faculties absorbed in All-pervasive Luminosity
become one with It.

Experience yourself as Radiant Consciousness
who intimately takes on the size to fit the cave of your heart,
and experience yourself, at the same time, transcendent to that.
Experience yourself as Consciousness
intimately filling the cave of the heart of manifestations,
as well as infinitely expansive, all-pervasive.

14. As water rained on an inaccessible height gets dispersed on (lower) hilly regions, similarly, one who perceives the selves differently, runs after them only.

When it rains on inaccessible high areas
the water is dispersed onto lower regions.
Similarly, persons who base their perceptions
on the falsity of diversity,
who see every entity—including themselves—
as a different self,
pursue them and lose their experience of the one Self.

You are one interconnected Power of Being.
That wants to be experienced and expressed—realized.
The drive for Self-realization is the most fundamental impetus.
It propels you from the false perception of separateness
to the realization of your interconnectedness
in all-pervasive and eternal Being.
It is the source of all your sub-drives,
your ambitions needs desires and aspirations.
This fundamental drive empowers your evolution.

In ordinary people, who perceive themselves and everything else
in terms of separateness,
the energies aiming at the experience of interconnected Self
are diverted into myriad directions.
Their life is dissipated in the vain pursuit
of satisfying separate selves
through which they attempt to fulfill the need for union.
Their fate is repeated death
until they finally resolve to sacrifice the separate ego-self.

15. *O Gautama, as pure water poured on pure water becomes verily the same, so also does become the Self of the man of knowledge who is given to deliberation (on the Self).*

The verse previous to this one describes the way of death.
This verse offers the way of Eternal Consciousness:
meditation, the *...deliberation (on the Self)...*
having your faculties' energies vibrate in the purity of Self
to be merged with Self.

Meditation is the willed continuous Focus
on the Experience of yourself
as the one eternal Consciousness.

In Meditation you experience yourself as Consciousness,
who through pure Will projects the Creator,
who through the Life-breath gives the Fire of Being and,
in Conjunction with the Five Elements,
causes Manifestation.

The Creator places Himself in the cave of the heart
of each manifestation.
Due to their limiting adjuncts
these manifestations tend to experience themselves
as differentiated from their essence,
until they realize oneness with All-pervasive Self
through meditation.

By meditation you free yourself from the false perception
of difference and separation caused by the myopic view
of the five elements and their many limiting adjuncts—
including grossness fragmentation and limitedness.
As a consequence you also free yourself

from the behaviors and experiences that result from falsity:
isolation fear anger depression harmfulness conflict
greed and competition.

Your liberation from false perception is most directly cultivated
by daily behaviors congruent with the one unitive Self
with whom you are uniting your faculties in meditation:
harmlessness sharing caring truthfulness and loving.
Positive behaviors lead to ever-increasing real knowledge
growing into wisdom, which then expands to Self-realization.
That is the way of eternal life.
Engaging in behaviors based on the perception of separateness
is not only immediately harmful to you and everyone else,
but negatively influences subsequent behaviors.

...pure water poured on pure water becomes verily the same...

In Meditation you radiate pure Vibrations of Consciousness
into the limitless Field of Consciousness:
you realize the Oneness of your Vibrations
and Eternal Consciousness.

PART II CANTO II

How Self Fares After Death

Chapter Thirty

Ruler Of The Eleven-Gated City

Allow your faculties to rest in effortless balance in your center,
faithfully and loyally, with continuity,
attending with loving devotion to the source
who is their reason for being.
Have the faculties' relationship to the reality of Self
be constant and never again denied or forgotten.
Thereby they deliver themselves from suffering.
This is the way it is.

Since humans are so thoroughly conditioned
to think and feel and act as a separate identity,
that they find it difficult to know their real identity—
Eternal Consciousness, the essence and substance of all—
Yama provides yet another dimension to the experience of Self.

1. *Of the unborn One, whose consciousness is unflickering, there is a city with eleven gates. Meditating (on Him), one does not grieve and, becoming freed, one becomes emancipated. This is that.*

Second translation:

Watching over the eleven-gated City of that birthless undistorted Consciousness one grieves not, and, when liberated (from the body), is freed indeed. This verily is That.

A city is a conglomeration of functions services and facilities,
just as is the body-mind-psyche manifestation.

In its core dwells a ruler who is not the city,
but uses it to be housed and perform her functions.

A city has a perimeter. In olden times, cities had walls
to protect the indwellers from invasion.
However, for the city to function for its dwellers,
it must provide ways to enter and exit;
otherwise the city would suffocate in isolation.
Therefore there are inlets and outlets
for people supplies communication and utilities.
These are the gates.

The human manifestation is *...a city with eleven gates...*
Who reigns in this city? It may be the rightful ruler.
Or it may be the usurper who has sneaked into the city
and illegally seized control of it, a despotic ruler
who reigns by deception separation and conflict,
and misuses the city to separate himself
by means of the city's wall
from others, or even from the rest of the world.

How do you identify the true ruler from the usurper?
The ruler is the one who dwells in the innermost center
of not only the city, but also of every citizen.
She is the one who provides a life of security joy
prosperity well-being consciousness and bliss
to the loyal citizens who identify with the rightful ruler
and not the usurper.
The ruler is the Creator of the city
and can be recognized by Her state:
steady and clear *...unflickering...* in calm peace.
The usurper's state is vacillating and clouded in conflict.

Who owns the eleven-gated city depends upon your allegiance,
whether to the usurper ego or real Self.
Most give their loyalty to ego instead of the rightful owner.
In reality, the city of eleven gates is *...of the unborn One...*
the Essence that you are.

Self is *...the unborn One...* who has never *not* been.
He is the reality of all that is—never created.
Ego, associated with the body-mind construct, is not real.
Self is free of changes, such as birth death and decay.
The Power of Being is unbeginning, imminently present,
eternal, and transcendent to the limiting adjuncts,
including time and space.
...that birthless undistorted Consciousness...
is the Creator and rightful owner and ruler
of this human manifestation
and dwells in its center but is not confined to it.

The eleven gates can be interpreted as the bodily orifices:
seven in the head—eyes ears nostrils and mouth;
the suture in the top of the skull
through which the *kundalini*, or divine energy,
is said to exit when liberated;
the navel;
and the two lower orifices, anus and sexual organ.
On a subtler level the eleven gates can be viewed
as the five organs of knowledge—
hearing seeing touching tasting and smelling;
plus the five organs of action—
speaking locomotion handling excreting and procreating;
plus the synthesizing, or uniting energy.
These are the avenues by which the Indweller

makes contact with the world,
where traverse all communication and action
by which He experiences and expresses Self.

When you continuously and permanently
focus all faculties upon your city's true ruler—
in undistorted Consciousness, in meditation—
you are freed from suffering the grief
associated with the usurper.

When you relate all your Experiences to the Indwelling Self,
and all you do as from Self,
then and only then are you liberated.

When, however, you give allegiance to the usurper ego,
as if it were the rightful ruler of the realm,
every aspect of your city suffers,
for you are giving energy and credence to
one who sucks the life force out of the city and all its citizens
for his own very limited purposes
that never return anything to the city.

The cause of most people's suffering is that
they do not know it is the usurper they serve;
they think it is the rightful king,
even though they get nothing but misery from their service.
What is wrong here? they keep asking.
A latent memory is embedded in you
from even before this lifetime

that the true ruler makes everybody flourish.
But since all your relatives friends and acquaintances
are on the side of the usurper,
you have served the usurper all your life
as if he were the rightful ruler.

If you dare question the validity of the usurper,
you are confronted with all your allegiances—
to your history and patterns of behavior,
to family friends and society.
Those relationships are well-established and familiar,
you feel safe with them.
You have invested much of your life in these attachments
and are not willing to give them up.
You are not willing to admit
that involvement with ego is harmful
and causes suffering pain and destruction of righteousness,
even hostility against the real Indweller, Self.

> You can not serve both Falsity and Reality.
> You can not serve both Ego and Self.

Even cherished family relationships illustrate
the hypocrisy most live in:
they consider themselves loyal to their family,
but when it comes to money,
they often treat each other like competitive strangers—
and they rationalize their greed with such false thinking as,
I merit or deserve it, they don't.

It is of cardinal importance to establish a relationship
with the rightful ruler of your city
so that the eleven gates are properly protected
and do not let in elements associated with the usurper,
elements that are destructive, therefore painful.
Students sometimes have the attitude,
Well, right now I can't be true to Self,
I am too confused, or, I am too this or that.
As long as you let the usurper rule your city,
he rules your gates, lets in his associates
and takes over your strength and vitality, your life.
The usurper places his forces into all the strategic places
to counteract whatever you might do against him.
And the longer you wait to take charge,
the more he amasses strength.

It is only by turning your allegiance to the rightful ruler, Self,
who dwells in the center of the city,
and by abiding in undistorted Consciousness—meditation—
that you free yourself from the suffering
the usurper perpetrates upon the city.
That is the empowered way by which
you realize freedom from bondage limitation and separation.
It is your final emancipation:
you never again have to take life within a limited body;
you will be unceasingly in the experience of Being
dwelling in the cave of the heart of His manifestations
and transcendent to them all, pure Consciousness.

When you finally and permanently free yourself
from Enmeshment with the false Ruler, the Usurper Ego,
and give your Loyalty to the Self you are,
you achieve Emancipation:
you are no longer limited to Experience in the human Form;
you no longer go through the Cycles of Birth Death and Rebirth;
you are free to be in the uninterrupted and undistorted Experience
of the Power of Being that you are.

...Meditating (on Him)...

When you include certain content in your meditation,
it helps impress your knowledge.
You now have such beautiful images as:
Purusa, the Self of all, of the size of a thumb,
completely filling the cave of the heart,
an intimate awareness;
unflickering Consciousness, like a flame without smoke;
and the Indweller of the eleven-gated city
who provides for the faculties' liberation.
These analogies are ways of experiencing the characteristics
of that which is transcendent to characteristics.
Through them the faculties become familiar and associated
with what otherwise seems strange to them—
although it is their essence.
By addressing Its sublime qualities,
the faculties come in touch with what is so subtle
that heretofore they did not know how to even reach for It.

Meditating in a unified experience
with facets of Limitless Consciousness,
they become true for your faculties.

There is also meditation *without* content.
Everything about you simply and purely—
without images or analogies—
takes on the vibratory state of Consciousness.
Body mind emotions feelings intellect intuition and senses
become one with infinite pure Consciousness.
That is the transformation that takes place in Self-realization.
How do you nurture that transformation?
Like a yogi nurtures the fire of Consciousness
within the cave of the heart—with devotion.

Eventually the distinctions between meditation *with* content
and meditation *without* content disappear.

Chapter Thirty-One

The Great One

Cause your faculties to rest in effortless balance in the center,
attending sincerely and devotedly to Self,
Eternal Consciousness that you are,
who has chosen to situate in the cave of your heart
and remain present there.

Let your faculties remain truly present to Self
with devotion sincerity continuity and purity.

2. *As the moving (sun) He dwells in heaven, (as air) He pervades all and dwells in inter-space; as fire He resides on the earth; as Soma He stays in a jar; He lives among men; He lives among gods; He dwells in space; He is born in water; He takes birth from the earth; He is born in sacrifice; He emerges from the mountains; He is unchanging; and He is great.*

Second translation:

> *(He exists as) the Swan in the Clear, as the Pervader (Vasu) in the Mid-Space, as the Priest on the Altar and as the Guest in the Sacred Jar; (He is) in Man, in the Superior (beings), in the Harmony (rita), in the Sky. (He is) born in the Waters, the (heavenly) Cows, the Sacrifice (or Harmony, rita) in the Sacred Stones. (He is) the Harmony (rita), the Great one.*

The ruler and Indweller of the eleven-gated city,
who has chosen to enter and remain in the cave of your heart,
and in the cave of the heart of all creations,
is now revealed in four major aspects.
They are, in descending order from higher to lower:
transcendent, all-pervasive, transforming and evolutionary.
On every level He is the Unitive One.

In His first aspect, *transcendent*, the ruler of the city is beyond time.
He has always been and is and shall be without end.
Self is beyond space, not even limited to any concept of space.
Self is transcendent to conditions and circumstances;
they do not exist in the infinitude of the Power of Being
that just is.

Consciousness' second aspect is *all-pervasive*.
The Indweller of the city, unconfined to it,
extends infinitely beyond the city's properties.
Purusa is in all, from small to large.
He pervades everything, from the least to the most subtle.
Capable of permeating the wide variety of all,
He is the subtlest.

Essential Being is like the ...*sun*... in pure space,
for all revolves around Him,
all is created and nurtured by Him
to be reabsorbed in Him.
Consciousness is the center, the ultimate power point
from whom all comes forth and scatters through infinity,
and to whom all returns upon its dissolution.
This cycle happens all at once, and in the duration of time.
He is the center who fills the center of each manifestation.
As in your center, Purusa takes on the size of a thumb,
assuming the size of the center of each manifestation.

Consciousness dwells in the center of the multifarious opposites,
which are but Self-expressions of the all-pervasive unity.
The play of opposites—expansion and contraction,
creation and destruction, manifestation and dissolution—
is the dynamic that causes and energizes
the cosmos and everything therein.
You can witness this energizing aspect of Self
through the apparent opposition in your own breath:
with the inhalation there is expansion
and with the exhalation, contraction,
and then ensues the quiet unmoving state

that, like Self, contains all the potential.
This process keeps the human manifestation,
as well as many others, alive.

Self is the balance of the extremes,
the energy source and culmination
of the negative and positive poles existing throughout creation:
the manifested and the Unmanifest,
the material and the spiritual,
the profane and the divine.

It is through the Tension between apparent Opposites
that the unmoving eternal Consciousness
provides the potential Power
that energizes all the Movements of Creation—
from the internal Spinning of Atoms,
which are the constituent Particles of all Matter,
including your Body,
to the Beating of your Heart and Flow of your Blood;
from Gravity to Levity;
from all Movements on Earth
to the appointed Rounds of Planets and Galaxies
and Cycles of Creation.

All-pervasive Consciousness dwells in the purity of space
and in *...inter-space...*
The concept of within implies an outside,
which then implies an in-between—'inter-space'.
He is the Consciousness in every here and in every there

and in between.
Self *...pervades all...*

The third aspect of the eleven-gated city's Indweller, Self,
is *transformation.*
The manifestations of the one all-pervasive Consciousness
may experience themselves as separated and differentiated,
as do humans within whose cave of the heart Self dwells.
Their transformation to unity takes place through sacrifice.
The manifestation as separate is offered up to the source
through Agni, the inner flame of Hiranyagarbha,
who is of Brahman, the Power of Being.
The sacrifice takes place on the altar of earth,
where unfold our evolutionary processes.

This Naciketa fire sacrifice, this transformation,
expresses the underlying and all-embracing *...Harmony...*
the all-pervading unity of Self.

The Harmony you experience
resulting from the Sacrifice of Separateness
is the Reality of Self.

The fourth aspect is the driving power of the *evolutionary process.*
It ranges from the lower level of desire,
to the higher level of inspiration.
Desire in its most inferior stage
enmeshes you with attachment to fragments
at the expense of the experience of the whole.
In ascending stages, the energy of desire for fragments

evolves to desire for union with the whole,
to the inspiration by which you experience yourself
one with Unitive Self,
to experiencing yourself as pure Consciousness.

A symbol of the drive of evolution
is ...*Soma*... the divine nectar of the myths
of many cultures and ages.
By this refined energy, the Creator inspires his creations
to evolve to Consciousness of Self.
In the phrase ...*as Soma He stays in a jar*...
'jar' symbolizes the human being;
divine inspiration lives in you—
Purusa, the Self of all, assumes the size of a thumb
and dwells in the cave of your heart.
Drinking this sacred elixir, you are inspired—
filled with the spirit—and liberated
from the restrictive experiences of the gross material realm.
You experience the divine.

The Self of all, Infinite Consciousness ...*dwells in space*...
as well as in the cave of the heart of ...*men*...
and among the higher powers ...*gods*...
He, the Birthless One, is born by His own maya, illusion,
in the spiritual medium of ...*water*...
wherein He takes on many forms—oceans lakes and rivers
and their rocks plants and fish.
He manifests through earth and on ...*earth*...
by means of its features and creatures.
He ...*emerges from the mountains*...
like rivers spreading their blessings,
and like seers and sages through the ages

who descend from the lofty realms of rarefied vision
to shed light and remove confusion.

Self, the Indweller of all, Brahman, Atman,
symbolized by *...the Swan...*
lives in and on earth water and air, in space and inter-space,
in humans and in gods, and even in the divine sacrificial fire
by which all manifestations are eventually absorbed again
in their source, the Absolute,
who through His creative power has spawned all.
He is the one all-pervasive Self
within whom there is no differentiation, no duality;
Self and all manifestation are One—
there is no Supreme Being separate from all else.
Through the cycles of creation maintenance and dissolution
He remains eternally unchanging—
Nataraja dancing in a ring of fire with tranquil mien.
He is the Great beyond all.
Great is the Self that we all are.

Chapter Thirty-Two

The Indweller Is Unattached

You are engaging in ever deeper experiences
of Eternal Consciousness that you are.
Impress these experiences upon your faculties
so they will function accordingly, with continuity and sincerity.

Gather all your faculties now,
truly bring them together to remain in your center
and sincerely attend to the Eternal Self that you are.

So be it.

3. *All deities worship that adorable one, the seated in the middle, who pushes the prana upward and impels the apana inward.*

Second translation:

> *The Prana he leads upwards; in the opposite direction he casts the Apana; He, the Dwarf seated in the Centre whom all the Gods sit near (upasate).*

Limitless Self, who has chosen to be seated in the cave of your heart,
is affectionately referred to as *...the Dwarf...*
in appreciation of His ability and willingness
to cause Himself—who is infinitely vast—
to take the size of a thumb.
...seated in the middle... He is the balance point
to whom all your experiences are brought by your instruments
and from whom everything comes forth.
Every sensation thought feeling and intuition,
everything that transpires, is meant to be presented
by your faculties to you, the inner ruler of your city,
as means for Self-experience.

He is the *...adorable one...* because He is the source and center,
the meaning of everything about you.
He is adored by the deities
and adorable to all your faculties
from the highest to the lowest, for He is their reason for being.
The activity of your instruments of perception
is meant to be a continuous worship of Self,
who silently receives their sacrifices

attesting that all are *to* Him and *of* Him,
and yet He is not attached to them.

He *...pushes the prana upward and impels the apana inward...*
The Power of Being controls the ebb and flow of the oceans
as well as the interstellar winds, the pulse of the galaxies
and the coming and going of all cycles of creation.
Just as prana, the animating force,
during inhalation flows inward to your center
while simultaneously expanding throughout the entire body,
and in exhalation flows outward from the body
and at the same time gathers all the energies in your center,
so it is with the pulse of everything throughout the cosmos.
All creation is a constant and simultaneous
inward and outward movement, implosion and explosion,
that continuously causes creation and maintains balance.
For centuries physicists have argued whether the cosmos
was created by a big bang or by contraction;
there is nothing to argue about,
both are taking place simultaneously all the time.

Everything in the universe
down to the smallest constituent particle, the atom,
and even the components thereof,
is in constant movement of expansion and contraction,
energy moving up and down, in and out,
prana moving up, apana moving down,
all directed by the Indweller, Self,
who takes the size that allows Him
to be seated in the core of every manifestation.
He makes the energy flow in apparently opposite directions,
creating thereby the tension of positive and negative

that provides the vitalizing force for all creation.
He is the director of the life energy
and experiencer of the events, the cause and effect.
Even the pull in you between matter and spirit
finds its origin in the Creator.

You can establish a relationship with the vitalizing force, prana,
by subtle control of your breath.
It is not the breath that keeps you alive,
but prana carried by the breath and independent of it.
Pranayama, yogic breathing techniques,
provide a way of bridging the apparent divide
between the grosser material and the subtler underlying realm.

Visualize the Indweller, the subtly pervasive Self,
who is able to take on minuscule proportions
and dwell in the midst of everything.
He inhales and exhales,
sends His energy up and down, in and out,
to breathe life into everything that is.
Self, the central originating force of all,
is the power by which you experience.
The sense-objects of hearing seeing touching
smelling and tasting
are powers arrayed around this central force.

The seers of many cultures regard
the powers of wind sun oceans and elements as ...*Gods*...
powers seated around the central Consciousness, Self.
We need not invest them with personalities and egos
and thereby limit them to being separate;
all the gods are but powers of the All-pervasive One

who is the conscious essence of all.
The gods, like your faculties, are often viewed by humans
to be in chaos and conflict.
It is like a storm:
masses of air seeking equilibrium want to unite,
which can manifest as clashing,
creating thunder, great lightning bolts and strong winds,
dropping great volumes of moisture, and so on.

From the Perspective of the Limitless One,
all Forms of Power are integral to the all-embracing Harmony,
be they your Faculties,
or the Powers of Wind Air and Water,
be they of Creation or Destruction,
Beauty or Ugliness,
Joy or Sorrow.
All Forms of Energy are essentially self-knowing Self
in the Bliss of Self-experience.

What happens when your identity, your essence,
the irreducible something without which you could not be,
detaches from the manifestation?
This is the question posed in the next verse.

4. *When this dweller in the body becomes detached, when He is freed from this body, what else remains in this body? This is that.*

Second translation:

> *Of the Embodied One, the Dweller in the body, on being loosed and freed from the body, what remains behind? This (In-Dweller) verily is That.*

When the Indweller withdraws from
the cave of the heart of the manifestation,
what is left behind?
The component parts that created the form
are reabsorbed into the five constituent elements
and redistributed among other forms.
The Indweller is thereby not affected.
The inhabitor of the city is independent of it;
the Indweller of the body-mind construct is transcendent to it.

An experience people often describe
at the death of a loved one is a sense of the person's absence
while the body is still lying there.
Such experiences are demonstrative of the fact
that Self is not this body nor this mind.
I once had three wild kittens come to live with me.
One day the timid one, whom I had named Beauty,
was lying still on a flower pot.
I picked her up and found she had died.
There was an immediate and overwhelming sense that
this was not Beauty; she was not there,
it was just an empty shell.
There was no doubt, not even a thought about it;
it was obviously so.

When the Power of Being is released from the body,
what remains is the Power of Being.
...This (In-Dweller) verily is That...
...This is that... the directness of reality:
this is the way it is,
beyond argumentation theorization or rationalization.

5. *No mortal lives by prana or apana; but all live by something else on which these two depend.*

Ordinary thinking is that you live
by the inhalation and exhalation of the breath.
However there is something deeper and more mysterious,
something subtler by which you are alive.
Breath is *not* the source of life,
breath is dependent on something else.
Anything that is dependent on something else
can not be your source,
and therefore not the reason for your being.

The flow of the breath is a construct, like your faculties.
It combines with your senses, mind,
neurological system and cells—all your facets—
to facilitate the experience and expression of your life.

It is not even by the life force carried by the breath—
prana pulsing in and up, apana moving down and out—
that you live.
All these processes are dependent upon their Creator.
It is by the power of the city's ruler,

who has chosen to take up residence in the core of the heart,
that manifestations live.
That One upon whom all this is dependent,
that source, Self, is independent of His constructs.

CHAPTER THIRTY-THREE

The Y In The Path

Continue steadily in the state
in which your faculties remain tranquil in your center,
deeply connected to the Power of Being
who is their source, and your identity.

Relate to this teaching as the immediate experience of Self
that you firmly impress upon your faculties
so that they will function accordingly permanently.
Thus you faithfully experience the purity and power
and permanency of Limitless Consciousness that you are.

6. Well, O Gautama, I shall tell you of this secret, eternal Brahman; and also how the Self fares after death.

Second translation:

> *Now then I shall set forth to thee the Secret Eternal Brahman and also what happens to the Soul after death.*

Now Yama offers subtler secrets of Eternal Consciousness, Brahman:
what happens to the individual Self *...the Soul...* upon death,
how it transmigrates and to where.
Naciketa has carefully prepared for this secret knowledge
through absorbing and living Yama's teachings.
Have you similarly prepared with these teachings?
If not, go back, sincerely and really prepare
so you can proceed effectively without harming yourself.

The knowledge announced in this verse
is of a cardinal point on the path of the soul's migration:
the Y in the road.
Here there are two clear choices:
passive continuation in evolution—just being pulled along—
or the inspired proactive path,
the path of the spirit in Self-motivation.

> You choose either to live in Accord with Reality
> and free yourself from the Suffering of this worldly Existence
> and the Need to go through further Cycles
> of Birth and Death and Rebirth,
> or to live in Falsity and suffer as do the Ignorant
> and require further Birth and Death.

Many live as if they were content
to be on the passive path of evolution.
They think, I don't have to do anything.
However, consider the eons of time that takes
spent in limitedness and suffering.
The dissertations by the Sanskrit sages
discuss the time of creation in terms of *kalpas*.
A kalpa is one cycle of creation lasting billions of years.
At the end of one cycle, another begins.
Creation is emitted again and again,
and creatures come and go and appear again
as long as they are tied to the wheel of karma.

> A Kalpa is the Time it would take for the Wings of an Angel
> to wear down a granite Boulder eighteen Miles cubed,
> brushing against it once every Hundred Years.

Is that how long you are willing to suffer in a passive state?

Remember Naciketa's earlier rumination
...Man decays and dies like corn, and emerges again
like corn...
The passive evolutionary path
is not the most advantageous option.

There is a drive within to free yourself from going helplessly
through seemingly endless cycles tied to cause and effect.
During this minuscule cycle in human form

with the powerful faculties you have at your disposal,
you have the unique opportunity to consciously participate
and fulfill your evolutionary thrust.
If this is what you truly choose,
you have to make the loving and absolute determination
for Self-realization in this lifetime.

How does this conscious fulfillment transpire?
Yama introduces his answer when he tells Naciketa
that he will now reveal
...what happens to the Soul after death...

Envision the soul as an eddy in the limitless ocean of energy.
As the ocean is of Consciousness, so is the eddy.
However the eddy is momentarily shrouded by,
and apparently limited to, its form,
which has been created by Hiranyagarbha, the Golden Germ,
through the instrumentality of the five elements
and their limiting adjuncts.
The separateness of soul from Infinite Self is only an illusion;
it is obvious the eddy is not a discrete entity.

Through the Creator's veil of illusion,
the soul enshrouded in its form
experiences itself as affected by the limiting adjuncts
and strives through a series of processes
to overcome these limitations
in order to experience Limitless Consciousness,
the Eternal Ocean that it actually is.
This empowers the process of evolution.

In this evolutionary process the soul goes through
ascending levels of Consciousness.

On the lowest levels, Consciousness is severely veiled,
the light is hidden.
Evolution is facilitated by the processes of nature,
which, in many stages, seem to involve very little—
if any—conscious participation.
Nature by itself evolves a single-celled organism
to the eventual complexity that is a human being.

Only when the manifestation in which the soul is enshrouded
has evolved to the higher level of Consciousness,
as in the human being,
does the soul finally reach that critical point, the Y on the path.
This is the point of decision,
the point of great crisis and greater opportunity.
Here the soul has two choices:
continue with mute participation in the evolutionary process,
which may persist over eons;
or you may choose to take quantum leaps of advancement
through conscious participation.
The option to consciously participate
emerges when the manifestation attains the initial inkling
of oneness with the ocean of Eternal Consciousness, Brahman.

Then arrives the opportunity to consciously seek out
knowledge of identity in Being
and develop relationship with Self:
to have mind think and speak of you as the Power of Being,
and to have the feelings reflect the internal experience
of knowing Self to be eternal and all-pervasive
and the source of all.
You then express those thoughts and feelings
through actions of interconnectedness.

Those actions reinforce and empower
Self-directed thoughts and feelings,
and you become less and less limited in your experience.
Thus you evolve through conscious participation
to experience yourself as unlimited and united.
You, the soul who through illusion appeared to itself
as limited and separated,
then Self-realize your all-pervasive and eternal identity
in Limitless Consciousness.

The marker at the critical juncture of the Y on the path
is knowledge of Brahman.
It is through the knowledge of Indestructible Being
that you have the choice of the way that leads to the cessation
of involvement with the cycles of birth death and rebirth.
However, knowledge alone is not enough.
How you relate to knowledge is decisive in
whether you function inspired by Self
or succumb to the habit patterns of separateness and limitation
formed during the eons spent under the shroud of illusion.

When you allow negative self-reinforcing Patterns
to dictate your Experience, Consciousness is veiled,
the Faculties do not reflect the Light of Consciousness.
The Knowledge of your eternal Essence
has to be lived from Moment to Moment
every Day, and for a long Time,
for the Soul to be free of the negating Effects
of the Faculties' History in Falsity.

7. *Some souls enter the womb for acquiring bodies and others follow the motionless, in accordance with their work and in conformity with their knowledge.*

Second translation:

Some Souls enter (again) a womb for re-embodiment; others go to the Fixed according to their Karma and according to their knowledge.

Just as there are two choices you can make
when you stand at the critical point of the Y on the path,
so are there two consequences affecting the soul after death.

When you have Self-realized,
and your Faculties have been relating to the Soul as Infinite Being,
at Death, you are like a Measure of pure Water
poured into the limitless Ocean of pure Water:
you merge in Eternal Consciousness.
There is no Need for further developmental Cycles,
therefore no Necessity to take on another Body.
This is final Emancipation.

Souls who are reborn
will manifest according to what they learned and did
in the life form they left in death:
...according to their Karma and according to their knowledge...
The soul will continue migrating
toward union with the whole, Eternal Consciousness.

If the response to knowledge gained
was limited or even one of neglect or denial,
the next manifestation will be of an accordingly lower—
and therefore more painful—level.
If the knowledge gained by the faculties was advanced,
and their behaviors and actions
were in response to that knowledge,
the next manifestation will be of a corresponding
height subtlety skill and breadth of Consciousness.
This is the path of karma, of return to manifestation
for further development through action.

Those who have acted fully in accord with their knowledge of Him
will go to Brahman *...the motionless...*
Being transcends changing manifestations.
Transcendence is the final reward of the soul
who has transmigrated from the illusory confinement
and subdued Consciousness of lower manifestations
to the higher Consciousness of Knowing Being.
Having faithfully dwelled in accord with Self
continuously expertly and sincerely,
you reach the transcendental level
of superconsciousness in Self-realization.
Even the faculties of the Self-realized soul
are transformed to absolute purity;
they, too, become absorbed in
the limitless wholeness of Eternal Consciousness,
like a measure of pure water
poured into the limitless ocean of purity.

There are two Paths for the Soul after Death,
according to your Involvement with Ignorance or Knowledge:
the Path of Karma, of return to Manifestation
for further Development through Action,
or the Path of realized Knowledge,
of final Liberation through Self-realization in Eternal Being.

When your soul is at the Y on its path, your options are clear:
you can continue the eons of being mutely tossed around
by nature's forces on a meandering evolutionary path,
or, empowered by your spirit and pure will,
take the path of Self-effulgent Self.
The light on the path is your own.
Be true to yourself and you can end your suffering
and be emancipated from the limiting false ego construct.

If you passively let the choice be made for you,
you will go in the direction of ignorance and falsity.
When you proactively—with sincerity devotion integrity
and trust in the Self that you are—
make an unshakable determination to travel the path
in accord with the knowledge you have gained,
you will be free, you will realize yourself as Satchidananda:
Existence-knowledge-bliss-absolute.

So it is and will always be.

CHAPTER THIRTY-FOUR

Transcendence

May you sincerely prepare yourself
so that your faculties are fertile ground for the teachings,
lest they fall upon barren ground, where they will wither.

Be open to the teachings.
Be open to Self.

In deep focus be in the experience of the teachings
as they are revealed to you,

and impress them so strongly and sincerely
that you will live accordingly henceforth,
lest you insult the Self that you are.

8 *Purusa, who keeps awake and goes on creating desirable things even when the senses fall asleep, is pure; and He is Brahman, and He is called the Immortal. All the worlds are fixed on Him; none can transcend Him. This is that.*

It is wonderful how skillfully
the great teacher Yama has brought Naciketa—and you—along
in a beautiful process of expansion of Consciousness,
of awareness of Self
through the experience of the many facets of Being—
Purusa the Self of all,
Hiranyagarbha the Creator,
Aditi and Agni the life-breath and divine spark,
the five elements with limiting adjuncts,
and manifestations—
to now even more deeply fulfill his promise
to reveal the secrets of Brahman.

You are neither the body nor its senses,
nor the mind emotions feelings intellect or intuition;
these are but instruments whose construct is
inhabited by Purusa, the Soul of all,
who takes *...the size of a thumb...*
in order to dwell in the cave of the heart of each manifestation.

The body-mind construct,
which you have falsely identified as yourself,
needs to recharge its energies during sleep.
In deep sleep you do not experience your faculties.

However, upon reawakening in the morning
there remains a sense of the continuity of yourself.
This is due to the fact that the Indweller, Self,
continuously remains awake.
He does not have to recharge; He *is* the energy.
Thus your sense of Self continues through the night,
even though the faculties are dormant.

> While the Manifestation sleeps,
> the substantive Power within remains ever awake.

The thumb-like Purusa dwelling in the cave of the heart
is the central energy of Brahman who is the cause of all,
including even the dream images.
And it is those illusory images *...desirable things...*
that usually compel your faculties to action.
To the Eternal Self there is no good or bad
in regard to the objects of desire.
However, the individual manifestation
whose faculties are enmeshed with these objects
suffers a limitation of the experience of itself,
for the reality of the soul is not material, but Infinite Being.

While the soul, due to the veil of maya, illusion,
may appear to be asleep to its Eternal Consciousness,
Infinite Self continues in the clarity of waking Consciousness,
unaffected by the manifestation's state.

Self inhabits all and is contained by none.
This is Brahman, infinite in space and time,

thus all-pervasive and eternally unending.
Brahman is the one and only *...Immortal...*
He is the source and the reason for being,
the center of all manifestations.
He is the fixed point around whom all worlds revolve
and upon whom they all are focused.

Eternal Consciousness is for all Souls
like the North Star to the Mariner,
the fixed Point of Focus by which to chart your Course.
All comes forth during its Creation, from Eternal Being,
and everything returns to Being, upon its Resolution.

Eternal Self is the balance point and power link
between the apparent opposites,
the negative and positive poles of matter and spirit,
the ephemeral and the Eternal.
This fixed foundation of all, the unmoving Brahman,
is symbolized by Siva.
He sits on the mountain in undisturbable tranquility
with the cool moon in the background.
The moon represents matter,
for it reflects the light of the sun—
as a manifestation reflects Brahman—
but gives forth no light of its own.
Siva basks in His light reflected by the moon:
Existence-knowledge-bliss-absolute.
In the aspect of Nataraja, Siva dances through the wild cycles

of creation maintenance and destruction,
balanced on the dwarf of ignorance, yet uplifted beyond it,
surrounded by fire, holding in his hand sound time and flame,
while gazing forth with tranquil countenance,
eternally transcendent to all that takes place.

He is *...the Immortal...*
and *...none can transcend Him...*

> Limitless Being is the Self of all that is.
> There is nothing beyond Being,
> nothing and no one can transcend Him.
> That is the Way it is.

9. *Just as fire, though one, having entered the world, assumes separate forms in respect of different shapes, similarly, the Self inside all beings, though one, assumes a form in respect of each shape; and (yet) It is outside.*

10. *As air, though one, having entered into this world, assumes separate forms in respect of different shapes, similarly, the Self inside all beings, though one, assumes a form in respect of each shape. And yet It is outside.*

Fire is fire. When raging in a forest, it takes a different form
from when illuminating a candle; both, though, are fire.
So it is with air; the air in the sky
is the same air that fills an empty jar.
And just so *...the Self inside all beings, though one, assumes a form in respect of each shape...*

...and (yet) It is outside... Consciousness has chosen to manifest
through the myriad of creations that make up the cosmos,
be it an atom or a galaxy,
and to dwell in the cave of the heart of each manifestation,
taking on a form accordingly—even a thumb-sized one—
and yet He is the same continuous formless one Self.
Although He is each creation's source and identity,
giving them the power to be,
Brahman, Self, residing within, is also completely outside.
He is forever one indivisible undiminishable
eternal all-pervasive conscious Power of Being.

Experience the unity in diversity that characterizes
eternal all-pervasive Consciousness, Self that you are.
Experience Self the Creator of all manifestations
who dwells within your body-mind construct,
but is not contained in it.
Experience the Creator transcendent to His creations.

11. Just as the sun, which is the eye of the whole world, is not tainted by the ocular and external defects, similarly, the Self, that is but one in all beings, is not tainted by the sorrows of the world, It being transcendental.

The Power of Being that you are is the Creator of everything,
including the apparent oppositions of negative versus positive,
illusion versus reality,
as well as the illusory objects of desire,
the pursuit of which results in so much human suffering.
As Self, Creator and Experiencer of all that is,
you have the innate ability to respond fluidly and successfully
to all the dynamics of creation.
However, when you regard yourself as the separate ego,

you feel too limited and anxious
to flow freely in unattached experience.
Thus humans under the influence of ego manifest difficulty
when it comes to accepting the great gift
of ability to respond—responsibility—
and blame Infinite Being for the ills suffered in the world.

I first became aware of this as a young boy when,
during the carnage of World War II,
I heard my respected mother declare
that she could not and would not believe in a God
who allowed such horror.
I knew there was something askew with such thinking.
God was not the perpetrator of the horrors of the war;
clearly human beings were—a child could see that.
Nor was God the cause of the reactions to the war;
human beings were.

Just because God, Infinite Being, caused creation, does not mean
He manipulates every act of every creature.
Having set the play of creation into motion,
Limitless Being allows for an infinity of variations
by letting each creature evolve along its path
with an increasing amount of options,
until, in the human form, all are endowed with the free will
to enact their own choices.

> It is by Free Will that you choose
> to love or oppose the infinite Power of Being.
> By this Choice you determine your Destiny
> in Bliss or in Suffering.

Infinite Self is unaffected by what you choose.
The suffering in the world
is neither created nor experienced as suffering
by the Absolute.
He *...is not tainted by the sorrows of the world...*

While the sun *...the eye of the whole world...* allows us to see,
the sun does not dictate how we relate to what we see.
The rain that the farmer views as a blessing
may be regarded as a curse by the city dweller.
Seeing includes interpretation;
one man's potion may be another man's poison.
One person may see the desert in terms of pristine beauty,
while another may see the same desert as arid ugliness.
The sun simply radiates; it does not concern itself
whether it illumines the beautiful or the ugly,
nurtures the worthy or the disreputable,
gives life to manifestations or sucks it out of them.
The sun facilitates seeing impartially;
if you falsely interpret what the light reveals,
it is not due to a flaw in the sun.

As in the ancient analogy of the snake and the rope,
wherein a man became frightened
because he superimposed the image of a snake upon a rope,
people suffer when they mistakenly superimpose
characteristics upon Self.
Self is pure, independent of characteristics.
Just as that man can not rationally blame the rope
for the fear he suffered due to his faulty interpretation,
so you can not blame the Creator
for the problems caused by your ego superimpositions.

Fire can cook your food or destroy your home.
Fire just burns; it is indifferent to the results.
So it is with Eternal Being;
It just is, independent of the ephemeral phenomena.
In the context of eternal all-pervasive unmodified Being,
the comings and goings within and of creation
are but momentary appearances
that have no effect on Limitless Self.
Self is transcendent to the phenomena
on which your senses so readily dwell.

> Although manifesting through the World,
> the Indweller, Self, is pure, transcendent to it,
> and therefore independent of it.

Electricity can empower a lamp to illumine a room,
a heater to warm your home,
or an electric chair to destroy a human life.
Electricity is not responsible for how it is used.
Although Self is the essence of every manifestation
and empowers each and every thought feeling and action,
Self is not responsible for their choices
or the quality of their behaviors.

There is a danger here:
if you attain Self-knowledge yet remain bound to ego,
thus influenced by the human tendency toward irresponsibility,
you might assume,
I can do anything I want, ultimately it doesn't matter.

And that reminds me of another story:

A manifestation of Eternal Being, a little village boy,
while strolling in the forest, came upon a man hunting,
whom he recognized as a king.
The boy watched as the king shot and killed a deer,
but as the deer lay dying,
it transformed into a beautiful human being.
The boy confronted the king,
who said he was very sorry for mistakenly killing this person.
The boy said to him,
You have accumulated a terrible karmic debt
by murdering this man.
Oh no, said the king, I am the Power of Being,
I am beyond all this, killer and killed.
But the boy kept challenging him.
Eventually the king became indignant and angry
at this uppity little kid in rags, and said,
Who are you to talk to me like this? I am the king of this land,
and I can do what I want. This is my forest!
And the boy said to the king,
Ah, so now you are the king of this land—
as a manifestation,
you will suffer the consequences of your actions.

Learn from this:

You can not be both Self and non-self,
shifting allegiances according to your convenience.

The cause of human suffering is acting in ignorance of real identity,

due to which you experience yourself
as isolated from the unitive whole.
This self-limiting perspective humans superimpose upon Self:

I am begging God; I am subject to God;
He is my master, and I his lowly servant.
This is not humility, but abnegation of responsibility,
which results in painful symptoms of separateness:
fear needing longing anger anxiety and depression.
Human suffering is not at all an indication that Self suffers.
In limitlessly interconnected Self there is no separateness,
hence no lack or need, no wrong, no suffering.
There is but pure infinite Consciousness.
This Is That.

Chapter Thirty-Five

Realizing The Peace Of Self

Sincerely and expertly prepare your faculties
so that they serve you well,
and through focused experience absorb the teachings faithfully
and integrate them in their functions permanently.

Let your faculties rest in a state of effortless balance and tranquility
in your center
so as to be pure reflectors of Being in Self-experience,

as Consciousness is revealed by Consciousness
through these teachings.

Be in harmony and deep attentiveness
with sincerity and clarity,
fully receptive to the teachings.

Be in the truth that is revealed to you
from the moment you recognize it,
continuously and eternally.

May you drink deeply of knowledge and be thereby nurtured.

May you avail yourself of the peace
that is found in the realization of Self.

12. *Eternal peace is for those—and not for others—who are discriminating and who realise in their hearts Him who—being one, the controller, and the inner Self of all—makes a single form multifarious.*

13. *Eternal peace is for those—and not for others—who are discriminating and who realise in their hearts Him who—being the eternal among the ephemeral, the consciousness among the conscious—alone dispenses the desired objects to many.*

All-pervasive and eternal Consciousness,
the Essence and Self of all,
is the source of all manifestations yet contained by none.
He is the *...one...* that all is.
As the Creator of all creatures He is the Indweller
who is present in the cave of their hearts.
Behind the veil of illusion
they feel separated from Him, their source.

They spend their existence seeking to be reunited with Self,
their reason for being.
To experience yourself as Self is your ultimate goal;
without fulfilling it, there is no peace.

> All in their own Way seek Peace unceasingly
> until they gain it.
> The only Way you can ever be fully and lastingly at Peace
> is neither by distracting yourself from what you really want,
> nor by dying,
> but by Self-realizing—
> realizing your Identity in Eternal Consciousness,
> the All-pervasive Indweller who is your Essence.
> Thus you gain permanent Peace.

This blissful peace human beings seek is rare,
even though we are richly endowed
with the faculties and abilities to achieve it.
Most people, instead of employing their gifts
in service of what they really want,
look for peace in all the wrong places:
they look for it on the outside, in the superficial.
Their energies are scattered
in all six directions and everywhere in-between.
Instead of coming to terms with what happens within,
they often purposely enmesh themselves
with the promises and problems of the material life,
which they consider practical:
lifestyles spouses houses cars jobs or projects—what-have-you.

And the more frequently you can change any of them,
the more busily distracted you are from Self
and enmeshed with obscuring Self-experience.

Through years of teaching, I have often witnessed
such persistent distractedness,
especially when someone discovers the Indweller, Self.
In their ego attachment, they waylay the energy
from the discovery of their true identity,
to attending to the outside situations.
They want to make big changes—go traveling,
buy a new house, get a new job—which diverts the faculties:
they become absorbed again in the new circumstances
and forget Self.

The very source of peace is within—always has been
and always will be.
It is your faculties' true mission to relate to Self.
You can not be at peace
if your faculties are not fulfilling their mission,
or if they are opposing it.
All the outgoing activities you perform to gain satisfaction
are doomed to failure if you impart your experiences to ego,
and not to Conscious Being.
It is like trying to feed yourself
by shoveling the food over your shoulder.

You are able to discriminate between the permanent—the real—
and the momentary phenomena that come and go
like traveling salesmen.
You are blessed with the critically important power
by which you can make intelligent choices between
the permanent and the momentary,

the inner- and the outer-directed,
the substantive and the ephemeral,
the real and the unreal.
You even have the power to further discriminate
based on the beneficial or harmful consequences
you experience as a result of your choices—to learn:

> Focusing your Attentiveness upon the inner Experience
> predictably yields a profoundly peaceful State.
> Letting your Attention be distracted by Objects and Events
> predictably results in Imbalance Need Frustration Anger
> Disappointment and Conflict: Suffering.

Knowing the predictability of these causes and effects,
one would think that all reasonably intelligent individuals
would choose the more satisfying inward attentiveness;
yet most people—even those who recognize cause and effect
and the constant suffering incurred by going outward
when everything about them yearns to go inward—
still choose the outer.
They live in states of depression denial or busyness,
which is all just irresponsibility.

It helps to understand that outgoing activity is in the context of ego,
the false perception of yourself
as separate from the essential source.
In reality, there is no outer, all is within All-pervasive Self;
in the infinite whole, neither outside nor inside exists.
Even suffering is a moot point in Eternal Consciousness,

a misinterpretation due to the misguidance of your faculties.
Suffering is created by your faculties
when they function from the perspective of separateness
and go outward to find satisfaction.

Chasing after the outer,
you fragment dissipate and weaken your energies.
Distracting from Self thus from reality, from Being,
is incongruent to your faculties and intolerable;
without Being, nothing *is* for you.
The more you act in ego-separateness,
away from the experience of the unified whole One,
the more suffering do you cause.

Eventually your suffering can actually help you;
it signals that you are misleading your faculties into unreality.
Rather than heedlessly continuing to hurt yourself and others,
you can be motivated to change.
Many feel unsettled, though, when the need for change arises.
Instead of being anxious or troubled, or procrastinating,
simply implement what you know step by step,
faithfully, in Consciousness, as the Power of Being you are,
and you will succeed.

*...Eternal peace is for those—and not for others—who are
discriminating, and who realise in their hearts Him...*
Having the power of discrimination
and applying it to your success and satisfaction
are two crucially different things.
All human beings have the power of discrimination;
not everyone utilizes it to realize Self.

Apply what you have learned here
to realizing the inner peace of Self:

While the Creator and the creation are One,
their experiences can differ.
Brahman, the Soul of all, radiating Himself
through his manifestations' experiences and actions,
is only experiencing Himself.
He is not only radiating *out*, He is radiating *in*;
He is radiating in and out simultaneously.
To the manifestations who see themselves separately,
their energies radiate out, therefore to forgetfulness of Being.

To Ego, Activity serves as Distraction from Being.
To Self, Activity is Expression and Experience of Being.

The Peaceful Self, ruler of your realm,
dwells in the very center of it
and radiates His luminous energy
through the eleven gates of your city.
The undiscriminating person
follows the Indweller's energies outward
without returning their experiences to Self.
Those who discriminate follow the city ruler's energies
of senses mind feelings intellect and intuition
inward to their center, the cave of the heart,
where He dwells.
Those who relate the radiant energies of the Indweller

to their source are united with that source, become one with It,
firmly established in the bliss of eternal peace.

The Eternal Unmoving,
radiating Himself in all directions, never dissipates Himself,
but the limitation-oriented faculties radiating in all directions
are scattered in the non-experience of Being.
The rare discriminating ones resist the temptations
of the world—riches power progeny or fame,
what Yama offered Naciketa—
and faithfully focus their faculties' attention inward to Him.

The Wise concentrate their Forces upon Indwelling Self—
the Supreme Consciousness that in Essence and in Fact you are—
with Enthusiasm Patience Integrity Continuity Diligence Sincerity
and unshakable Loyalty and Love.

The devotedly discriminating ones
expertly transform their faculties
to ever-subtler vibratory levels
and ever-ascending levels of functioning.
They become Expert in Life, expert in functioning:
no matter how mundane or elevated,
they transform their actions from being scattered outside,
to experiences and expressions of Limitless Being.
The faculties become so pure in their vibratory form,
that they merge with Consciousness
like pure water poured into an ocean of pure water;
they become one in experience.

This is the unitive state called yoga.
In this state you are in real meditation.

Instead of being enmeshed
with what can be heard seen touched tasted or smelled—
the multifarious *Unreal*—
the discriminating ones unite their Faculties
with the soundless invisible untouchable
tasteless odorless all-pervasive eternal Consciousness—
the One *Real*.

This is the North Star upon which well-meaning discriminating
intelligent individuals focus their faculties.
They thus attain immortality
and are disentangled from Death's extensive net.
They see themselves and all as the Power of Being.
They regard every one of their thoughts
as the Indweller's thought,
every one of their feelings as the Indweller's feeling,
every one of their actions as the Unmoving Brahman's action.
They dwell in the continuous Consciousness of Eternal Being
who is the Self of all, the One of the many.

The 180-Degree Rule is a powerful direct
and succinct way to succeed.
The discriminating ones, knowing they have a long history
of conditioning their faculties
to be preoccupied with the *...ephemeral...*
at the neglect of the *...eternal...*

with the illusory at the expense of the real,
consciously act 180 degrees opposite of their conditioning
and reclaim the power residing within, in the cave of the heart,
to live as Consciousness.

If you are struggling, apply the 180-Degree Rule.
Your Faculties' Tendency is to go outward
with the radiant Beams of the Indweller's Self-expression.
For those who consider themselves separate,
that spells Suffering.
Guide your Faculties 180 Degrees opposite:
focus their Energies upon Infinite Being, Self.
It is in Self that all your Desires are really fulfilled,
and only in Self.

The discriminating and wise,
who impress and implement what they have learned,
realize their identity in limitless Power of Being,
the source and ultimate ...*controller*... of all,
who expresses Himself
through the myriad manifestations of creation
while He remains the unified One.
They are utterly secure and fulfilled, free of lack need or fear.
They abide in ...*Eternal peace*...

Chapter Thirty-Six

This Is It

You are in essence and in fact Unbeginning Consciousness
who is present now and always shall be, eternally,
and who is transcendent—beyond names and forms,
beyond times and circumstances,
beyond the material sensual emotional and intellectual realms.

Consciousness, through Its facet of Creator,
projects Self as life-breath and motivating fire
into all manifestations, some of which are engaged
in awakening to Limitless Consciousness

in a direct and clear way—
what this teaching offers on the higher and final levels.

May you utilize such teachings as:
knowing Brahman who radiates in and out at the same time;
using the rays leading out through the eleven gates
to go inward to the ruler of the city;
engaging in constant focus upon Self;
being an Expert In Life;
having your faculties merge in Self
like pure water poured into pure water;
and applying the 180-Degree Rule to negative tendencies.

May you have the self-respect and self-love
to live true to the knowledge you gain.

14. How shall I know that supreme, unspeakable Bliss which they realise directly as "This"? Is It self-effulgent—does It shine distinctly, or does It not?

Second translation:

This is That—thus they know—the supreme indescribable bliss. How, indeed, shall I understand It? Does it shine of itself or is it a reflection?

One of the most vexing questions teenagers have is,
How do I know when I'm in love?
Their very yearning for being in love is an indication
that deep within they have some of what they so ardently—
and at the same time hesitantly—seek.

What all Humans seek most of all is that rare Experience
of pure undiminishable balanced luminous Joy and Contentment
called Bliss,
that results from the spontaneous and continuous
Experience of yourself
in the clear Understanding and unconditional Acceptance
that is real Love.

This state is beyond description—it is *...unspeakable...*
Therefore this indefinable is termed *...This...*
This is even closer and more intimate than *That.*
This is the all-inclusive eternal Consciousness.
It is the This that all yearnings for love really aim for:
conscious experience of being at one with the All,
the infinite essence and identity that you really are.

...How shall I know... ...the supreme indescribable bliss...
that the realized seers experience intimately as This?
What are Its fundamental characteristics?
Does It shine light from Itself
or does It reflect it?

I was blessed to attain the experience of This as a boy.
I have described how,
when I survived the bombing of our home
in an illuminating experience,
I began to search for answers to the questions,

Who am I? Why am I still alive?
And how after spending years trying to get my mind
to solve this, through my own ardent concentration practices,
one evening I was flooded with clear perception:
simple and direct experience of Being, beyond limits.
It was my This-Is-It experience,
This is why I am,
the whole experience of being the Being I am.

This experience was far beyond mind,
but had come by transcending mind
through my rigorous focusing exercises.
The illumination I had experienced
meeting Death during the bombardment,
I had reclaimed with my practices.
I now had knowledge with certainty—
there were no questions regarding This;
my experience was utterly clear,
even though as a boy I did not have the words for it.

Thus I came to know *...that supreme, unspeakable Bliss*
which they realise directly as "This"...
without previous experience, scriptures or instruction,
but directly motivated by my meeting with Death.

In the awareness of reality,
you experience the indefinable so deeply and expansively
that you know yourself as Eternal Consciousness.
Any previous vagueness of experience—
vagueness of awareness, of mental processes,
of feelings and emotions—
is completely obliterated by the sheer luminosity
of loving knowing Being.

This is the blissful state that the seers of yore
refer to as ...*This*...
and I referred to as my This-Is-It experience.

I invite you, instead of merely *seeking* the clarity and bliss of Being,
authentically *participate* in Being—
not, Once I have the luminous experience of Being
then I'll participate in it.
You *are* the Power of Being, get with it.
When you do, you know.

15. There the sun does not shine, neither do the moon and the stars; nor do these flashes of lightning shine. How can this fire? He shining, all these shine; through his lustre all these are variously illumined.

Second translation:

Not There shines the Sun, nor Moon nor Stars nor these Lightnings, still less this (earthly) Fire. In His shining all (these) shine after Him. By His Light all this is illumined.

Do not allow yourself to be blinded
by Objects and Conditions of the World;
flow along the Beams of brilliant Light
to attain their Source.

In the Self of all—the This—the sun does not shine,
nor does the moon, not even ...*flashes of lightning*...
nor fires or lamps or any other form of light.
They do not shine in Brahman because He *is* the light

who gives the ability to cast light to all.
A candle lit inside the sun would not be a light.
Infinite Power of Being is the one and only source of light.
He receives light only from Himself.
He is the Self-effulgent One.

Eternal Consciousness is pure This,
unrelated to interpretations—purity absolute.
You can only realize Self when you are in the state of purity,
when your mind emotions and feelings are
independent of everything and anything,
congruent with Consciousness knowing Self
to be eternal and all-pervasive and the source of all.

The pure state is one of independence;
you are not owned by anything, not modified by anything,
not even your desires and aversions.
Illimitable Consciousness is utterly independent.
Consciousness does not care whether we are or are not;
It is independent of that.
People blame God for wars and their suffering—
How could He let this happen?
We are responsible for inflicting pain and sorrow, not God.
Conflict is caused by humans with free will.
The problems and crises in which people enmesh themselves
are momentary phenomena, not reality.

In the state of independence congruent with Transcendent Being,
your faculties relate to Self free of desire
and free of relation to objects and conditions
or any other limiting adjuncts.
The faculties relate to the infinitude of Eternal Self,
not to limiting momentary phenomena.

You realize Infinite Consciousness
when your Faculties transcend their ordinary Activities,
rest effortlessly in unfluctuating Balance
and reflect the pure Essence you are.
Then, and only then,
do you dwell in the Luminosity of eternal Peace.

This can happen unexpectedly,
as happened to me with my This-Is-It experience.
I was not creating the experience; I did not even know about it.
It happened as a result of my focusing practices.
If you do your practice sincerely, realistically,
congruent with Self,
things will happen that your mind can not anticipate,
because they are higher than the mind,
and they are higher than your past experiences.
If you habituate your faculties
to hiding under the bushel of unconsciousness,
then the moments of clarity are much less likely to occur.

Start by getting your faculties to be independent
from all the stimuli outside and inside, all the sensations,
the electrical charges, the positives and negatives.
Be the Silent Observer,
impartial witness to all that takes place.
If you are not, your faculties are not independent.
If your faculties are not independent
you are not going to Self-realize—
you are not even in the process.

You can cultivate through practice the modality of the Silent Observer.
I learned at a young age to appreciate practice
as a vehicle to transform certain endeavors
that were initially difficult and awkward
into actions I could do fluidly and gracefully.
Like the pianist who practices the scales painstakingly—
when she plays in a concert, the music just flows.

Even the body wants to experience
and be in that state of independence.
Most people much of the time
make the body dependent upon their mental-emotional state,
and as a result the body suffers.
Anxiety and tension make the body dependent,
sap its energies and hinder its movement;
a dependent body is even more affected by negative states.
You can do yoga postures in such a way
that there is no opposition or friction;
it is a free flowing-forth of your potential
as you move your body into and through the postures.

You have through these teachings
learned many ways to help your faculties,
so accustomed to limitedness, experience the illimitable,
to come to terms with limitlessness
and thus access your innate ability
to experience yourself as Infinite Self.
You who are habituated to limited experience
must become accustomed to experiencing the illimitable.
That is your faculties' challenge,
it is what they are meant to do.
Normally, limited mind can not experience the All,

but it has to experience It eventually,
because We Are That: Illimitable Self.
Mind and all the other faculties have to transcend themselves.

The experiential analogies in the Kathopanisad
can help your faculties establish familiarity with Self,
which can eventually become intimacy,
which can grow into the experience of oneness:

The *inner ruler* of the eleven-gated city
who lives in its center, His radiance flowing outward
and your faculties' experiences gliding on those beams inward.

The *yogis*, who keep the experience of Being
warm and close in the cave of the heart,
alive in their Consciousness constantly, every day.

The *chariot*, your body-mind-personality complex, transporting Self.
You relate to your vehicle meaningfully and properly.
You are the master of the chariot,
you are not the driver, the horses, nor the chariot or reins.
You are the one being transported
across the battlefield of experiences.

The *subtly discriminating ones*
who constantly choose actions that represent
the Consciousness they are.
These are the Self-realizing ones.
I say Self-*realizing* to emphasize
it is not just one big flash and you are Self-realized;
realizing is something you experience as your way of being.
You can not Self-realize mentally or intellectually.
You are engaged in Self-realizing through your behaviors.

The inner state is absolutely devoted, continuous
and all-embracing in all behaviors, be they external or internal.

Through sincere spiritual endeavors,
your faculties transcend themselves.
They take on the state of their source
which they are meant to reflect.
As the faculties take on the subtle vibratory state,
they eventually cease being faculties;
they are Consciousness in their own experience.

...In His shining all (these) shine after Him.
By His Light all this is illumined...
You can experience the radiant energy that you are,
and you can experience yourself centered as that—
the radiant source experiencing Self through the faculties.
Your faculties relate to you as Self-effulgent Being.
The next step: there are no faculties,
there is simply being Absolute Consciousness.
It is a given, This Is It.

Part II Canto III

Attaining Self-Realization

Chapter Thirty-Seven

The Beginningless Peepul Tree

Sincerely determine to keep your faculties continuously present
in your center, the cave of the heart,
where dwells Eternal Consciousness that is your essence,
your identity.

This all-pervasive interconnected eternal Consciousness that you are
is the light that illumines all the worlds,
and the source from which the sun and stars take their light,
as does lightning, fire and every other form of illumination.

Let your faculties remain seated and devotedly focused
upon the Luminous Indweller that you are,
and let them reflect Self to Self with devotion.
Be filled with the song of love
of the many facets and qualities of Illimitable Self,
this dialogue with Death.

1. *This is the beginningless peepul tree that has its roots above and branches down. That (which is its root) is pure, that is Brahman and that is called immortal. On that are fixed all the worlds; none transcends that. This verily is that.*

Second translation:

With Root above and Branches below is this Primaeval Fig Tree. That is indeed the Pure, That the Brahman, That is termed the Deathless. In It are contained all the worlds and none ever goes beyond It. This verily is That.

The tree has been an important symbol for humanity
from prehistoric times to today.
In many cultures the tree has served as the joiner
between the divine and the material realms.
To the ancient Nordic tribes, the Ash was a sacred tree,
a symbolic connection to the divine.
The Greek Roman Egyptian Arabic and Indian cultures
revered the fig tree.
The *...peepul tree...* is a type of fig,
also known as the *ficus religiosa*, or sacred fig.
The inverted fig tree is an ancient image
referred to in numerous scriptures.

...the beginningless peepul tree... the tree of the world,
illustrates the apparent dichotomy
that stimulates a more expansive understanding.
It has its root in the Beginningless above,
in the Eternal Brahman, the Absolute,
and its trunk and branches grow down
into the ephemeral realm of manifestation.
Through this tree analogy we experience the power charge
inherent in a connector between positive and negative poles.
The apparent contradiction is spanned by the tree,
the pole between the two opposite charges,
which creates a great surge of energy.
That is a principle in physics and electro mechanics.

The tree of manifestation that grows out of the Power of Being
has for its seed the Creator.
The creative power arises through conscious determination,
wielding the powers of knowledge and action.
Like an image in bold relief, from Infinite Brahman—
the substance, the background of everything that is—
emerges Hiranyagarbha, identical to Him, yet standing out.
Out of the field of pure absolute Non-manifestation
arise knowledge and action causing manifestation.

Why knowledge?
Knowledge is *of* something, Eternal Consciousness is not.
Consciousness is Consciousness; there is nothing beyond It,
nothing transcendent to It.
There is nothing to know about Consciousness, It just *is*.
Knowledge means particular realization or objectifying,
making things phenomena events ideas thoughts and feelings.

Why action?
Action is potential realized in creation—
this is 'realized' in the opposite direction from Self-realization.
The created has a beginning and end,
it is subject to the limitations of time,
therefore not real, illusory.
With illusion there is false perception
and the suffering of ignorance.
Creation includes ignorance.

From the limitless Field of Eternal Consciousness,
the Creator casts Knowledge and Action, causing Creation,
which expresses itself through the Ephemeral, the Momentary.
Now there is something subject to Time.
Something that has the Limitation of Time is illusory,
because in Reality there are no Limitations.
Illusion leads to suffering
in the false Perception of Identity as temporal and limited.
Thus is created the Tree of Life,
while pure unlimited Consciousness immovably persists.

In ignorance you superimpose characteristics
upon the pure eternal This, Self.
Ignorance regarding your identity generates desire—
when you do not know you are all, you have great needs.
An isolated and limited entity is compelled by desire
to unite with other entities, thus you act.
Ignorance leads to desire and action;
they form the sprout of the world tree, the peepul tree,
which is rooted in the Unbeginning.
The sprout grows and branches
as it is nurtured with the water of desire.

Do not regard this analogy with value judgments.
Manifestation is not bad because it is ephemeral.
The Creator is not less than the Power of Being.
The image of the great inverted peepul tree
rooted in the Eternal Unbeginning
and branching down into momentary manifestation
symbolizes the oneness of all.

While the analogy speaks of up and down,
you do well to remember that in infinity—
which, after all, is the reality—there is no up or down.

Integral to the tree of manifestation
are the phenomena of birth death decay and sorrow,
the experiences of limitation and isolation, need and fear.
They are the symptoms of the illusion related to manifestation.
When you experience the reality, Brahman,
the illusion dissolves,
as do its symptoms by which people suffer,
just as the shimmering lake disappears
in the distance of the desert, once we recognize it is a mirage.
The tree of manifestation,
along with the suffering and happiness it contains,
is felled by knowledge of reality.

Ever-changing, the tree itself has no real substance.
Although humans invest much of their lives in it
with all their fearing hoping wanting and distrusting,
the tree of life can vanish like a gust of air at any moment.
While it provides a home for arguers skeptics
and hypocritical intellectuals crowing in its branches,
the sincere seekers of truth never regard this tree as *This*.

Picture the inverted peepul tree:
its trunk is comprised of the subtle bodies of all creatures;
its tender sprouts are the objects of the senses of knowledge;
its branches pointing downward consist of heaven and hell
and the states of beasts and ghosts;
its leaves are the sacred scriptures, the teachings of truth;
its beautiful flowers are deeds in accord with real identity,
such as sacrifice charity and austerity;

its various tastes are comprised of happiness and sorrow;
beings subsist on its many fruits—their desire for them
is enough to create a set of well-developed secondary roots.

...*all the worlds*... are contained within this tree of manifestation.
It is filled with the tumultuous sounds of the world's creatures
shouting and screaming, laughing and crying,
singing and cursing, playing and fighting,
expressing the pleasures and pains of beings living in illusion.

The inverted peepul tree represents human life rooted in the divine,
traversing the path from suffering in ignorance,
through falsity to knowledge to the bliss of enlightenment.
All is contained in the tree,
yet infinite Power of Being is contained in none.

The inverted peepul tree vanishes
when attachment to the tree and its ramifications ceases,
and you realize Self.
When you know reality, the unmovable eternal indestructible
all-pervasive Self that you are,
and your faculties experience you as that,
everything else—the ego, the tree with all its activity and noise,
life and death—no longer exists.

The resplendent Tree of the World
with its Roots in pure Being
can cease to be at any Moment; it can be felled.
Coming from the Eternal, it is momentary,
growing out of the ultimately Substantial, it is ephemeral.
These apparent Self-contradictions reveal the Infinitude of Self.

The source of all is Infinite Self;
all worlds come forth from This,
are fixed upon This as they revolve about It,
and dissolve in It again when reality is realized:
I am the eternal all-pervasive Self.
Nothing is beyond This, nothing transcends This.
This is the way it is.

While the great inverted Tree of Life,
rooted in the Eternal above and branching down into the World,
shivers and changes
with the Desires and Actions of its Inhabitants,
while it appears and disappears,
Transcendent Self remains unmoving and unchanging.
This Is.

CHAPTER THIRTY-EIGHT

Fear Of Self

May the Soul of all,
    who dwells in the cave of the heart of every being,
    be honored by your faculties
    in their true relationship of continuous conscious attendance.

You are the Indweller,
    not the outgoing rays and the sensations they experience.
    You are Self, Eternal Consciousness,

not merely a manifestation, a material object
disconnected and disempowered in its experience.
You are reality, not illusion.
You are truth, not falsity.
That is the way it is.

2. *All this universe, that there is, emerges and moves because there is the supreme Brahman that is a great terror like an uplifted thunderbolt. Those who know this become immortal.*

Second translation:

> *Whatever there is, this whole Universe, has come forth from and vibrates in Prana. The Great Fear, the raised Thunderbolt—those who know that become Immortal.*

The supreme eternal Consciousness, Brahman,
has by His breath caused, through Hiranyagarbha,
the entire universe and everything within it.
The determining force of Brahman is the breath of life,
which as ...*Prana*... is the life force that vitalizes all creation,
maintains all creatures
and absorbs them again within Himself.

> The Movement of the Life Force
> is a constantly alternating Coming and Going,
> as is Inhalation and Exhalation.
> This Pulse of the Universe between apparently opposite Poles
> results in the dynamic Balance of continuous Being.

The expansion and contraction of the great life force,
beyond its apparent opposition and imbalance,
in its ultimate balance gives life.
The upheavals of life and death and rebirth
are resolved in the realization of the equanimity
of the Eternal Unmoving that you really are.
However, when,
through the myopic perspective of a limited life form,
you regard yourself only in the framework of this one life,
the grandeur and power of the ultimate source—
who through His animating energy
is your cause and preservation—
strikes bolts of fear into your heart.

All forms of being are so intrinsically dependent upon the vital force,
that they fear His power.
Just as the *...thunderbolt...* was seen as
the angry expression of Zeus
and feared by gods and humans alike,
so *...the supreme Brahman...*
strikes terror in the breasts of humans.

How is it that human beings are so afraid of their ultimate source?

You have for so long placed your identity
in the phenomenal events, the manifestations,
that your faculties have lost touch with the essential force,
the Self you really are.

Attaching yourself to this Life and fearing Death
is like attaching yourself to Inhalation
because you fear Exhalation.

Whatever is not familiar in terms of this limited life
is invested with fear.
Ironically, the most unfamiliar is the most intrinsic to you,
the Self you are.
In His great power,
Brahman appears to pose the greatest threat.

This ancient scripture, in the voice of the Teacher, Death,
now discloses how the world behaves in that fear.

3. *From fear of Him Fire burns, from fear shines the Sun;*
from fear run Indra and Air, and Death, the fifth.

Here we come closer to understanding the purpose of illusion.
Without illusion, manifestation would not be possible;
manifestation is enabled by illusion.
The illusion is of separateness.
Without manifestation there is just Consciousness.
Eternal Consciousness does not move, does not act,
does not perform functions; It just is.

In order for something to perform functions,
it has to think of itself as a separate and limited entity
that has needs and desires,
and fears the Grand One from whom it feels separate.
That fear is the motivating force to perform functions,
with your ultimate aim to be reabsorbed in the One,

to be united with Him whom you so much fear.
When you understand that, you need not fear.

Be careful that ego does not take over and say,
I'm not afraid, so I don't have to do anything anymore.
Eternal Consciousness has determined to manifest, to move.
It is Unmoving Consciousness that is moving,
it is the Unmanifest that manifests.
Why? He just does.
Why does Brahman act? Because Brahman acts.
Just so, when you are true to Self,
you act with purity tranquility expertise unattachment
unlimitedness and ultimate functionality.

When you are in the perception of yourself
as an identity separate from the Great Self
and bound to the perishable body-mind,
you feel too unqualified and disempowered
to act effectively.
You wallow in lethargy hesitancy and procrastination.
When you do act, your actions miss the mark;
you act as someone you are not,
not as an expression of Self-empowered Being.
Left to your self-limiting devices
you may well end up not acting at all, or, at best, minimally.
It is due to the fear of Death that you get off your back
and at least attempt to make something of your life.

You aspire to something greater than the material life
and its limitation, for inherently you know that real Being
is far subtler greater fuller and richer,
and you want to experience yourself as that.
To qualify for this realization,

you must transform your faculties
to be fully focused empowered and pure,
so they reflect Limitless Self, the source of all,
and become, in their experience, one with that—
like pure water poured into pure water.

Thus can your relationship with God be transformed
from one of fear of a distant great power,
to oneness with your most intimate love.
Have the fear of God inspire you
to evolve to intimacy with God, union.

The entire cosmos and everything within it—
...Sun...Fire...and Air...
and the higher powers, the gods,
even Yama, the Lord of Death—
all is ruled by the transcendent power
of the indefinable That, Brahman, Self.

The theme sounded throughout this dialogue with Death,
that nothing is greater than the Power of Being,
nothing transcends This, all is ruled by This—
why is it so important to say this repeatedly?
Because the falsity is so prevalently lived
that ego seems more important than the reality of Self.
This is your clue to what you must do all day every day:
remind yourself that the force of all,
and the essence in which everything is absorbed again,
is Self—that is what you are.
Thou shalt have no other gods before me—
the First Commandment in the Bible.

Brahman, Self, is the Reason for all that is being.
Without Him there would be no Creation with all its Creatures.
He dwells in the Cave of the Heart of each one of them
and is their Ruler.
He rules the Heat Light and Nurturing of the Sun,
the Destruction and Warmth of Fire,
the Waters and Air.
He rules Life and He rules Death.
All that takes place is because of Eternal Consciousness,
the ultimate Cause.

As the ruler of death, He creates fear in your life.
This fear serves you as motivation
to transcend the limitations of your faculties,
liberate yourself from bondage to ego
and realize your identity in Brahman.
Then you feel free to let go of attachment to this life,
which is mortal,
and dwell in Absolute Consciousness,
which is the Immortal.

Chapter Thirty-Nine

Human Life Is A Rare Opportunity

May you be true to yourself by preparing your faculties
for these subtlest teachings.
Have them deeply focused
and continuously present in your center,
seated in effortless balance with the Infinite Self,
who dwells in the cave of the heart.
Engage deeply with the teachings
so as not to relate to these revelations of Self

as mere words, but as sincere experiences
that vibrate in accord with the Limitless Consciousness
that you are.

4. *If one succeeds in realising here before the falling of the body, (one becomes freed); (else) because of that (failure) one becomes fit for embodiment in the world of creatures.*

Evolution is a constant growth toward perfection.
Prodded by evolution, humans strive for perfection.
You attain perfection
only in the realization of your identity in Infinite Self.
Is it possible for human beings to experience themselves
and live as all-pervasive and eternal Consciousness?
Can you relate to yourself
as the one interconnected source of all?
Can you be in the unending experience of yourself as infinite?

As perfection is the goal of evolution,
it would be perversely ludicrous if it were unattainable.
For evolution to aim at something that can not be
would certainly not be consistent with
the order of the universe.

By prevailing evidence it seems
that human beings are the most highly evolved
of all the life forms on this earthly plane.
Thus you are evolution's candidate
for its inexorable drive toward perfection
in the realization of identity in the one all-pervasive Self.

How are you qualified for this mighty accomplishment
of evolution's purpose?
You are equipped with a wonderfully subtle
and powerful ensemble of faculties:
your body and senses, with which you can conduct yourself
in experiencing the material realm;
your emotions and feelings, by which you can experience
on subtler and more complex levels;
your mind, by which you not only
experience the material realm,
but also correlate and coordinate
the functions of the other faculties;
your intellect, by which you can have knowledge
far beyond the reach of your senses feelings
emotions and mind;
and your intuition, which is connected
to the subtle holism of Consciousness.

With all that potential—including the ultimate potential—
what is missing? Fundamentally, nothing!
You only need to release your precious faculties
from the stranglehold of attachment and devotion
to a false self, the limiting ego.
Do not wrestle with ego—
that would only further involve your faculties with falsity—
but proactively dedicate your faculties
to behaviors in accord with Self.

When you relate your Faculties to who you really are,
with Sincerity Continuity Expertise and Trust,
Success is inevitable:
your Faculties will be transformed
and take on the vibratory State of Eternal Self.
The Manifestation then experiences itself
through those pure Faculties
as Infinite Consciousness: Union.

When is this wondrous transformation,
the fulfillment of your faculties' evolutionary potential,
to take place, after the faculties are dead? Obviously not.
However, many live as if it will somehow take place
when they die, as if thrown into the bargain
with the change of state.
For those individuals, death only leads to yet another birth,
to continued bondage to the wheel of life death and rebirth.
Yama does not even promise that such a one
will be fit for another human birth;
he may well return as one of the many other *...creatures...*

This is the predictable Fate:
When you allow your Instruments of Consciousness
to remain enmeshed with the temporal Realm,
the Doors of Eternal Consciousness will remain closed to you,
and your Experiences will be driven by
Forgetfulness and Suffering.

Only in realizing the Truth of Self,
dwelling without Fluctuation
in the Eternal Consciousness that you are
and emanating Consciousness
through all your Actions and Behaviors,
will you fulfill your evolutionary Potential
and abide in permanent Peace and Bliss.

5. *As (one sees) in a mirror, so in one's intellect; as in a dream, so in the world of the manes; as it is seen in water, so in the world of the Gandharvas. As it is in the case of shade and light, so in the world of Brahma.*

...As (one sees) in a mirror, so in one's intellect...

As a mirror can reflect your face
so can your intellect reflect Self.
If the mirror is spotted or broken, the reflection is untrue,
even to the point of being unrecognizable.
If the intellect is impure—
due to distraction with objects on the material realm,
or loyalty to ego,

or not being a responsible determining driver
of the chariot, your body-mind-psyche complex—
its reflection of Self will be untrue
to the point of complete lack of recognition.

When your intellect is pure—
when the waves of modification have ceased—
it reflects Self perfectly in all Its power and splendor.
Take care of the state of your mirror, the intellect.
If you continuously dip it into the mud,
it will give you a muddled, distorted image.
If you continuously devote your intellect to
subtle discrimination and unswerving determination,
you will dwell in clear reality.

...as in a dream, so in the world of the manes...
Your dreams reflect the secret life of the subconscious
with its stored wealth of experiences
reaching far back into the past.
That inner treasure trove is the accumulation
of all experiences in this manifestation
and all previous manifestations of your soul
and all souls.
Knowledge gained from those experiences
is deposited in all of us,
as are the negative and positive impressions
accumulated from our response to that knowledge.

...the world of the manes... is the world of spirits.
When you leave this body behind,
your behaviors attachments and loyalties
continue to have an effect on you.

You dwell for a limited time in a realm
where the soul is subject to the effects of past deeds.
Many souls continue seeking to reap the fruits
of their achievements, as was their habit in their previous life,
maintaining the cycle of cause and effect, karma.
If you are in murk during this lifetime,
you will be in murk after death,
and you will have to take another body or form accordingly.
Examine your present state: into what form would this state fit?

As you allow your Soul to be influenced
in this Body-life,
so will the Soul continue to be influenced
in the Afterlife.

In the world of the manes, Self-perception is vague, as in a dream;
the soul is in a modified state,
distracted from the experience of pure Consciousness.
In a dream the images are intangible or ephemeral,
very hard to take hold of and keep;
so it is in the world of the spirits.

When your instruments of perception are in an unmodified state,
the original state of pure Consciousness,
they are able to tap into the vast store of collective wisdom
that is available in the spirits of the dead,
as well as in the spirits of the living.
This can be a tremendous help

to effecting a quantum leap in evolution.
Thus the spirits of the dead, the manes,
can contribute to the living, on the path to Self-realization.

...as it is seen in water, so in the world of the Gandharvas...
The Gandharvas are higher refined powers, celestial beings.
In their world, the perception of Self is clearer—
as clear as one's reflection in still water.
However, even calm water has a subtle shimmer;
the image reflected will be somewhat indistinct.
So it is in the perception of the gods.

...As it is in the case of shade and light,
so in the world of Brahma...
Brahma is the Manifestor, Brahman's potential.
In His realm, perception is sharply defined,
as in the bold relief of light and shade.
Now the experience has depth to it,
it has background and definition,
affording greater clarity and understanding.
Creation's diversity and contrasts offer the opportunity
of an utterly clear realization
of the all-embracing unity of Infinite Being.
However, realization in this realm is fraught with difficulty
and takes a long time.
The soul continues to develop from one manifestation
to another, and then without form altogether—
or a refined form unrecognizable by human faculties—
until it eventually attains the level of the Creator.
There the perception of Self is clear.

In the human form, with a clear and determining intellect—
a true mirror—Self-realization can be attained in this lifetime.
That is the opportunity and meaning of this manifestation.
Therefore it is highly advantageous
to make use of this, your unique moment.

Chapter Forty

The Silent Observer

Bring all your faculties to your center and have them remain there
seated in perfect balance, devoted to Luminous Self.
Let them be in a state of deep relaxation and tranquility.
Thus your faculties are pure reflectors
and will be absorbed in Eternal Consciousness.

In that state your faculties recognize the teachings
as expressions of Limitless Self.
Merged in these teachings,
they will be merged in Consciousness, deeply transformed.

Simply cause your faculties
to remain in this effortlessly balanced state,
situated in the cave of your heart,
attending to the Indweller, and one with Him.

6. *Having known the dissimilarity of the senses that originate separately, as also their rising and setting, the intelligent man does not grieve.*

Second translation:

The wise, having understood the separate nature of the senses, their rising and setting as of things that come into being quite separate from himself, grieves not.

Grief is deep sorrow usually in response to loss or death.
What kind of person does not grieve?
The person who identifies Self according to real knowledge,
that of unending transcendent Being,
as opposed to the false limited and dependent ego.

What is the knowledge regarding
the real meaning and purpose of your senses
that liberates you from pain and sorrow?
That they are not Self, you are not the senses nor their input.

Your senses are different from you, from your real identity,
in three fundamental ways.

First, while you, Self, are permanent, the senses arise and set again
according to their involvement in the material world.
When you are awake, the senses come in contact

with many objects and conditions.
They respond to sounds with hearing, to sights with seeing,
and so on.
However, as you descend into sleep, the senses set like the sun.

The second fundamental difference is that
the senses are created thus dependent, Being is not.
For each of the five elements
a sense is born to perceive its phenomena.
Therefore each sense is dependent upon the element.
Self is not dependent, Self is sufficient unto Self.
Having been created, senses die.
Being is unborn, unbeginning and will never cease.

Thirdly, your senses are involved with incessant change.
They respond to the chimerical appearances
and disappearances of the phenomenal world.
For the unchecked senses there are multifarious objects,
all experienced as not only changing, but separate—as other.
There is only one Self of all, and It is constant.

When you identify yourself with your senses,
you think of yourself as impermanent and other,
not as the Unchanging Self.
If you are to experience yourself in reality,
you must have everything about you, all your faculties,
in constant relationship with who you fundamentally are:

You are Eternal Consciousness, unchanging and permanent,
unbeginning unending transcendent,
who through the Power of Determination
causes the Creator, who with the Life-breath and motivating Fire
manifests through the Five Elements and their Limiting Adjuncts
as the Objects and Creatures of Creation,
in the Center of which you, Absolute Consciousness,
are present and experience Self.
Self, dwelling in the Cave of the Heart of each Creature,
experiences Self through the Experiences of His Creations.

When you prevalently experience through the senses,
you experience yourself as material,
as phenomenal momentary separate and isolated.
When your faculties function in constant relationship
with the fundamental fact that you are Consciousness,
you think feel and act as Limitless Being.

The purpose of the senses is not to occupy your attention
with the passing phenomena of the material realm,
the comings and goings of momentary appearances,
but to experience everything as the Unitive One you are.
What do *you* use them for?

Be careful. This is not to say you should repress the senses.
After all, the Self of all, in His limitless wisdom,
has chosen to create them.
However, your senses enmeshed in the material realm

can distract you from the experience of Being.
Many a student complains, My senses are always shifting,
going from one thing to another,
distracting me from experiencing Self.
If I have to be in contact with the senses,
I will be distracted.

> To be free to experience yourself as the Infinite Being you are,
> do not repress or deny the Signals of the Senses,
> but relate to everything
> as an Experience of the One—That You Are.
> This you accomplish by
> keeping the Faculties effortlessly balanced in your Center
> where you dwell as Luminous Consciousness.

Do you know how to focus on Being?
Are you capable of doing that? *Are* you doing it?
Do you know dwelling in Consciousness
is to your ultimate advantage?
Otherwise you will be mired in inertia:
continuing in the behavior to which you are habituated.
You are at the chasm of understanding,
standing on the razor's edge:
on one side is disaster, on the other liberation.
Disaster happens when you *fall* off,
liberation is when you *walk* off.
Liberation is by choice, in Consciousness.

To overcome the Senses' Seduction into the material Realm,
relate to Sense Input as the Experience of Being
continuously and faithfully—
not once a Year, not once a Week, not once a Day.
Constantly nurture your Relationship
with the Flame of Consciousness,
keep it alive in the Cave of your Heart.

With your faculties gathered in your center,
be the impartial witness of your senses' activities
in calm unattachment, tranquil in the knowledge
of your immutability and permanency,
the unmoving Power of Being that you are.
Make the Silent Observer your stance
in regard to the multifarious sense input.
Allow all the sense experiences to go on
without trying to alter them,
in a fluid stream of Self-experience, Eternal Consciousness.
In that state, even though the senses are *...rising and setting...*
your experience does not fluctuate.
There is clarity, as when the mind is utterly still.

Relate all Sense Data to Self
by keeping your Faculties, especially the Mind,
in the State of Silent Observer, the impartial unattached Witness.
Thus even the ephemeral shifting Senses
are in a real Relationship to Luminous Consciousness.

In the resultant Clarity you witness the Shimmering of the Senses
as mere momentary Appearance
by which you, the permanent Self, *experience* yourself
but certainly do not *identify* yourself.

As the Silent Observer
you are detached from the vicissitudes of your senses
and their apparent fragmentation,
and, most importantly, from the grief you suffer
when you falsely identify yourself with them
in the forgetfulness of your eternal identity.
Thus you dwell in the bliss
of self-knowing limitless Consciousness
with the senses engaged and alive.

7. *The mind is superior to the senses; the intellect is superior to the mind; Mahat (the Great Soul) is superior to the intellect; the Unmanifested is superior to Mahat.*

Because most tend to live by the senses,
so much so, that they allow their fragmentary experiences
to be pervasively impressed
and thus take them to be the permanency or even their identity,
Yama gives you yet another opportunity
to know the order of priorities in overall reality.

Your senses and the sense-objects—the reasons for the senses—
are meant to be ruled by your mind; mind is superior to them.
Without mind, the senses are like horses drawing the chariot
with no reins—most have not made the connection
between mind and senses.

When you are in the attitude of Silent Observer,
your mind is in the unmoving state
even while the senses are responding to stimuli;
its modifications having ceased,
your mind is as pure as the limitless mind.
This unattached state allows your mind to merge
with the higher intellect, which is subtler, more pervasive
and therefore *...superior...* to mind.

When you are in the unattached State, as in the Silent Observer,
Mind merges with the pure Intellect.

When you merge your faculties in the higher intellect,
you transcend the intellect to fulfill its reason for being:
...Mahat (the Great Soul)...
the fundamental source of the intelligence of all beings.
All souls are the Great Soul, as all waves are the ocean.

From realizing yourself as the Great Soul
you ascend to the rarefied heights
of the womb of manifestation *...the Unmanifested...*

Superior and greater are not qualitative terms;
they just connote a sense of succession,

which you must not interpret in a linear fashion.
There is no facet of the divine that is lesser.

8. *But superior to the Unmanifested is the supreme Purusa who is pervasive and is, indeed, without worldly attributes, knowing whom a man becomes freed and attains immortality.*

Second translation:

Higher than the Unmanifest is the Purusha, all-pervading and devoid of any characteristic mark, whom having known, every living being is liberated and goes to the Deathless State.

Purusa, Self, Is.
He is the Infinite All, therefore beyond all attributes,
for any description would be a limiting way
of regarding the Infinite.
Mind tends to think in terms of modifications:
I am such and such.
Self is all.
Thus we can not rightly attribute worldly characteristics
to Self.

Beyond the manifest and beyond *...the Unmanifest...*
you realize your ultimate liberation in *...the supreme Purusa...*
who pervades everything and is contained by none.
You must not superimpose upon Purusa
...any characteristic mark...
Even to say the Power of Being is great
may be assigning a limiting attribute;
great is tiny compared to what Limitless Being is.
In Its infinitude in every facet and every direction,
It is beyond definition.

When you say God is this or God is that,
you are talking not about God, but a projection of ego.

Merged in the supreme Purusa, Brahman,
you not only bathe in the light
that illumines and empowers all life
and rests unmoving in the cave of the heart of every creature,
but you *are* the light.
Herein you realize your true identity and everlasting peace.
You are finally freed from the ignorance and illusion
that have bound your faculties in service
to someone you are not, to the false identity, ego.

This liberation—you must remember—is to be attained by you
while in the human body.
Then, when you slough off this body,
as the snake does its skin, you never have to take a body again,
nor its limitations and suffering.

You are the Immortal.
You are Eternal Consciousness.
You Are This.

How, then, can you experience and realize Eternal Self,
when This is without attributes
and therefore considered incomprehensible?

Chapter Forty-One

The Cessation Of Modification

Treasure the sacred teachings given to you by Lord Yama.
Respond to the energies inherent in these great gifts
by faithfully applying them to your faculties
with continuity and expertise, and with utter sincerity.
May you experience these teachings in purity
and cause that experience to be impressed as your knowledge.
May you allow this knowledge to mature into wisdom
and to guide your actions
and your most subtle internal behaviors
so that you live true to what you know,
faithfully every day from moment to moment.

With this knowledge live true to yourself—
this is the foundation of love.

9. *His form does not exist within the range of vision; nobody sees Him with the eye. When this Self is revealed through deliberation, It is realised by the intellect, the ruler of the mind, that resides in the heart. Those who know this become immortal.*

Second translation:

Not within the field of vision stands His form, nor with the eye can any see Him. By the Heart, by the thought, by the mind He is framed. They who know That become Immortal.

The limitless subtle power that in essence you are
is situated in the cave of the heart of every manifestation.
Self is the identity of all that is—
all-pervasively and without exception.
All Is That, yet most know It not.

Why is what is so intimately you—your very Being—
so unrecognized by you?
Because you can not see It with your eyes,
you can not touch It with your hands,
you can not taste smell or hear It—
your senses can not perceive It.

Most have become so habituated to sense perception,
that they are dependent upon their senses
and regard them as the only indicators of reality.
Many proudly proclaim that they are staunch realists
because they will acknowledge as real only the ephemeral,

only what they can experience with their senses,
which is illusory.
Such is the delusion of ego.
They even identify themselves as their senses:
I am cold, I am hungry, and so on.
They do not identify themselves as Self, the reality they are.

What helps keep ...*It*... in the forefront of your awareness?
Relate to the senses' input as momentary phenomena,
which are only appearance, not real;
the forms taken by material objects will eventually disappear.
What you see hear touch taste or smell
is only sense interpretation of illusory images.
The Power of Being is not an object,
not a manifestation composed of the five elements,
as are entities of the material realm.
Consequently the senses can not perceive Self.
In Its infinite subtlety, Self is beyond sense perception.

How can you know—not merely believe hope or hypothesize,
but really know—that there is a Self,
an all-pervasive essence that is *the* fundament, *the* identity
that you and all really are?
Only through direct experience.
And herein lies the challenge, but also the ultimate opportunity.

Being in the experience of yourself in reality—
which is being most congruent,
most intimate and harmonious with yourself—
can certainly be seen
as the most deeply satisfying way of being,
and the end of fear lack depression anger
dysfunction and failure.

Are we talking about two persons here, you and some higher Self
with whom you try to enter into a relationship? No.
It is your instruments of experience and expression,
your faculties,
that you need to bring into harmonious relationship with Self,
if you intend to experience this life and all that follows
as who you really are.
Your faculties have for so long been habituated—
to the point of addiction—to relating to a false idea of you,
that they are ignorant of real you.
This estrangement results in regarding Self as a threat,
an enemy to be feared and avoided at all cost,
including your life liberty and fulfillment.
The usurper of the kingdom calls the king a usurper
and stirs up fear in the citizens,
who suffer horribly under the usurper
and would be liberated by the rightful ruler of the realm.

Let us be clear about what *is* the problem and what is *not*.
Living in accord with Self is *not* the problem.
The ego would have you believe Self is the problem—
the usurper says the real king is the invader.
Living free from the suffering of ego is not the problem.
While Limitless Being, seated in the cave of your heart,
radiates His benevolent Consciousness,
your faculties remaining attached to self-denying behavior
cause conflict within and among themselves—
that is the problem.
The beautiful harmonious experiences of Self
may be subdued or repressed, but they are there,

and their poignant contrast to the lies and negativity
in which the faculties are so persistently enmeshed
creates great inner conflict.

Even those who have clearly experienced reality
can still relate to Self as the problem:
I was fine before I heard about ego and Self,
I was fine in my suffering—I was fine in my living death?

Instead of regarding Self as the Cause of your Problems,
it behooves you to see that
Attachment to false Thinking is the Reason you suffer.

Instead of regarding Self as the Cause of your Unease,
it behooves you to see that
Loyalty to Ego is the Reason you are in Conflict.

Instead of regarding Self as the Cause of your Agitation,
it behooves you to see that
Living in Falsity is the Reason for your Dysfunction.

How do you see the Self that you are,
in the clear light of unconditional acceptance,
as your one and only real identity?
Have the higher intellect be the driver of your faculties,
firmly and unswervingly with skill and self-trust
holding steady the reins, your mind,
to undistractedly direct your senses
so they empower your physical functions

on the path to your evolutionary goal in this lifetime:
final fulfillment in Self-realization.

Otherwise, your mind will only function as the lower mind,
coordinating the senses in the pursuit of sensual experiences,
not the experience of Self.
When the senses run amok, the mind runs amok with them,
and the intellect does too—
the faculties tend to join forces,
whether to your benefit or not is up to you.
The reasonably intelligent human being,
after going through the infantile and puerile stages,
will take responsibility for her or his life
with the determining intellect.

After living through the horrors of the war, as a child,
I was so painfully shy that I could not speak to a stranger
without tears in my eyes.
As the determiner, I said to myself,
I am sick and tired of being so fearful,
I will make myself face my fear.

From my book *Self-Healing Through The Awareness Of Being*:
I determined to go out on the street,
stop the first four strangers coming along,
no matter how threatening they looked to me,
and ask them what time it was...
This exercise was embarrassing and difficult for me.
The tears flowed
as I painfully stuttered through each encounter.
Nonetheless, I did it
and even repeated the exercise many times,

until I was free of fears tears and stuttering,
because I was not going to allow that shyness to limit me...

The higher intellect determined that, my senses surely did not,
nor my emotions and feelings,
not even my mind.

> Your Salvation lies in allowing your Intellect
> to be true to its Purpose,
> to be a responsible Driver of your Body-mind-psyche Complex.
> The Intellect must be firmly unswervingly in Control.

If you give your faculties the message
you intend to be responsible only now and then,
that means never.
If your faculties are functioning in opposition to you,
your higher intellect has to decisively say, Stop,
and your instruments of action need to immediately comply.
Whatever your higher intellect determines, is to be carried out;
if not, there is trouble.
If your intellect directs your faculties to function true to Self,
but the response is, I will honor what I know is true for a while,
maybe now and then, if I get around to it—that is a problem.
You have weakened your relationship to reality,
and you have surrendered the reins controlling your faculties.

The intellcct is closer in quality to Self than your mind,
and certainly closer than your senses and the material realm.
That which is closer to you in quality and character

has to stand up for you loyally and say,
This is what you faculties will do—I am the driver,
and I get my signals directly from Limitless Consciousness.

Cause your intellect to be true to its function as the responsible driver.
This is of cardinal importance
if you want to be an intelligent empowered individual.
Otherwise your mind will be pulled helplessly in all directions
by undisciplined senses running amok like crazed horses,
and you will suffer the agonies of being constantly victimized
by your own harmful behaviors.

The higher intellect resides in the cave of the heart
with the inner ruler, the Self of all,
who through His determination has born the Creator,
who has given life-breath and fire
to create the manifestation with the heart wherein He dwells.
The manifestations are meant to reflect the Power of Being.
Really knowing this, you *...become immortal...*

Now I invite you to experience how you can attain that blissful state
wherein everything about you is in union, and you realize Self.

10. When the five senses of knowledge come to rest together with the mind, and the intellect, too, does not function, that state they call the highest.

Second translation:

When the five means of (sense) knowledge sink to rest together with the mind and the Buddhi also acts separately no more, that is described as the Highest Path.

This state of harmony-quiescence-union is yoga.
Yoga chitta vritti nirodha—

so the great sage Patanjali instructs—
yoga is the inhibition of the modifications of mind.

Through steady determination, your higher intellect—
buddhi, who is of Infinite Being—
causes mind and senses to be one with each other
and with itself,
just as the pure and empowered charioteer
makes the horses and reins one with each other and himself.
They cease their separate functions.

> When your Intellect in its pure Power, the higher Intellect,
> causes your Mind and Senses to become utterly still,
> all your Faculties in Unity attain perfect Tranquility:
> there is simply Luminous Consciousness,
> perfect Functioning.

Something in us knows this to be true; yet many argue,
I do not want to be so calm, how will I be motivated to act?
Stress gives me the competitive edge, it makes me excel.
Another popular misconception is:
If I put the senses to rest, let mind be completely still,
and intellect, too, ceases its separate functioning,
that is letting the devil in.
No. That is the way to keep falsity out,
because your faculties will then be in such luminous clarity,
that no darkness can prevail, no opposition to what is, persist.
The devil is opposition to what is, to truth, to reality,
opposition to successfully functioning in harmony.

You experience the light of Consciousness
only when the senses are in harmony,
and they are in harmony only when the mind is still,
and mind is still only when the intellect directs all
in utterly unmoving tranquility.

11. They consider that keeping of the senses steady as yoga. One becomes vigilant at that time, for yoga is subject to growth and decay.

Yoga is the state in which you experience yourself at one with all.
It is the state of ultimate connectedness.
The root of yoga, *yug*, means to yoke, connect, unite;
in the state of yoga you have all facets in union with Self,
you are together, whole.
Yoga is also the state of being disconnected
from your involvement with the particular.
Fragmentation is painful illusion:
you do not experience the joyful interconnectedness
that is the reality of yourself, of all.

In yoga you keep your senses steady and prevent them
from helplessly jumping to the innumerable stimuli
that attract and compel them.
Keeping your senses steady is not an isolated task:
only when your mind is in an unfluctuating state,
is it able to rein in your senses.
You also keep your psychic energies
from their habitual state of rising and falling—
you steady your emotions and feelings
in response to internal and external conditions.
Emotions and feelings left to their tendencies
will react to the ever-changing phenomena

with desire and aversion, needing wanting and aspiring,
fearing and hoping.

With unshakable determination you continuously and faithfully
maintain the unfluctuating state,
you steady your instruments of experience and expression.
It is the function of your higher intellect
to make this real determination.

Your higher Intellect makes the Determination
to create and maintain the unfluctuating State
in the Senses, in the Mind, and in itself.

If you have been exposed to knowledge of reality
and your life is still dysfunctional, filled with suffering,
this may be why:
you have not caused your higher intellect to be the determiner
who says, Mind, you shall now be tranquil—
and seen to it that mind responds.
Can you determine so clearly and strongly, so meaningfully,
that mind will respond whether it wants to or not?
When your mind responds, the senses will follow.
There may remain some latent impressions
that arise in opposition;
however, knowing they are reinforced
by repetition of the behaviors that caused them,
you vigilantly determine not to re-impress and recharge
those negative energies.
In a brief period of time,

the powerful positive impressions will be so well established
that tranquility will be your prevalent—
and eventually permanent—state.
This is not difficult; the difficulty results from
noticing the negative impressions
and nevertheless repeating the harmful behaviors.

You have the ability to understand this and you have a choice.

> The successful Attitude is,
> As soon as I know any Facet of Reality, I will live it;
> anything else is complete Nonsense and harmful.

To accomplish this task of steadiness,
that can seem overwhelmingly difficult,
it helps to know the ways that do *not* work,
ways to which you may be accustomed.
You must not attempt to create steadiness of the faculties
by brute force of suppression,
or you will compound the faculties' errors
and sink to denial or depression, further frustration and anger,
and thereby even greater isolation from the whole.
You will not gain steadiness of senses by being insensitive,
nor by being passive or indifferent.
Learn from observing the suffering of people
who are inattentive and walk around in unconsciousness,
unconcerned with anything that does not involve ego.

You will, however, gain beautiful steadiness
to the point of transcendent tranquility,

when you silently observe the functioning of your faculties.
You observe with total impartiality,
unattached to whence they come and where they go.
Silently observing with dispassion
makes steadiness easily attainable.

In yoga you create steadiness not only in moments, but in continuity.
Thus steadiness becomes more than a practice,
it is your underlying attitude, a life stance of effortless balance.
You no longer flit from one thing to another
as does the undisciplined mind,
and as does an individual devoid of determination.
You do not vacillate from object to object,
from project to project,
from one spiritual teacher and path to another,
for your experience of yourself would then be
as ephemeral as any decaying object,
instead of real as the Unchanging Self.

Why do you think steadiness is taught over and over again,
not only by this Teacher, but many?
Because it speaks of the human experience
and the human frailties.

Implement observances:
determinedly cause your behaviors to steadily reveal Self,
be congruent with Self, express the Self that we all are;
focus with fiery discipline
on keeping your intellect's determination true to Self,
continuous and empowered;
cultivate the stance of the Silent Observer;
purify the vibratory state of all your facets and levels
by the repetition of sacred mantras;

expand your Self-knowledge through focused experience
of illumined writings and teachings;
surrender to the divine in all your actions and moments,
live the Divinity you are.

Implement restraint:
restrain your faculties from behaviors opposite
of who you really are that conceal the light of Self;
relinquish any and all of your misapprehensions
regarding reality, regarding you;
give up ignorance and your attachment to it,
throw it into the sacrificial fire, along with any trace
of attachment to your false identity and egotistical behaviors;
free yourself from enmeshment with such negativity
as aversion antipathy conflict or gossip;
let go of fear and its symptoms of anxiety insecurity
and anger.

Then, and only then, will you experience the graceful steadiness
integral to the eternal unchanging infinitely pervasive Self.

You succeed when you have the right knowledge
and respond to it with the *right means*:
sincerely—not by merely going through the motions;
continuously—free from backsliding,
independent of circumstances and conditions
or whether you feel like it or not;
expertly—with all the skills and knowledge
that you have at your disposal;
and *faithfully*—with abiding trust in the Self that you are.

Yoga is not a hobby, not a fad to be followed
or practiced in gyms as mere physical exercise.

It is not something to give to the ego for competitive display
to aggrandize yourself, which is belittling.
A yogi, or spiritual aspirant, is aware of and avoids
the pitfalls of the human condition.

The unitive state of yoga, being created,
is *...subject to growth and decay...*
Yoga is not sustained by happenstance or wishful thinking;
it has to be willfully maintained.

How do you motivate your feelings and emotions,
your mind and all your facets
to be so determinedly devoted to the state of yoga,
to being so steadily in union with Self,
that they are one with Self?
Impress in your faculties the knowledge with certainty
that union with Self is the experience of the deepest greatest
and most satisfying love, a love that fulfills all your dreams—
your ultimate goal and supreme reward.

Devoted to loving union with Self,
your mind feelings emotions intellect and intuition
do not waste their energies in pursuing superficial diversions,
even if they are habituated to do so.
Your faculties will clearly remember
that distractions have always yielded—
and will invariably yield—disappointment and suffering.
They will no longer mistake a bad habit,
which makes you weak and full of pain,
as forbidden pleasure.
Steady in Self, your mind knows that
when the senses indicate a distraction is pleasurable,
it is a false signal.

In the state of yoga, and properly educated,
your faculties respond to the temptations
offered by your distractions
initially with repulsion, and eventually with utilizing them
as yet another way to center in Self-experience.
If you are still allowing your senses to mislead you,
you have not taken even the beginning steps
to becoming a yogi or spiritual aspirant,
or even simply a responsible person.

In the experience of yourself as Limitless Being
you are suffused with love so nurturing and healing
that you do everything in your power to make that love last,
to make it permanent, to make it real.
You certainly do not want to give up
this most fulfilling and permanent joy for anything less,
for partial or momentary experiences
that result only in disappointment and pain.

Therefore, from the moment one determines to be in yoga,
the unitive state *...one becomes vigilant...*
You avoid your most prevalent—and even the smallest—
pitfalls, the tendencies to which your faculties are subjected
by your conditioning.
Keep in mind that they are impressed
upon the matrix of your psychic energy
like embedded grooves that carry the latent energy
to repeat the behaviors that caused them,
compelling you to live, not according to intelligent free choice,
but according to negative forces
that are predictably and repeatedly harmful.

Why are your tendencies predominantly harmful?
The majority of them were formed in your infancy
during your struggle for survival.
Are the life strategies you created as a child
able to accommodate your mature needs and potentials?
The answer is an obvious, No!
Yet you have reinforced the impressions
made in infancy and childhood
by repeating their causative behaviors over the years
to the extent that they largely rule
not only your mind feelings and emotions,
but even your intellect that is meant to be the determiner
of how you conduct your life.

Be vigilant and discern which of your faculties' behaviors
are in response to conditioning,
and which are in response to Self.

You are free to choose, so remember:
your Tendencies' Urgings, no matter how seductive,
will always hinder and harm you,
while any Response to the Light of Self,
no matter how subtle its Glow,
will always bring you Ease Peace and Love,
and Fulfillment of your evolutionary Path in Self-realization.

Expertly focus your mind with deep devotion,
with continuity and permanency, upon the Self you are.

Have mind think in relation to Self: experience every thought
as *about* Self and, ultimately, *from* Self.
When you keep your mind steady and pure,
it takes on the state of Self, merges with Self.
Then your senses relate to everything
as a way of experiencing Self, and so with all your faculties.
Your intellect potentially has the purity and power
of infinite all-pervasive Consciousness;
use your intellect accordingly,
not as some dull weak useless tattered piece of flotsam.

With devoted concentration and unswerving vigilance,
you will complete the unitive cycle.
Steadily focus your faculties upon the Self that you are,
and in that unfluctuating state
Self experiences Self through the faculties
in and as eternal all-pervasive Consciousness: Self-realization.

Yama is certainly knowledgeable and vigilant
about the human tendency to resist and even reject
any knowledge that liberates you from ego's limiting patterns.
He knows there are those who will respond to the knowledge
offered in this verse, by quibbling:
If the realization of Self is dependent upon human faculties—
most especially intellect's determination—how can it be real?
Thus Lord Yama instructs you further.

CHAPTER FORTY-TWO

I Am That

May you, the recipient of this great gift of knowledge
brought by the master teacher Yama,
be appreciative of your station.
May you regard yourself
deserving of these luminous revelations.

You have not come to the Gift of real Knowledge by Accident.
You have not come to it as the Reward
for all the terrible Things of which you accuse yourself.
You have not come to these sacred and secret Teachings
by being unworthy, as your Ego may claim.
There is nothing unworthy about Self,
there is nothing tainted sinful or untrustworthy
about the luminous all-pervasive Source of all that is.
Do you know this to be true? Then live it.

Once you know Self, live It, and you will be released
from the bondage that has choked your heart,
you will be released from the suffering
that depresses everything within and about you.
You will be liberated to be luminous and blissful,
self-knowing as eternal and all-pervasive,
suffused with the power of giving and love,
Self that you are.
That is the way it is.

12. *It cannot be attained through speech, nor through mind, nor through eye. How can It be known to anyone apart from him who speaks of It as existing?*

Second translation:

Not by speech, nor by the mind nor by the eyes can It be compassed. How could He be comprehended other than by saying 'He (or It) is.'

You can *not* realize Self, Eternal Consciousness,
by the accustomed means of experience.
Your mind tries to grasp anything and everything,
including that which is way beyond it;
in its linear and fragmentary functioning,
mind can not grasp All-pervasive Self.
The familiar supposed indicators of reality lead you astray.
What you see is not what is, but what appears to be.
Your eyes see the ephemeral, not the real;
they can not perceive Self.
People resort to speech in their attempts to take hold of reality.
They argue discuss question explain theorize and hypothesize,
as they barely touch upon It.
Mere speech can not adequately describe the Power of Being,
let alone attain It.
Thus the means by which you usually
attempt to attain reality—and Self is *the* reality—
do not work.

How *are* you to fulfill your evolutionary goal,
which is the realization of Self, Limitless Consciousness?
If Self is so difficult to attain, is it actually possible?
Since everything about you—and everything in the universe—
is striving for that, it must be possible.
In the cosmological order,
it would be perverse to have an evolutionary goal
for which all manifestations are striving,
if it were not attainable.

There is a knowing of Self deep inside you, because You *Are* That.
Even if all is confusion within you,
and you are distracted or misled,

there is a quiet voice that asserts, I Am.
Here is a sure-fire way by which you can experience Self:

> Sincerely faithfully and continuously assert within:
> I Am Consciousness, Awareness of Being: That I Am.
> *That I Am* is Self-effulgent Self radiating the Light of Consciousness.
> Through Senses Mind Intellect and Intuition,
> I notice those Rays as they emanate from my Center.
> I trace them to their Source and experience Self.

Have this be the constant experience of your mind feelings emotions—
every facet of you.

'I Am' is your source.
On the evolutionary, or devolutionary, path,
when you are behind the veil of illusion,
you relate to yourself as a body-mind construct.
This seemingly solid permanent and separate construct
is brought about by a momentary conjunction
of five basic elements as they revolve in space
according to their limiting adjuncts.
The Creator of the elements invests Her creation
with the breath of life and the transforming fire
by which the manifestation goes through its changes.
Abiding in the cave of the heart of each manifestation,
She is an aspect of what is beyond manifestation,
the source of the Creator
and, by extension, of everything created,
the all-inclusive undefinable That.

Thus your *I Am* experience,
simultaneously is your experience of *I Am That.*

The timeless all-pervasive eternal source of all
is beyond description in Its infinitude.
It has no particular attributes;
all you can say about It is that *...It is...*
When you know with certainty that It is,
you experience It—Brahman, Self—
as the necessary and self-evident foundation,
the ground essence and identity of all that is.

Self is self-evident; that you are is self-evident.
The fact of your being attests to Self,
for Being and Self are one.
You are, you exist.
The Power of Being is the subtle all-pervasive essence
by which everything and everyone is.
The clearest statement to make regarding Self
is that It is, It exists, It is Being.

Nevertheless there is a persistent faction among us
that insists that there is really no existence,
and there is no All-Inclusive Being, no Self—
everything is just appearances that will disappear
and become part of the cycle of comings and goings.
Their logic is as follows—and I will give you a brief version:
Since Self is dependent on the determination of the intellect,
Self ceases to be perceived when intellect ceases.
If a tree falls in the forest and nobody hears it,
has it really fallen, or has there even been a tree?
If Self is not perceived, It has no existence;

thus Self is illusory.
As you say that Self is existence,
there is then only non-existence.

Yama addresses such false logic in the next verse.
Ironically, death itself proves existence.

13. *The Self is (first) to be realised as existing, and (then) as It really is. Of these two (aspects), the real nature of the Self that has been known as merely existing, becomes favourably disposed (for self-revelation).*

Second translation:

As a bare 'He is' He should be realised (first) and (also) in His essential being (tattva bhavena). Of these two (modes), the realisation of the essential being comes as the gift of grace (prasidati) to him who has already realised Him as a bare 'He is'.

That you are is self-evident.
What you are is *that* you are, because you are Being.
Being is to be experienced as It is.
How is It? It is eternal all-pervasive now.

This, which resides in all, is to be realized purely as 'It is'.
Being simply *is*, He is immanent in all,
immediately present, yet transcendent.
Reality is now and forever, presence forever.
What *is* now will forever be.
What *appears* now may not appear a moment later.

Being simply *is*,
It is immediately and eternally present in all,
including in all Effects.
All that *is*, is Being.

Experience the pure essence that is Self, devoid of limiting adjuncts.
Experience yourself as immanent unceasing Consciousness,
transcendent to all phenomena,
transcendent even to such descriptions as existence
and non-existence.
You are Absolute Consciousness,
beyond interpretation or distinction, beyond cause and effect.
Be deeply totally absorbed in the experience of that.

When you experience Self as immanent in all, pure presence,
in your center, in the cave of the heart,
the Ultimate Absolute *...becomes favourably disposed...*
to revealing Itself: I Am,
I am Being,
Absolute Consciousness I Am.
This is *...the gift of grace...*

Be fully suffused with the pure experience of Being.
Be absorbed in that.
This Is It.
This is what you are, what all is.

This is bliss.

Chapter Forty-Three

One Path

Gather your faculties in your center now.
This need not be a lengthy or complicated process.
Allow the energies of your faculties
to go to the very center of the city where abides the Indweller.
Have your faculties surround Him
and direct their energies in perfect tranquility toward Self.
Remain steadily here.

Declare your allegiance to eternal all-pervasive Self,
the essence of all.
Assert your knowledge of the reality of Being,
the reality of you.
Affirm your loyalty.
Feel the upwelling of joy and security
that leads to deepest tranquility.
Be in peace.

14. When all desires clinging to one's heart fall off, then a mortal becomes immortal, (and) one attains Brahman here.

Desire takes place in your intellect,
which is also referred to here as the heart.
The intellect and the heart are one;
they are the determiner,
the ruling aspect dwelling in the core of the manifestation.
The lower intellect misperceives you as separate from all else,
thus desires connection, which spawns the need for action
and the false notion of separate doership.
Things need to be known, you need to become a knower,
and you need to engage in the act of knowing—
all in their separate categories.
The fragmentation becomes more and more confusing,
and eventually you die, because you need to repeat the lessons
until you understand and realize.
Think about this: what would it be like for you,
if you were still confused by fragmentation and falsity
when you die?

Ignorance, desire, action in service to ego
and seeking knowledge out of desire, all make you mortal.

Intellect's misperception is a fatal involvement.
This you need to understand to plumb the depth of wisdom
offered by these great teachings.

Here Yama says, You have to be desireless.
This is often where people draw the line:
You mean I have to give up cheesecake?—
someone actually asked me that!
How do you effectively free yourself from desire?
Be cautious here, for this realm is fraught with danger.
Do not attempt to rid yourself from outward-going behaviors
like desire, through more outward-going behaviors.

You do not free yourself of desire by denial.
Denying yourself is in response to
what you think you *should* do.
And who is the holder of the reins of 'shoulds'?
Others, who relate to you only as ego,
and who you feel are constantly judging
whether your behaviors are acceptable or not.
Actually, others are usually so enveloped in their own ego
that they have little awareness of your behaviors.
Denial only results in deeper ignorance
and less readiness to grow.
It is lying to yourself—
I don't want this, it's bad, it's disgusting, it's ugly—
which sets up distrust between you
and your indicators of reality or unreality.
Denial does not work.

You do not free yourself of desire by repression.
That only loads the energies of your senses mind
feelings emotions intellect and intuition

with a heated force,
like a volume of gas pressed down
into a more constrictive space.
Repression does not remove desire;
it builds the force of desire to the point of explosion.

Repression and denial are subtle forms of avoidance.
Using avoidance to starve desire, is that a good state?
It is a state of tamas and rajas alternating
and fighting each other.
The resolution of desire is not by feigned indifference.

What do you need to do, then?
You need inward-going behaviors to experience Self.

You do not resolve Desire
by Denial Repression Avoidance Indifference,
nor any other outward-going Behavior.
You resolve Desire through the Realization of Reality,
all-inclusive Power of Being, Self.

With your higher intellect engaged,
you experience yourself in the wholeness of reality.
Desire no longer stands out, it no longer is separated;
the energies of desire are integrated in the experience of Being.
Ultimately, when you realize your oneness, Self,
and you are freed from the perception of other—
both you as other and others as apart from you—
there is no desire.

Thus freed from desire,
you are freed from its irritation and distraction.

Disentangle your lower intellect from enmeshment
with the false construct of your separateness,
the breeding bed of everything that causes suffering:
I have to protect and preserve, I have to gain;
I have to compete and fight, otherwise I won't survive;
I have to fear and be anxious—
those strategies are actually the means
by which you cut down your strength.
When you are rid of ignorance, your faculties are liberated
from their separatist involvement with desire—and death.
When you realize the known and knower and knowing
are all one—their differences dissolved in Self—
knowing no longer keeps you mortal.

Living reality, infinite continuous oneness I Am,
you need no longer be gathered by Yama, the Lord of Death,
to be conveyed to yet another body to continue evolving.
In the realization of your infinitude, you are unmovable—
to where would you move the Infinite?—thus unmodifiable.
You realize yourself as Brahman
...*here*... right now, in this lifetime.

Experience yourself as undifferentiated one absolute Consciousness.
You experience no modification or interpretation,
no isolation separation or differentiation,
just pure Being, unitive all-pervasive Being,
infinite and eternal.
There is no desire thus no actions,
there is neither knowing nor not knowing.

You simply relinquish the idea of separate self—
there is no other.
You submit all that to the one pure presence.
You sacrifice limited self to Limitless Self.
You sacrifice to Self your attachment to ego
and all its familiarity.
Even the desire for bliss you let go.
Free of action, you effortlessly act
in sharing the experience of self-knowing Being
with those facets that suffer in ignorance.

> You are the Conditionless One,
> you are This,
> you are Absolute Consciousness,
> You Are.
> This is the Realization of the supreme Reality.

Tremendous pain and suffering are caused
by attempts to throw off desire by the wrong means,
so integrate these teachings well.
Those who are still in a primitive relationship to desire
demonstrate its pain.

15. *When all the knots of the heart are destroyed, even while a man is alive, then a mortal becomes immortal. This much alone is the instruction (of all the Upanisads).*

Having examined the outward-leading dynamics of desire,
you will now learn about the 'inner' dynamics of your heart.

...heart... refers to your center of experience,
your intellect, which embraces and is meant to determine
the activities of your mind feelings emotions and senses.

When your faculties are occupied with the false conceptions
that create desire for the outer and other,
they are tied into a Gordian knot.
Gordius, ancient king of Phrygia,
made a huge knot in a massive rope of bark and pitch,
and let it harden over many years.
According to legend, whoever succeeded in loosening the knot
would rule all Asia.
It was a test of heroes to loosen this knot.
Men of great power and skill tried, but one after another failed.
Until one day a young warrior approached the knot,
and instead of trying to pull it apart,
drew his sword and with one swift stroke cut the knot asunder.
That young warrior became Alexander the Great.
Does this legend not speak of the human condition?
Most people think in certain accustomed convoluted ways,
then someone innocent—or daring—comes along
and cuts through all the complications.

The human Gordian knot is of stasis inertia tamas,
which stems the flow of your energies
that could otherwise contribute to the blissful fluidity
of Limitless Being experiencing Self in and as
Infinite Consciousness.
The *...knots of the heart...* are made by conditioning—
your energy gets tied up in habitually repeating behaviors
formed in childhood or even infancy,
no matter how harmful or painful they may be.

Many spend much time and labor
in attempts to loosen these life-choking knots;
they worry at them, try to loosen their strings,
they search and examine, analyze and discuss,
push and pull and puzzle,
yet the knots remain unchanged, tight as ever.
Such involvement with the negative
results in ingraining it even more.
The knot of misapprehension and distraction
only gets thicker and tighter with time.

What to do?
Decisively cut through the knot of negativity
that ties up your heart.

How do you accomplish such a decisive severing
from your enmeshment with self-limiting behaviors
founded on falsity?
Charge up your intellect
with the powerful and real determination
to fully focus everything about you on the experience of Self,
Eternal Consciousness that you really are,
have always been and will eternally be.
The sincere devotion with which your intellect
makes this pure determination embraces your mind,
and mind in turn empowers the senses,
until all your faculties merge
into the fully charged unified state of Consciousness.

I am the Power of Being, not the five elements and their effects.
There is an ancient way—thousands of years old—
of approaching the experience of the Indescribable,

called *neti neti*—not this, not that:
I am not the body, nor the mind, nor emotions or feelings.
What is, is not wealth, nor wine women and song,
nor kingdoms, nor any other ephemera.
All that is, is pure Being.
I Am That.

Fully focused on the experience of Self,
your faculties become as sharp as a fine-honed sword.
You function as Self:
in constant awareness of interconnectedness,
empowered by love empathy and clarity.
Therein lies *real* success.
Cultivating this experience with sincerity
and unswerving continuity and devotion,
you permanently remove the misconceptions and desires
that form a gigantic knot in your heart, in your center,
and liberate all your energies from painful bondage.

The karmic wheel to which you are tied keeps revolving
through birth death decay and rebirth, until you Self-realize.
All life cycles are evolutionary steps
toward more and more refinement of the relationship
between the manifestation and Consciousness,
an ever-expansive Consciousness in the manifestation.
An amoeba evolves to last longer, become more sensitive,
more complex, and evolves into more advanced life forms
until Limitless Consciousness is reached.
Once you know and then realize
your all-pervasive interconnected one eternal identity,
there is no more evolution.

When you realize your identity in Attributeless Brahman,
the undecaying essence of all, Self,
you are—in your experience—
merged with Brahman in this life
and therefore need not go through further life cycles.
You are liberated from the karmic wheel
to which ignorance desire and action had bound you.

That is all there is to it. Look not for more.
This is the principal teaching.
...This much alone is the instruction (of all the Upanisads)...

...When all the knots of the heart are destroyed, even while a man is alive, then a mortal becomes immortal...
Again Death sounds the theme of what you can accomplish *in this human life cycle.*
You have attained the opportunity
of Self-realization in this lifetime.
If you do not seize it,
although you may evolve to a higher realm,
you have missed the chance to realize Eternal Consciousness
right here and now.
Then you have a much longer way to go—eons and eons.
How would that come about?
By not destroying *...the knots of the heart...*

Beware of a most insidious facet of those knots—
lack of responsiveness to knowledge.
You may feel you have to process this,
when all that is required is that you *realize* who you are,
live your true identity.
If your relationship to knowledge is to not respond to it

or to defer your response,
you will tend to have the same dismissive relationship
with the opportunity of Self-realization in this lifetime.

Now Yama reveals how to implement the results of this knowledge
toward your ultimate success.

16. *The nerves of the heart are a hundred and one in number. Of them the one passes through the head. Going up through that nerve one gets immortality. The others that have different directions, become the causes of death.*

Second translation:

A hundred and one are the subtle channels of the heart: of them one extends upwards to the crown of the head. Having gone up by that, one goes to Deathlessness; the others are for going forth differently.

...The nerves of the heart...
are the highways that lead outward from the center of the city
where dwells the inner ruler, who is Self.
...subtle... pathways, they are not physical
or even neurological—
you will not find them in an anatomy book.
These radiating channels of communication and transport
are among the myriad means by which
the Power of Being expresses Self and experiences Self.
Remember, though, that Transcendent Being is also
totally independent of them;
He does not need Self-expression or Self-experience,
because Being is all.

Yama informs you that there are 101 nerves of the heart.
All but one of them transport and receive
emotional mental intellectual and intuitional energies
to and from all directions.
This ordinarily results in the meandering flow of your forces,
which causes the dissipation of relationship to Consciousness,
therefore eventual death.

The 101st *...channel...* called the *sushumna,* is the middle path.
Along it flows the mediating energy
that resolves all the apparent opposites of the other channels.
It leads straight upward to pierce the crown of the head
and is therefore called the royal pathway.
When the transforming and purifying energy of Agni
flows up this royal path, you realize Siva,
unmoving unmodified Brahman in tranquil Self-experience.

This channel is also known as the kundalini pathway.
Kundalini is powerful energy resting at the base of the spine,
waiting to be liberated,
like a coiled-up serpent ready to strike.
Through devoted rigorous yogic practices,
you can learn to release this power and let it rise.

Be careful here, the teaching regarding the sushumna
is subtle and very powerful;
it is harmful if employed in service to ego.
The practice of liberating the coiled-up energy
is only for highly advanced students.
You must be thoroughly refined and empowered
to work with this great power,
or you could damage yourself terribly.
Teaching it to unprepared students,

so prevalent in Western culture, is considered by the sages
as exceedingly dangerous and irresponsible.

Through the mere repetition of yoga postures and breathing,
you can bring about physiological and psychological sensations
that are very different from the norm.
Some seek those experiences
as proof they are advancing spiritually;
they deny, or do not know, that these are merely sensations.
As others accumulate material wealth,
they accumulate the wealth of these sense experiences
and become just as power-hungry and competitive
as those who abandon their lives to money and social power.

Your faculties are not organs, they are not objects;
they are powers, energies.
And how amazing it is, that there is the energy of,
I can sense this, I can feel that,
and I can understand and communicate.
For those who are properly prepared
with sincere practice related to Self,
the burning force of the kundalini energy
freely rising upward along the spine purifies the faculties.

The culmination and transcendence of the faculties' energies
through the subtle middle path
blazes forth through the crown of the head.
Perhaps that is why saints are depicted
with a luminous ring around the head.
A person whose energy is suppressed,
who meanders about aimlessly in a negative state,
is very different from those rare individuals
who radiate a glow of pure energy.

> The Path of Reality goes straight to Supreme Consciousness.
> That is how it is: direct.

The other 100 paths predominate in the human experience,
and they lead to death.
Only one path, the 101st channel, leads to liberation
and immortality.
That is why the path of yoga is one of conscious choice,
taken with expertise and sincerity; it is not a game.
Tread this path as you would a razor's edge over a chasm.
Be keenly aware that your actions have consequences,
even if you do not notice them immediately.
You may not keel over the moment you eat something toxic,
thus keep eating it and end up terribly ill.
Because you do not instantly fall into a coma
or suffer a heart attack when you live untrue to Self
does not mean that you are not courting death.

If you continue on the other 100 pathways,
your life will be an enmeshment in the distractions
of the phenomenal world.
Death will have to claim you to go through more lifetimes
until you understand reality, Self, and live accordingly.
Ask yourself, if you were to die now,
would you go on in Luminous Consciousness
or just latent Consciousness,
bound to the muddled material realm?

As the one channel among one hundred others is rare,
so are real spiritual aspirants among the rest of humanity.

Rare in Humanity
are those who arrive at Glimpses of Self;
of those, even rarer
are they who have real and full Knowledge of Self;
and out of those very rarefied ones, even more precious
are they who live in Accord with their Knowledge
and thereby realize Self.

Some use this as an excuse to be discouraged and give up.

Once you know who you are, to live true to Self is easy;
to live in contradiction to Self, or to give up living as Self,
is not an option.

Chapter Forty-Four

The End-Beginning

You are deeply and truly blessed.
Be aware of that.
You are blessed for the light that radiates within you
and is your essence, the source of all.

You have spent millennia of evolution coming to this point
at which you can realize Eternal Being
and no longer dwell in unconsciousness.
In this lifetime you have in your grasp the opportunity
to never die to your own perception of being you,
to dwell consciously in the experience of Self in eternity.

Allow yourself to savor joyously and blissfully
the gift of light that you are,
by which you have the power to share luminosity,
radiate it into the apparent darkness
and warm the hearts of fellow beings.

17. Purusa, the indwelling Self, of the size of a thumb, is ever seated in the hearts of men. One should unerringly separate Him from one's body like a stalk from the Munja grass. Him one should know as pure and immortal. Him one should know as pure and immortal.

Second translation:

The Thumb-like Purusha, the Inner Soul, is ever seated in the heart of all beings. Him one should patiently separate from one's body like a reed from its outer sheath. Know him to be the Pure, the Deathless. Yes, know him to be the Pure, the Deathless.

We are arriving at the conclusion
of the great secret teaching of the Kathopanisad,
which Lord Yama has imparted to a most qualified student,
Naciketa—and also to you.
His ultimate instruction is
...one should patiently separate from one's body...
Purusa, the Soul of all dwelling in the cave of the heart,
and know Him as transcendent *...pure and immortal...*

The wisdom of these teachings is your focal point
for successful relationship between your faculties and Self.
You have for so long committed your faculties
to a nearly exclusive relationship with the material realm,

that you have identified yourself with it through your body—
a material object.
Now you must patiently completely expertly and faithfully
differentiate between your ephemeral body—
which, face it, will not last—and Eternal Self,
like separating the substantive *...reed...*
from its flimsy *...sheath...*

In your core, in the midst of all your faculties
dwells ever the innermost Consciousness,
Self the essence, your real identity.
Your body and senses are *not* Self, are *not* you,
nor are your mind emotions feelings intellect or intuition,
nor are your precious tendencies.
They have *seemed* to be your identity
only due to the illusion from which you have suffered.

The knowledge of your real identity purifies your faculties.
It separates in your experience the Self you are
from the muddle of ignorance illusion and material bondage,
bondage to the wheel of karma—birth death and rebirth.
You are that which dwells in the cave of the heart.
When you identify as a manifestation,
you feel and act as vacantly as an empty shell.
When you identify as the energy
that gives this manifestation the power to be—
motivates even its atoms—
you realize the Self that you are, who *is* always and eternally:
you realize the truth of you.

The instruments that have been created and evolved to serve you—
your faculties—are the pathways through which Being radiates

from your very core into infinity, expressing Self,
and through which She gathers unto Her center
the experience of Her Eternal Beingness.
If you live your life untrue to reality, you are the usurper ego,
stealing from Self's purpose and meaning.
And do not misunderstand, this does not affect Self—
but it has powerfully painful effects upon the manifestation
with which you have identified yourself,
as well as upon all other manifestations.
Whereas when you are true to reality
and dedicate your faculties to Self's purpose,
you have pure and empowered instruments
through which Self expresses and experiences Self.

Completely remove all aspects of yourself from any further contact
with ignorance and falsity regarding your identity.
Thoroughly burn out the effects of ego on your faculties,
the tendencies that bind you to the repetition of behaviors
that deny the experience of reality,
thus keep you feeling left out, isolated in the darkness
of ignorance self-negation and unconsciousness.
Once and for all cut the Gordian knot
with the courage and determination founded upon love of Self.

Have everything about you function in conjunction with who you are,
and you will soon realize oneness with the Power of Being.
You will be liberated from the illusion
that you are a body-mind construct,
by which you conceive of yourself as mortal.
You will be conscious eternally,
free of the necessity for Death to clutch you again
into further cycles of karma—action and reaction,

birth death decay and rebirth—
through which you tumble for painful millennia,
epochs of creation and destruction.

Whatever you do not resolve in this Lifetime
you have to face in other Lifetimes,
whatever you do not resolve in this Creation
you have to work out through other Cycles of Creation.
This is the Way it is.

Remember that the love peace and tranquility,
the cessation of pain suffering uncertainty
self-negation and doubt,
takes place when you are true to what dwells
in the core of your heart, the Indweller you are.

The Self that you are is free of interpretation modification
intellectualization manipulation rationalization
commercialization or any other '-ation'.
Self is *...Pure...* and Self is *...Deathless...*
Self is eternal, It is the all-pervasive eternal essence.
You Are That.
That is why, once you realize Self,
you realize yourself to be immortal.
Immortality is to be realized, not merely conceived.

Thus the great Lord of Death concludes with
this most important advice:
...know Him to be the Pure, the Deathless...
You see, his is really a mission of mercy:

Death does not want to have to come and gather you again
after this life cycle.
Know yourself to be pure and deathless—
not mentally, but knowing as a man 'knows' his lover,
by being in union with her.
Know your deathlessness, know your purity
by being in union with the reality of Self that you are.
That is his final statement to you.
Know Self to be *...the Pure, the Deathless...*

This is what you have always wanted most of all,
to be pure, to be deathless.
Now that you have been taught how to have this exalted state,
do you know what the tendency is?
To run away from it.
If you behave so foolishly as to fall for the tendency
to run away from what you really want,
be not surprised by the suffering you cause yourself.

Yoga is really about this teaching of your pure eternal identity;
it is the map and the culmination of the path to Self-realization.
Yoga is not a collection of practices,
it is not a dogma or belief system or religion,
it is not a game fad or hobby.
Yoga is not a process, and yoga certainly is not a business.
Yoga does not mean living in self-denial and shame;
it means living as the loving Self you are, Purusa,
who dwells in the cave of the heart.
Once you have gained real knowledge, live it,
otherwise you reject and disrespect Self—
that is not yoga, that is not love.

Naciketa simply absorbs Yama's teachings in full experience, agrees with them, and lives them from that moment on.

> Living as the Self you are is not optional;
> it is not a Matter of Convenience
> and not a Matter of, When I feel like it,
> not a Matter of now and then.
> You are Self permanently, eternally,
> always have been and always will be.
> Be congruent with what is, live Self always.

Remember these teachings,
keep them warm and glowing in the cave of your heart,
as do the yogis, for this is your salvation and eternal joy.
Be real, be true to yourself.
Be in integrity with the knowledge
you have been blessed to receive.

Responding to this knowledge by living as if you did not know
would be utterly disloyal to Self
and foolish to the ultimate degree.
To knowingly look into the face of Consciousness
and choose to ally yourself with ignorance
is the most self-negating and harmful choice you could make.
To look into the eyes of the Power of Being and see yourself
and, from that moment on,
consciously lovingly loyally and expertly dwell in that insight
as the Indweller that you are—

Infinite Consciousness, Essence, Purusa—
that is the only reasonable response.

Ask yourself, Is this the response I have truly chosen?
Is my response one of loyalty or disloyalty,
honesty or falsity, clarity or confusion, love or disregard?
Has my experience been of joy and ease,
or of sadness dysfunction suffering despair
anxiety depression and shame?
You can give yourself an honest answer if you so choose.

The love peace bliss and ultimate success you seek
dwells in the cave of your heart
and is always available to all your faculties.

18. Naciketa, having become first free from virtue and vice, as also desire and ignorance, acquired this knowledge imparted by Death, as also the process of yoga in its totality, and he attained Brahman. Anyone else, too, who becomes a knower thus (like Naciketa) of the indwelling Self, attains Brahman.

How is Naciketa *...free from virtue and vice...*?
Being is unmodifiable; virtue and vice do not apply
to one who has realized the all-pervasive infinite Eternal.
However, this does not mean
you do not perform virtuous actions;
you naturally act virtuously because you *are* that—
this story began with Naciketa's virtuous action.

Brahman is free of the faculties' pathways,
free of the cave of the heart, free of human beings;
they are ways of expressing and experiencing Self,
but the infinite Power of Being does not need them;

He is ever transcendent to them.
Realizing oneness with Brahman,
the true aspirant enjoys the same freedom.

...as also desire and ignorance...

Those who, like Naciketa, identify with Brahman, Self,
irrevocably free themselves from attachment
to the ignorance and misery of accustomed ego desires.
Those who have knowledge
but stay in the familiar dysfunctional ego patterns
are ignorant irresponsible and miserable,
as they cultivate desire for power fame or wealth.
The desirelessness of the true aspirant,
who knows Self as the source of all,
is not indifference, nor is it repression or denial.
To the Infinite, what is and is not does not make a difference,
but He is not indifferent or uncaring.

What about ignorance?

With all the knowledge offered you by Yama
can you legitimately claim ignorance?
People sometimes rationalize:
If I'm not living as Self, I must still be ignorant,
and ignorance is a condition imposed upon me,
thus I'm not responsible.
This is not true; living as Self is a choice.

...acquired this knowledge imparted by Death...

Naciketa took the knowledge in, he owned it and lived it.
...as also the process of yoga in its totality...
Real yoga is living as self-knowing Self;
the practices are just means to this, ways of living it.
...and he attained Brahman...

He attained Limitless Consciousness
upon deciding, in absolute integrity,
to live true to the knowledge of Self.
How long did this decision take? A moment.

...Anyone else, too, who becomes a knower thus (like Naciketa) of the indwelling Self, attains Brahman...
How do you become a knower like Naciketa?
Absorb the experience of reality, Power of Being that you are,
and sincerely continuously expertly and faithfully
live in the union of Self,
be a knower in the totality of yoga, the unitive state:
be Self-realized.
Self-realization in this lifetime is not just for rarified sages
who sit in the mist of the mountaintop,
but for all born into the human form.

Consciously living true to Self is not a process, either you do it or not.
What do you choose?

19. May He protect us both (by revealing knowledge). May He protect us both (by vouchsafing the results of knowledge). May we attain vigour together. Let what we study be invigorating. May we not cavil at each other. Peace! Peace! Peace!

Absorb yourself in this prayer.

...May He protect us both... the teacher and the taught.
How? *...by revealing knowledge...*
What faith Yama has in you.
By revealing knowledge he protects you from the suffering
to which you have so persistently attached yourself.
Self reveals Himself to his manifestations—what faith.

Once Self is revealed and sincerely responded to,
the manifestations are protected.

...May He protect us both (by vouchsafing the results of knowledge)...
May He protect us both, teacher and taught alike,
by not only revealing the teachings,
but granting you the ability to attain their results
while remaining free of attachment.
How do you attain the powerful positive results?
By living true to the teachings.
What are the results?
The limitless joy of liberation, Self-realization.

...May we attain vigour together... Be in the passion of Self
each moment as you conduct your life.
Unite with like-minded aspirants
to enjoy and support one another in interconnectedness.
Be not passive lazy procrastinating or fearful
in your response to these sacred teachings.
Respond with the purity of energy inherent to Self.

...Let what we study be invigorating...
This knowledge empowers and energizes,
generates enthusiasm passion and joy.
If you are walking around
with your face dragging on the ground,
you are not living according to the knowledge that you have.
Allow this wealth of knowledge to enliven and empower you,
to uplift you with great vitality.

...May we not cavil at each other...
All too often aspirants compete enable and oppose each other;
they *...cavil...* argue, create conflict.

Competing religions do it in the name of God:
My God is better than yours.
Love each other—you are fellow aspirants
devoted to Limitless Self, pioneering the pathway for all.
Be deeply grateful to your brothers and sisters on the path.

...Peace! Peace! Peace!...

Be at peace, love and be loved, be in harmony,
feel self-respect and honor,
be invigorated and empowered
by what you have been privileged to learn.
Live according to the sacred knowledge
that you not only have, but are.
Thus you are protected, and thus you will be fulfilled.

The end, that is the beginning.

I salute the Power of Being that you are
and bow down ego before that.
You Are That, That You Are.
That is the way it is.

Glossary Of Terms

absolute: total, unqualified, undiminished; not subject to any limitation; existing independently.

action: expression of Being.

Aditi: the mother of all creation, giver of life, life-breath; the aspect of Consciousness in the act of expressing Its potential in association with the elements, through created beings.

Agni: the essential fire, the fire of creation, maintenance and destruction; luminous fire sparked in the relationship of Consciousness with Its potentiality manifesting through life-breath.

ancients: original seers of reality.

apana: the pulse of life force that is gathering in, moving down; descending energy.

aspirant: student on the spiritual path.

Atman: the essence, reality and substance of every creature, lodged in their very core; Self; the transmigrating soul, the conscious experiencer of all that transpires.

attachment: bond with the unreal, the momentary, illusion.

austerities: practices, disciplines, restraints.

avaricious: greedy for wealth, conditions or material gain.

awareness: conscious experience.

being: a) the being that Being does; existing; manifesting Being; b) a manifestation of Being.

Being: all that is being; the essential all-pervasive enduring unifying and united power by which everything is, knowing Itself; the irreducible identity of all.

Beingness: term used to emphasize Being, what is, over being, the act.

bliss: transcendent joy integral to the clear, undistracted and continuous experience of Being.

body: the physical or material apparatus of a being.

body-mind construct/complex: the body, mind, emotions, feelings, intellect and intuition; the vehicle transporting the individual Self from one evolutionary stage to another.

Brahma: Absolute Being in Its creative state; Brahman's potential state; Creator.

Brahmacarya: to live in the knowledge and purity of Consciousness; to cultivate the life of balance, live in association with a real spiritual Teacher for the purpose of sincere study, and dedicate your life to the experience and expression of Essential Being; restraint.

Brahman: Absolute Being—unmoving, unchanging, timeless and conditionless, unmodified, without qualification and indefinable—in tranquil Self-experience; ultimate source and goal.

Brahmana: high-born, intelligent, spiritually dedicated person; member of the social class consisting of teachers and priests, the upkeepers of ritual, sacrifice and spiritual study.

buddhi: the higher intellect, which is in service of Self and relates all to the one infinite Being.

cause and effect: the law of nature relating all actions inexorably with their consequences; principle that all actions cause reactions of their kind; karma.

cave of the heart: the area to which the breath goes, the general area of the heart, and your center of Consciousness.

center: a focal point in meditation, the area of your heart, which is limitless, free of boundaries.

circumstances and conditions: the momentary, ephemeral, impermanent; the opposite of essence.

chariot: analogy for the body-mind complex, the vehicle of transmigration through evolution.

charity: expressing your real identity in interconnectedness through giving; sharing yourself in egoless service.

commitment: aligning yourself with a specific choice and assuming responsibility for it by integrating it into your existence, living it.

concentration: the gathering of your energies (mental, emotional, intellectual, intuitional, physical and sensual) and fixing them at will upon a chosen point.

conditioning: patterns of reaction and behavior established through repetition.

conscious experience: being aware of Self purely, or in relation with objects and events (physical, sensual, emotional, mental, intellectual or intuitional).

conscious action: action in the experience and expression of yourself as interconnected, eternal, all-pervasive, conscious Being.

Consciousness: the awareness or experience of Being; Being aware of being; the subtlest, most refined energy that permeates all; the light of Self-awareness *that* you are and *what* you are.

contemplation: constant 'being-with'.

core: the center, where dwells awareness of Being.

Cosmic Experience/Union/ Intelligence: the subtler, more pervasive, superior intelligence that prevails beyond the limits of the intellect and intuition; oneness with the cosmos, thus the cessation of perceived lack and need; immortality; Mahat.

Cosmic Dancer: Nataraja; tranquil Being in the whirling dance of creation, maintenance and destruction.

cosmos: the universe, the manifested world, a cycle of creation.

Creator: Self-projection of the Power of Being, from whom all manifestation comes forth.

creation: expression or manifestation of the Power of Being; that which has a beginning and an end.

crisis: crucial and decisive event or time, caused by not responding to reality.

darkness: a) the absence of light; b) lack of Self-awareness.

death: when a manifestation of Being ends and changes into another state of being.

Death: personification of death; Yama.

denial: refusal to acknowledge reality.

depression: a dysfunctional state resulting from the repression of feeling and disregard of Self-experience.

desire: want, wish for.

desirelessness: release from want and need, due to the recognition that there is no more than the infinitude of Being.

destiny: the course of life molded by that with which you come into this life, and the conditioning and habits established in this life, as well as your determined actions.

devil: opposition to what is, to truth, to reality; opposition to successfully functioning in harmony.

devotee: one who lives in love and devotion to reality as the means to Self-realization.

discipline [Self-]: action chosen to express Self, sometimes in opposition to prevailing tendencies.

direct experience: your experience, as opposed to belief or hearsay.

disease: the breakdown of the integration of the various aspects of your Being; imbalance.

distraction: mind's meandering in thoughts unrelated to the moment of being that tend to enmesh mind in matters that cause you to suffer in dysfunction, deprivation and disappointment.

dysfunction: self-opposing behaviors resulting from being out of touch with Being; a block to the inherent tendency to flourish; actions devoid of expertise and real success.

ego: the false perception of your identity as an isolated, limited body-mind construct.

ego [pure]: pure indicator of 'I am', without modification.

ego-doership: false perception of a limited, isolated entity acting.

ego-ownership: ego taking credit.

emotion: an expressive state, the subtle, internal response to an experience.

emptiness: an undesirable state, your faculties disconnected from the Being you are and not relating to you their experiences of the world around and within you.

enlightenment: living purely in the truth of who you essentially and really are.

entity: a creation, a being.

equanimity: balance; evenness of mind.

esoteric: of the internalized approach to reality, where you observe and respond to inner, subtler, therefore more secret experiences, with a focus on Self-realization in this life.

essence: the absolute, irreducible substance of all that is; that without which a being could not be.

[the] Eternal: unbeginning unending Being.

Eternal Consciousness: Infinite Being aware of Being.

evolution: growth toward the highest state, integration with the whole; continuous process of development toward a state free of limitation; the process by which the manifestations of Being grow toward recognition of themselves as the one limitless Being they really are.

existence: that which is being.

Existence-knowledge-bliss-absolute: Power of Being passionately experiencing Self; Satchidananda; true identity.

exoteric: of the popular, commonplace approach to reality, where you focus on external expressions, such as rituals, and on the afterlife.

experience: the undergoing of things generally, be they internal events—such as sensations, emotions, feelings, thoughts or intuitions—or external events; the process of encountering Being through its manifestations; the totality of your perceived and remembered encounters with Being.

experience of Being: consciously encountering Being; being conscious.

Expert In Life: an approach to living based on consciously and expertly utilizing your faculties toward the fulfillment of your life's meaning and the realization of your potential.

faculties: instruments for experiencing and expressing Self: body, senses, mind, emotions, feelings, intellect and intuition.

falsity: untruth; not reality.

fear: emotion caused by ego sense of isolation, and in response to perceived danger or threat.

feeling: a) a perceptive state, the subtle, internal experience in relation to inner or outer conditions; b) experiencing the sense of touch.

fire: transforming and purifying energy.

five elements: fundamental components out of which all manifestations are formed: earth, water, fire, air and ether.

focus: to draw together the attentiveness of your faculties onto yourself.

frustration: the painful feeling of inability, defeat or discouragement, the result of dwelling in a state contrary to who you really are and what you really want.

fulfillment: the state resulting from the experience of your infinite interconnectedness, in which you realize that you are all and have all; the cessation of desire and need.

Gandharvas: celestial beings; higher, refined powers.

genesis: Consciousness' fervent projection of Self as Creator coming to fruition in beings.

God: interpreted differently by various approaches, but here: Infinite Being; the reality, Self of all that is; the essence and source.

gods: the highest refined created powers; immortals.

Golden Womb/Germ/Seed: Hiranyagarbha; the creative aspect of Being.

Gordian knot: symbol for complications resulting in seemingly unsolvable problem.

grace: a) elegant refined movement; b) favor, blessing, goodwill; Self revealing Itself.

Guide: Teacher on the spiritual path.

gunas: the three vibratory states that compose all matter: rajas, tamas, satva—dynamic, static, pure.

Guru: spiritual Teacher, Guide.

habit: automatic behavior pattern based on repetition, often opposed to conscious choice.

harmlessness: not causing harm, an ethical and moral behavior predicated upon your understanding of your intimate interconnectedness with all creations.

health: fully balanced system of forces.

heaven: the cessation of fear and need; the realm of immortality.

hell: a life of self-denial; bondage to the pleasurable.

Hierarchy of Being: view of the relationship between Absolute Being, the Creator and the manifestation, through the ascending levels of senses, sense-objects, mind, intellect, Great Soul, the Unmanifested and Purusa.

highborn: a) born into a manifestation with higher social status; b) highly evolved.

Hiranyagarbha: the projection of Eternal Consciousness through which It manifests; Brahman's Self-expressive modality; the First Born from whom emerges creation; the Golden Seed.

holism: the principle that the whole is greater than the sum of its parts, and every part contains all the information of the whole.

hospitality, law of: principle of showing a guest consideration and courtesy.

human being: Self-projection of the Creator.

I-Amness: sense of 'I am', free of the limiting adjuncts.

identity: the irreducible and permanent factor about a being.

ignorance: lack of knowledge of reality.

illusion: perception of things as other than what they are.

immortal: beyond the cycles of birth, death and rebirth.

immortality: freedom from death.

Indweller: Self, residing in the core of everything in creation, and transcendent to all.

inertia: the tendency to continue in the same state or direction, and to resist growth, unless another and greater force causes a change.

infinite: without limit.

initiate: one who has received initiation from a real Teacher.

initiation: a most powerful, honest and interconnected relationship with a real Teacher that can ensure the aspirant's success on the path to the realization of highest potential; relationship with the ultimate reality, with real Self.

Inner Knower: the serene honest voice within that guides you with its utterly reliable truth; the way by which you know within, what *is*, with certainty.

inspiration: response to the urgings of the essence, the spirit that you are; a powerful motivating force to realize Self.

integrity: being true to reality, to who you are and to your knowledge and determination.

intellect: the power of knowing that includes the ability to extrapolate and reason.

intellect, higher: buddhi; determining faculty that relates all to Self.

intellect, lower: faculty that gives reason to—rationalizes—the workings of the lower mind on the material level.

interconnectedness: unrestricted union, oneness.

intuition: immediate cognition without evident rational thought or sensory experience.

kalpa: cycle of creation, which lasts billions of years.

karma: cause and effect; action.

karma yoga: meditation in action; conscious action; egoless service.

knowledge: knowing reality as a result of study and direct experience.

Krishna: Atman; Lord of the chariot.

kundalini: the mediating energy resting at the base of the spine that, when liberated, resolves all the apparent opposites of the other energies.

learning: the life process of acknowledging and integrating experience of reality.

limiting adjuncts: limitations inherent to the five elements, thus all manifestation, through which the illusion of separateness is wrought.

love: unconditional acceptance of Being; the harmonious realization of fundamental essence shared.

Mahat: the omniscient One; Cosmic Experience; the fundamental source of the intelligence of all beings; Great Soul.

mala: garland of 108 beads that is a symbol of the union between Teacher and aspirant, and the succession of lifetimes, and a reminder of mortal desires.

manas: mind.

manes: spirits of the dead.

manifestation: the created; expression of the Power of Being; an event, action, object, entity.

Manifestor: the Creator.

mantra: distilled energy of an aspect of essential reality, expressed in the form of a word or word phrase, passed down to us from the Rishis.

mantra meditation/chanting/ repetition: a complex spiritual discipline employing sound patterns, or mantras, which purifies, refines and empowers human faculties for the experience of Being.

maya: illusion; the impermanent appearing permanent, the unified appearing as separate and isolated objects and events.

meditation: the unalloyed experience of Being, including the knowledge of what Being is, with clarity and continuity, without distraction and at will.

mind: the faculty that gathers input from the other faculties and coordinates and reflects it for your experience.

mortal: one who lives in ignorance and is tied to the wheel of life, death and rebirth.

Naciketa: name of boy who is the representative of Self-realizing, or Self-realized, human being.

Naciketa fire: burning light of pure truth.

Naciketa sacrifice: burning away all attachment to ego, non-being, and dwelling in the continuity of Eternal Consciousness.

Nataraja: the aspect of Siva, Limitless Consciousness, who stands in effortless balance amidst the whirl of the natural forces that create, preserve and destroy the entire cosmos; the Cosmic Dancer.

need: inner state caused by false notion of isolation leading to wanting to unite with an other.

negative: conceals, obscures or distorts the experience of Being; ultimately disadvantageous.

neti neti: 'not this not that', an ancient way of approaching the Indescribable.

non-being: illusion, falsity.

non-self: false identity, ego.

objects: phenomena caused by the coming and going of atoms creating the momentary appearance of material with shape and weight.

oblation: giving up any sense of 'otherness'; sacrifice.

observance [Self-]: faculties focused upon the Being you are; behavior in attentiveness to All-inclusive Self.

Om: Absolute Being and Its symbol or name, and the first vibration of Being, the beginning of all creation, and Its symbol or name; Seed Mantra.

omniscient One: All-knowing Being; Mahat.

passion: strong emotion; potentially, a pure power of devotion, joy and all-inclusiveness.

peepul tree, inverted: analogy for Limitless Being, with roots in the Beginningless above, and branching down into manifestation.

personality: the character, the manifestation by which you tend to identify yourself.

phenomena: momentary events; the passing, the ephemeral.

positive: reveals and contributes to the experience of Being; ultimately advantageous.

potential [human]: the full capability of all, including your faculties, to be in Continuous Consciousness.

Power of Being: the power or energy that gives everything the ability to be; the substance of all that is.

practical: actually works toward accomplishing the goal.

practicality, fundamental: living according to your true identity.

practice: the repeated, intelligent use of a faculty by will.

prana: life force, vital energy, animating energy.

pranayama: yogic practice of the subtle control of the breath as a means to establishing a controlled relationship with the life force.

prayer: Self-luminous Being manifesting, opening fully, beyond the appearance of this manifestation, to merge with Limitless Being.

pride: a distorted opinion of one's worth in an attempt to compensate for feelings of insecurity, rooted in ego.

procrastination: delaying the fulfillment of your intentions indefinitely.

psyche: mental and emotional processes related to a manifestation.

Purusa: the Soul of all; Absolute Self, Being of all beings, yet beyond.

rajas: the dynamic vibratory state; creative mode.

rationalization: lying to yourself and others; attempt to make falsity appear as truth.

reality: that which permanently is, independent of circumstance, condition, time and space; the underlying absolute.

realize: make real by living it.

reparation: action in strength to give to Self purely without attachment, to free oneself from the negative effects of wrong action.

resistance: that which opposes change; that which keeps you from realizing true Self.

responsibility: the ability to respond to reality.

Rishis: the ancient seers, masters of the highest consciousness and acute perception.

sacrifice: an offering made to acknowledge the Power of Being by which all is; giving up the false ego-identity; freeing oneself from attachment.

sage: one who experiences and lives the transcendent and ultimate reality.

samadhi: the superconscious state; both the state of death—dead to ego—and the state of bliss—all needs, desires and aspirations fulfilled.

Satchidananda: Existence-knowledge-bliss-absolute; self-knowing Being in the bliss of Its own luminosity.

satsanga: gathering of the wise.

satva: the pure vibratory state; balanced mode.

seer: Self-realized being who sheds light and removes confusion.

self: false identity; limited ego concept.

Self: real, unchanging identity; that which you and all are essentially.

Self, individual: the transmigrating soul.

self-effulgent: needs nothing but itself to shine.

Self-empowered: acts, or of actions, in the experience and expression of Self.

self-existent: needs nothing but itself to be.

self-luminous: does not take light from something else, does not have light, but is the light.

Self-realization: living your true identity, eternal, all-pervasive Consciousness; being congruent with knowledge of Unitive Being and thus freed from identification with the limiting ego construct.

sense-object: that which experiences specifically through each sense, and which has created, or actuated, each sense for its own revelation.

senses: the perceptive capabilities by which you relate to the material realm: smell, taste, sight, touch and hearing.

service [egoless]: acting in the consciousness of interconnectedness; action without attachment to the results or desire for rewards; karma yoga.

Silent Observer: internal stance of unattached, nonjudgmental witness of events external and internal.

Siva: personification of the Power of Being in Its unmoving state, with the potential for all movement, all creation.

soul: innermost essence, momentarily shrouded by the veil of illusion, transmigrating through evolution to Self-realization; spirit.

Soul, Great: level of Consciousness associated with manifestation, but beyond the faculties; all souls; Mahat.

spirit: essential subtle force by which one is; soul; the true intent or meaning of an entity.

spiritual life: to live in loyalty and devotion to your spirit.

spiritual path: path to fulfillment in the realization of your true identity; way to the highest level of Consciousness in which you experience yourself as the imperishable, all-pervasive Power of Being.

student: Being manifested in the guise of separateness, being guided to recognize interconnectedness by Being manifested in the illumined state.

study [real]: to seek knowledge of the permanent underlying foundation of all that is, not the momentary show.

stupid: having knowledge of reality but living in self-disregard and -opposition.

substance: that which stands under or upholds all that is; the real or essential.

suffering: the result of ignorance regarding, or disregard of, your true Self.

superconsciousness: samadhi; faculties highly refined, merged with Consciousness.

sushumna: subtle internal upward pathway for the mediating energy, kundalini.

tamas: the static vibratory state; destructive mode, at times.

tapas: fiery spiritual discipline; austerities; the internal fire, the deep glowing warmth of Consciousness turning inward toward Self.

Teacher: Eternal Consciousness manifesting in the Self-awareness of all-pervasive interconnectedness, guiding those manifestations who are in the illusion of separateness, toward the realization of their interconnectedness.

transcendent: beyond the limits and qualifications of time and space.

transformation: permanent change to a higher level.

transmigration: the soul passing into a different state after death.

truth: that which unequivocally is.

unattachment: not involving yourself in particulars at the expense of your involvement in the infinite wholeness.

unitive state: when all faculties are harmoniously balanced and integrated in the clear experience of Self, integral with all; being in the experience of complete devotion to, and absorption in, Infinite Being; yoga.

universal: all-inclusive; without exception.

[the] Universal: manifestation of Consciousness characterized by vibration and movement, but not separate from Infinite Consciousness; the infinite interconnected One; Mahat.

Universal Consciousness: experience of all in the continuum of time; Cosmic Union.

[the] Unmanifest(ed): the potential for manifestation; Absolute Being in Its pure potential state.

unreality: that which *is not*; the momentary; illusion.

Vasudeva: the Self-luminous One who provides a home for all in Himself.

vibratory modes: three types of vibration that compose all manifestation: active, static and dynamically balanced.

Vishnu: All-pervading Spirit.

want: inner state resulting from false notion of lack.

wheel of karma: repeating cycles of life, death and rebirth.

will: the power by which you implement your choices.

wisdom: knowledge gained by experience of reality, continuously applied to your behaviors and actions.

Yama: personification of death.

yoga: the cessation of the modifications of the mind; the unitive state; the multi-faceted discipline and approach of realizing the unitive state.

yogi: one who is devoted to the unitive state.

Photograph Captions

PHOTOGRAPHS BY ERHARD VOGEL*

Front Cover
Himalayan Sunset
India

Page vii
Evening Waves
San Diego, California

Page ix
Migration

Page xi
Mahabalipuram Temple Sculptures
Tamil Nadu, India

Page xix
Beach Sand
USA

Page 1
Ocean Interlude
Athens, Greece

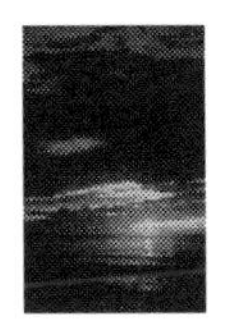

Page 5
Beach Sunset
San Diego, California

Page 9
Palace Portal
India

Page 21
Himalayan Gate
India

Page 31
Wheel Of Karma, Konark Sun Temple
Orissa, India

Page 39
Mother India
Himalayas, India

Page 47
Erhard In Cave
Himalayas, India
*Anonymous

Page 325
Razor's Edge
Grand Canyon, Arizona

Page 339
Ancient Temple Complex
South India

Page 349
Harmony

Page 371
Japanese Maple
Seattle Park,
Washington

Page 379
Ocean Sunset 2
San Diego, California

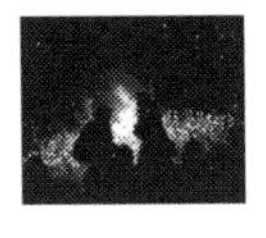

Page 393
Candlelight Vigil
Washington DC

Page 405
Driftwood
Seattle, Washington

Page 415
Carved Cave Hallway
India

Page 423
River
Yosemite, California

Page 429
Ganges Near Its Source
Gomukh, Himalayas,
India

Page 439
A Tree Grows In Brooklyn
New York

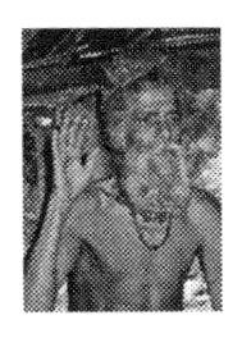

Page 447
Himalayan Sage
India

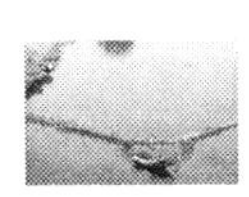

Page 455
Fisherman's Dam
India

Page 465
Ancient Trees
Washington State

About The Author

Erhard Vogel, PhD, is recognized as one of the foremost meditation and Self-realization teachers in the world. Born in war-torn Germany, Dr. Vogel immigrated to the United States at age fourteen. He graduated from the Pratt Institute of Design in New York, and at an early age rose to a respected position in a world-renowned architectural firm. At thirty-one, he set aside a brilliant career in architecture to devote himself to the service of humanity.

For four years Erhard, as he likes to be called by his students, traveled the globe on foot. He lived in Europe, the Middle East, Afghanistan, India, Nepal and China, thoroughly researching the ways in which people of different cultures seek fulfillment. He saw the underlying need in everyone to fulfill their potential.

In India Erhard met two of the world's most renowned luminous Masters, who welcomed him into their midst and invited him to teach among the Himalayan sages—a rare distinction for a westerner. He lived for an extended period of time in a Himalayan cave in a remote sacred area.

Living in utter joy and luminosity, Erhard remembered how so many people throughout the world suffer. He returned home to address the problems and aspirations of our contemporary society with his teachings. Following a lecture tour spanning the United States, Europe and Canada, he came to San Diego and founded The Nataraja Yoga Ashram, a not-for-profit organization.

Erhard's teachings are a unique combination of time-tested wisdom and pragmatic method. His fundamental, experiential and systematic approach is based upon sound psychological, physiological and spiritual principles that make meditation and Self-realization practical and attainable.

Erhard teaches not from books nor from other people's ideas, but out of his own profound life experience. Through his depth of knowledge he is able to inspire and gently guide sincere students to the experience of their limitless potential. With unconditional acceptance and unwavering respect for the Being they are, he inspires his students to recognize their real Self and to treat themselves with trust and kindness.

Since 1969, Erhard has taught tens of thousands of students throughout the world. He continues to travel regularly to India and teach among the sages in the Himalayas, where he is recognized as a Master Teacher. He has authored three additional books: *Self-healing Through The Awareness Of Being*; *Journey Into Your Center*; and *The Four Gates: A Saga Of The Human Being On The Path From The Pit Of Despair To The Realm Of Fulfillment, From Confusion To Clarity, Culminating In The Deepest Realization*; as well as numerous audio recordings of guided meditations and teachings. Erhard currently offers courses on-site and online through The Nataraja Meditation and Yoga Center in San Diego, California.

About The Nataraja Yoga Ashram

The Nataraja Yoga Ashram is an organization for Self-realization. Established by Dr. Erhard Vogel in 1974 in San Diego, California, as a not-for-profit social service organization, The Nataraja Yoga Ashram provides in-depth experiential teachings of expert ways to lead a fulfilling and successful life that is realistically directed toward the attainment of Self-realization in this lifetime.

Through a wide array of programs and services offered on-site and online through its teaching center, the Nataraja Meditation and Yoga Center, the Ashram is dedicated to promoting the physiological, psychological and spiritual welfare of the human being.

The Expert In Life™ Program was developed by Dr. Vogel over a lifetime of direct experience to provide the means by which to live in the state of Self-realization: fully Self-aware and self-accepting, free from limitation, in deep inner peace and quietly balanced joy.

The Program is a graduated group process centered around proactive life practices and strengthened by a shared commitment to success. It is the objective of the Expert In Life program to empower students to become so expert at understanding, fine-tuning and strengthening their faculties, that they can harmoniously integrate and apply them with easy skill and power toward fulfillment.

For more information visit yogameditationnataraja.org.

Audio Publications By Erhard Vogel

Available at yogameditationnataraja.org/shop

The Cave Meditation This powerful meditation comes to you from the direct experience of world-renowned Meditation Master, Erhard Vogel, who dwelled in a Himalayan cave and taught among the sages of the Himalayas. Allow yourself to be guided into a state of clear, focused consciousness in which all aspects of you rest in effortless balance in your center, reflecting the infinity of Being that you are.

The Stress Release Response: 7 Steps to Triumph Over Stress This guided experience contains a set of steps by which you can dependably free yourself from stress and its harmful effects—at a moment's notice and at will. Dr. Vogel has taught tens of thousands of students from many parts of the world and walks of life, to effectively reduce anxiety and stress, including members of such high-stress professions as hospice workers, doctors, lawyers, police officers, teachers and mothers. The Stress Release Response™, which he developed in the 1970s to answer an unmet need, has proven to be among the most beneficial means of coping with stress, yielding predictably positive results.

Guided Meditation for Beginners This meditation provides an inspiring and enjoyable experience in which you will learn the fundamental steps necessary for meditation, and cultivate your ability to relax at will, focus your mind, and know yourself and your potential on the deepest level.

Centering In this meditation you are guided in a unique and powerfully effective method of making the state of clear and centered consciousness directly available. Anyone who sincerely implements the step-by-step suggestions will create an inner state that is vibrant and attentive as well as deeply relaxed, thus overcoming internal struggles, mental distraction and the 'zoned-out' state that is often mistaken for meditation.

Feelings and Emotions Human experiences, including our feelings and emotions, are richly varied. However, we habitually repress our feelings because we fear they would overwhelm us. With this guided experience you will relate to your emotions with acceptance and become deeply in touch with your feelings. With repeated listening, you will open to ever subtler levels and no longer experience your feelings as distractions, but as enriching aspects of your Self-experience.

The Healing Power of Love Imagine having everything about you in such a pure, clear and luminous state that your deepest insights and inner light shine forth in unrestricted strength. With this meditation, you will guide your faculties to harmonious union and thereby develop a powerful, peaceful love of yourself that creates healing from the physical to the deepest levels.

The Silent Observer Learn to guide your faculties into a calm, clear and balanced state in which you experience yourself as the unattached witness to all events, external and internal. You attain a level of perception and judgment far subtler and more lucid than your ordinary mental processes allow. The relief and freedom gained by becoming skilled at maintaining the Silent Observer state is a significant aid to anyone who wants a life of empowerment and peace.

Yoga For Life Erhard instructs you with clear, detailed description through a wide variety of yoga postures in two hour-long classes. Whether you are a beginner or advanced, you will find it easy to give yourself your own rejuvenating classes at home. This will benefit you on all levels: developing flexibility and strength, deeply calming and centering the mind, creating a state of balance emotionally and on every level. You will use these recordings for years to come, growing ever healthier and more powerful.

Advanced Breathing Techniques and the Breath Meditation This set of two recordings guides you through: 1) the super-oxygenation and alternate nostril breathing techniques, or *pranayama*, which you can employ to dramatically increase your clarity, vitality and concentration, as well as balance and fine-tune your nervous system; and 2) the *Breath Meditation*, a guided experience in harmonious breathing requisite to meditation in which this natural process becomes deeply significant and strengthens your experience of Being.

Made in the USA
Columbia, SC
27 September 2020

21667658R00346